EDITED BY
SARI BOTTON

GOOD BYE *to* ALL THAT

WRITERS ON
LOVING AND LEAVING
NEW YORK

SEAL PRESS

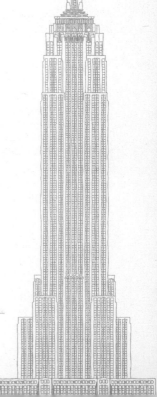

About the cover: The front cover illustration was drawn by artist James Gulliver Hancock (jamesgulliverhancock.com), whose distinctive work has been exhibited in galleries worldwide. His book, *All the Buildings in New York,* features drawings of iconic and everyday buildings in New York, from the Flatiron and Rockefeller Center to the brownstones of Brooklyn. He lives and works in both Sydney and New York City.

Meghan Daum's story was originally published in *The New Yorker* and later in *My Misspent Youth: Essays.* It is reprinted here with permission from Open City Books.

Portions of Melissa Febo's story were originally published on the New York Times Opinionator blog, "Townies" and in Salon.

GOODBYE TO ALL THAT
Writers on Loving and Leaving New York

Copyright © 2013 Sari Botton

Published by
Seal Press
A Member of the Perseus Books Group
1700 Fourth Street
Berkeley, California
www.sealpress.com

Library of Congress Cataloging-in-Publication Data
Goodbye to all that : writers on loving and leaving New York / [edited] by
Sari Botton.
     pages cm.
ISBN 978-1-58005-494-2 (pbk.)
1. American literature--New York (State)--New York. 2. Women authors,
American--New York (State)--New York--Biography. 3. Women--New York
(State)--New York)--Biography. 4. New York (N.Y.)--Biography. I. Botton,
Sari, 1965- editor of compilation.
 PS549.N5G66 2013
 810.8'0327471--dc23
 [B]
                              2013016147

10 9 8 7 6

Cover design by Erin Seaward-Hiatt
Interior design by Tabitha Lahr
Interior illustrations: title page © artisti/123rf.com; pages iii, v, vi, ix, x © Pavel Sivak/123rf.com;
    page xiv © Oleksandr Melnyk/123rf.com
Printed in the United States of America
Distributed by Publishers Group West

"All I mean is that I was very young in New York, and that at some point the golden rhythm was broken, and I am not that young anymore."

—Joan Didion, "Goodbye to All That,"
Slouching Towards Bethlehem

For Clarisse

And for Maggie Estep (1963–2014), a great talent, a generous
spirit, and an inspiration—who first made it seem super cool to live
in the East Village, and then just as cool to leave it for upstate

CONTENTS

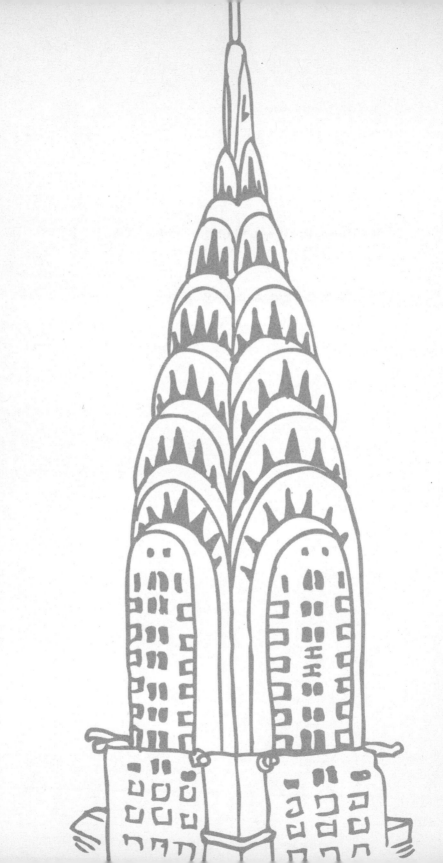

INTRODUCTION

I n the early 1990s, when I was in my mid-twenties, if someone told me I'd someday leave New York City and move to Upstate New York, I would have told them they were crazy. I thought of myself as a lifer, and anticipated that I'd stay in the city forever.

But in 2005, after we were evicted from our under-market loft in the East Village and couldn't afford even a studio at the going rate, my husband and I felt strangely relieved to leave a city that seemed to be changing more rapidly than we could keep up with, and where living had become completely unaffordable for us. We moved to a depressed town in New York's mid-Hudson Valley, just under two hours from the city.

It was only a short time before we met a slew of other New York City expats. Many of them were fellow writers and editors struggling to stay afloat in the new, shrinking publishing economy, just as I was. Trading the high cost of living in New York City for the significantly lower cost of living in a depressed rural area helped.

I'd cross paths with them at cafés (often cafés established by yet other expats), and as we got to know each other, we'd compare notes on what prompted our respective exits from the city.

In time, I started to notice a recurring theme, regardless of the particular circumstances that finally led to each person's departure:

they had all, after once being enamored with the city and excited by its literary scene, over time become largely disenchanted with both. Enough so to leave.

It's a common narrative arc, a story that's been told over and over, but nowhere is it more evocatively or relatably told than in Joan Didion's iconic essay, "Goodbye to All That," included in her 1967 essay collection, *Slouching Toward Bethlehem*.

In telling the story of her own eight years in New York City, from her starry-eyed arrival at twenty to her bleary-eyed departure at twenty-eight, Didion inimitably captures something universal and timeless about coming of age as a young adult in New York, particularly one with literary aspirations. She somehow makes the precise specifics of her own experience recognizable to even those who lived in New York thirty or forty years after she had.

"Goodbye to All That" seems to remain relevant to one generation after another no matter how far in time we get from 1963, the year Didion left Manhattan for Los Angeles. It is considered by many to be the gold standard of personal essays, the one that so many writers count among their favorites, and which many aspire to replicate. (In fact, contributor Meghan Daum says she wrote "My Misspent Youth"—the title essay of her 1999 collection by the same name, reprinted here with a new introduction—as an homage to Didion's essay.)

"Goodbye to All That" came up so many times in conversations with my upstate colleagues that it occurred to me it might be interesting to get a bunch of writers I admire to write their versions of "Goodbye to All That," their stories of loving and leaving New York City, and how the time passed before them in between.

At first, I was going to reach out only to writers who had left New York City permanently, as Didion had, and as I seem to have— "permanent" being a relative term. If I'm not mistaken, Didion lives there now, again, and if I win the lottery, you can bet the first thing I'll do is get an apartment there, as well.

But as I shared my idea with city-based writer friends, many of

them asked to be included, too. They wanted to write their versions of Didion's famous essay—about how they left New York for a time, thinking they were done with it, but then, like Didion, eventually returned. Or about their love-hate relationship with literary life in the city, and how the challenges make them frequently contemplate saying goodbye.

And so you have before you the personal essay collection that resulted from those conversations. Here I've strived to collect stories that vary in viewpoint, and in specific details, although some overlap is inevitable. (It is a wonder that some of the other writers and I didn't run into each other when we were all sneaking into the city on our own, as teens.) I don't want to give anything away before you've had a chance to read the stories. So I won't single anyone out.

I'll just say that it's a great group of stories from great writers. There are some who are very well-known, like Cheryl Strayed, Dani Shapiro, Hope Edelman, and Ann Hood, among others. And some are pretty much debuting, like Valerie Eagle and Eva Tenuto.

With their unique stories, they join me in paying homage to one of the most resonant and memorable personal essays ever published. I count myself lucky to have wrangled them all into this project, and to join them here.

—Sari Botton

YOU ARE HERE

HOPE EDELMAN

ike so many New York stories, this one begins with real estate.

Picture a four-floor brownstone on the north side of Washington Square Park. A golden number "24" nestles inside a stained-glass panel above the front door. Two high school girls sit on the front steps, eating thick slices of Ray's Pizza off paper plates, careful to keep the viscous gold oil from dripping onto their jeans.

It's the fall of 1981, the beginning of their senior year. This morning they took the bus thirty-five miles from suburban Spring Valley into Port Authority, then rode the A train to West 4th Street. It's a Saturday afternoon, early October, low-hanging sun, thin slice of chill in the air. The leaves are just starting to give it up for the year. The dogs across the street at the Washington Square dog park yip and chase each other in endless loops. At the park's central fountain, tight clusters of Rasta musicians rhythmically beat their sticks and drums.

An old woman smothered in layers of wool pilots a grocery cart full of blankets along the sidewalk. She stops in front of the girls and stares at their fat pizza slices. Her hair is dull steel and matted, her eyes a cloudy gray.

"Eat yer vegetables!" she barks.

The girl on the left, the tall one with the sad smile—that's me—is startled into silence. Her mother died three months ago. No one's been paying attention to her vegetable intake since then. She looks at her pizza and wonders, *Do mushrooms count?* But the girl on the right, the delicate one with rippling, russet hair and a splash of freckles across her nose, tips her chin back and laughs. That's Heidi, my best friend, fellow lover of books and words.

The bag lady disappears around the corner. New York City is filled with random, quirky moments like this, chance collisions that just might change your life. This kind of thing never happens in Spring Valley. Spring Valley is strip malls and wine from twist-top bottles, black Trans Ams full of muscled Italian guys shouting, "Yo!" from the backseats. There's nothing sophisticated about Spring Valley. Real life, vibrant, urban, creative life, starts with a 212. So naturally, Manhattan is where the girls want to be.

We'll be writers here one day, they believe. And why not? They're seventeen. Everything is possible. Heidi says she'll come home to her fabulously handsome husband in their Upper East Side penthouse and kick off her Manolo Blahniks. (Yes, they existed in the '80s.) The other girl has no idea what a Manolo Blahnik is, but it sounds exotic and therefore desirable.

"Perfect," she says.

Her future plans lean more toward a leather messenger bag and a fitted tan trench coat, wooden bookshelves lined with hardcovers, and amber whiskey in cut-glass highballs full of ice. It's decidedly more Lion's Head than Elaine's, though under the trench coat might, *might,* be a little black dress. She's still thinking that part through.

But one thing she knows for sure.

"I'm going to live *here*." She slaps the concrete step at her side. This brownstone has history. This brownstone has permanence and solidity. This brownstone has authenticity. It's a place a real writer would live.

"Right *here*," she repeats.

The girls have no way of knowing that in thirty years, both of

them on the West Coast by then, they'll look back on this October day and wonder, *Was anyone ever that young?* And they'll realize with sweet amazement, *Yes. We were.* And they'll marvel that of all the dreams they had that day, of everything that happened later and everything that didn't, my apartment in that brownstone was the one wish that came purely, perfectly true.

To get from Spring Valley into Manhattan took me ten years and three thousand miles. The story isn't that unusual, I suppose: suburban kid so enamored with New York she couldn't commit until she felt ready for its risks and rewards. I could have applied to NYU for college, but I knew I lacked the sophistication, the social finesse, the kind of tough exterior Manhattan would demand of me. When my mother died, my sense of stability disappeared along with her. My father was a kind man, a good man, but he relied on Scotch—lots of it—to soften his grief. I chose a college in the Midwest, the one farthest from home that accepted me. I couldn't chance failing in New York yet, or letting the city fail me. It was the only place I knew I belonged. If I couldn't survive there, I would have no place else to go.

After college, an entry-level editorial salary wouldn't cover New York rents, and moving back to my father's somber house was out of the question. I took a magazine job in Knoxville, Tennessee, where $15,000 a year paid for a one-bedroom apartment. Three years later, I was accepted to a graduate nonfiction writing program in Iowa, and headed back to the Midwest.

It seems romantically itinerant to me now to have pulled up stakes and moved on as each opportunity arose, but really, it was all part of my grand plan to get back to New York one day. New York was where the real writers were. New York was where all the agents and publishers and magazines worth reading were. New York was where the aspiring writers wanted to be in the 1990s. Well, there and Prague.

There were relationships in Chicago and Knoxville and Iowa City, but none that would have led me back home. And no man could compete, in my mind, with the lure of a summer night in Greenwich Village with the air still warm enough at midnight for sundresses and sandals, streetlights casting a silver glow on sidewalk diners sipping from glasses of dark wine at red-checkered tables, full taxis gliding beneath traffic lights flashing candy-colored cycles from green to yellow to red. All those years when I thought I wanted a man to love me, what I really wanted was the romance of being a writer in New York. I ached for it like a woman pining for an unattainable love.

The "writer" part came sooner than I'd imagined. For ten years I'd been searching for a book about girls whose mothers had died, wanting to know if the persistent sadness and emptiness I felt was normal. In my last year of graduate school, I decided to write it myself, and in a remarkable twist of luck and fate, the book proposal went to auction in New York on April Fool's Day 1992. The resulting contract finally gave me the stamp of legitimacy I felt I needed to move back. In my mind, I wouldn't be returning to New York as her servant or minion. I'd be meeting her as an equal.

Ten years, two degrees, seven addresses, and a book contract: that's what it took to get me home.

I arrived on the Upper East Side in the summer of 1992 with a freshly printed master's degree, a desktop IBM computer, and seven cartons of books. My first apartment was on East 64th Street between First Avenue and York, a 610-square-foot, one-bedroom flat—enormous by New York standards—rent stabilized at $760 per month. My aunt, who'd lived there for twenty years, offered it to me when she left New York. My advance check wouldn't have supported me in Manhattan for the eighteen months I needed to fin-

ish the book, and so it was my aunt's generosity, as much as the book contract, that made New York possible for me.

Yorkville was an unlikely neighborhood for me to land in, but my gratitude was immune to geography. Every morning as I walked up First Avenue, I passed a parade of perfectly coiffed ladies in peach and turquoise Chanel suits walking pouffy little dogs named Genevieve and Charlemagne. My short cotton sundress paired with brown motorcycle boots raised eyebrows, but I didn't mind. East Side, West Side, above Houston, below Canal—what did neighborhood matter? The sidewalks I walked on were *New York* sidewalks. I could hardly believe my good fortune.

This was 1992, 1993, a tremendous time to be writing nonfiction in New York. Memoir hunger was rampant. Young writers with personal stories of trauma, loss, or just generic dysfunction were in high demand. It's become cliché to romanticize publishing's glory days of the 1990s, but for many the decade really was a charmed, abundant era. The city was brimming with journalists, essayists, screenwriters, and novelists still able to survive on their craft, boosted by the dot-com boom's new need for paid "content." Manhattan was a living flowchart of creatives. For a while I dated a *Daily News* reporter I met at a book party at the Lion's Head. I joined an urban writer's room in Greenwich Village, where I took coffee breaks with office mates whose names had studded my bookshelves for years. That spring I played second base on the National Writer's Union softball team. We were flat-out the worst team in the Publishing League, but who could blame us? Stick a bunch of young writers in Central Park at dusk with the 57th Street skyline rising majestically from the trees, and they're not thinking, *Line drive to left field.* They're thinking, *Holy crap. I'm really* here.

What I'm trying to convey is the sense of reverence a working writer could feel in the New York of the early 1990s. The pulse of everyday life in Manhattan felt like the very heartbeat of Western civilization. I never took living there for granted, not for a single day.

And then.

One afternoon in early 1994, with my book finished and in production, I returned home to find an eviction notice taped to my front door. *We've been alerted, unauthorized tenant*—that was its gist. Building management gave me one week to leave. Having already paid that month's rent, I bargained it up to three. Real estate brokers were the only way to find decent apartments in Manhattan. They charged horrendous finder's fees, but then you were done with them. The first broker I called had a one-bedroom available on 14th Street, the northern border of Greenwich Village. We agreed to meet that evening.

When I arrived at his office, a fax was coming through. The broker read it while I waited. I watched his face register mild surprise.

"You mind if we stop here first?" he asked. "It's out of your price range, but it's a brownstone right on Washington Square. They don't come up often. Actually, I've never been in one before."

A brownstone? Washington Square?

"Just out of curiosity," I said, "what's the address?"

He checked the fax. "Number 24."

In his bulky blue parka and tweed cap, the realtor looked more like a high school social studies teacher than a Manhattan broker. If I were to call back the next day to discover he didn't exist, that he'd been an angel come to earth for just one night, I'd believe it.

"How much out of my price range?" I said.

The apartment at 24 Washington Square North was the back half of the uppermost floor, atop three flights of elegantly carved stairs. Its main room featured two skylights and a kitchen against a wall; the compact bedroom looked out on the Empire State Building. At less than 500 square feet, the space was "cozy" in realtor-speak, and in that peculiar New York fashion, rooms that had once housed lesser servants were now an enviable place to live.

In the three months between move-in and book release day, I started creating my first permanent home. The brownstone's original details, circa 1830s, called out for objects of that era. At an outdoor antique booth near Astor Place, I found an inexpensive walnut hall table. I bought half-price walnut picture frames on Madison Avenue and filled them with photos of my ancestors, hardy immigrants from Czechoslovakia and the Ukraine. On frigid February nights, as the radiators clanged and pumped out excess heat, I sat warm and content in my snug cocoon, surrounded by images of the great-grandparents and third cousins who'd helped populate Manhattan's Lower East Side.

This was early 1994. Bill Clinton was in the White House, Rudy Giuliani newly settled in Gracie Mansion on a pledge to clean up New York. A 7.0 earthquake rattled my sister's house in Los Angeles, but in New York I was safe and secure. My days began with a mug of freshly brewed coffee and *The New York Times*. When I came home at night after coffee at Café Reggio or a foreign film at the Angelika Theater, I'd see the Empire State Building glowing in whatever colors corresponded with that month's holiday, like a joyous, communal beacon.

And then.

My book was released in early May, just before Mother's Day. It launched with a segment on the *Today* show and a *New York Times* review. Which should have been my tipoff.

If I'd known more about publishing, I might have known that a *Today* segment meant to unlist my home phone number in advance. I would have known that a seventeen-city book tour, even in the age of seventeen-city book tours, meant the publisher expected a significant Return On Investment. I might have known that when the marketing director said, "Fasten your seatbelt," she did not mean it in jest.

I thought I'd sell a few thousand copies, including a bulk order from my grandma. Instead, I arrived at bookstores in Charlotte, North Carolina, and Salt Lake City to find hundreds of women standing in the aisles. I'd wonder which writer I'd just missed seeing. Then I started getting a clue.

It was as if an entire culture had woken up to realize early mother loss had never been discussed before and had to be discussed, starting now. The book's publicist fielded more media requests than the calendar could hold. "Make them fit," she said. I tried. I did a *People* magazine shoot outdoors in Central Park in 104-degree heat. When Nicole Brown Simpson died in June, leaving two children behind, I spoke to a magazine reporter from a pay phone at the tow pound on Pier 76 while trying to retrieve my stolen car. The rest of the year went much like that, and the next.

New York was where book publishing and media came together, the hub of the publicity wheel. Editors, producers, news outlets, television networks, national magazines, and speakers' bureaus all radiated from its critical mass. Media-friendly, articulate young women with compelling stories that could move books were golden. (Think Elizabeth Wurtzel. Think Lucy Grealy.) I was grateful for the attention. God, I was grateful. What writer wouldn't be? And because I was so grateful I said yes to everything, all of it. Invitations for fundraisers, keynotes at conferences, appearances at hospices and universities and bookstores to tell my story of mother loss and recovery again and again. As the book climbed *The New York Times* bestseller list, I basked in the spotlight of attention, with no sense of what it might cost me later.

Because this kind of attention as a memoirist almost always comes at a cost. Telling one's story so frequently and on demand turns the story into a commodity, potentially a very lucrative one. The more handsomely one is compensated for being a screw-up who's redeemed, or just for being a screw-up, the greater the motivation to (1) remain screwed up, and (2) talk about it to the point of self-obsession. I knew I was in deep trouble about eight months in, at dinner with a group of friends, when I found myself feeling inept and bored when the conversation turned to a subject other than me.

My story became its own organism, separate from me. I added

parts to jazz it up, took out anecdotes that fell flat in crowds. I started losing track of what had been embellished and what was actually true. It stopped seeming to matter. Performance mattered. Reviews mattered. Sales figures mattered most of all. After two years, I found myself exhausted in a way I had never known possible, taking pills to combat anxiety attacks that otherwise woke me in a raging panic nearly every night. New York had become a hard place to live—how had I never noticed this before? It was beastly hot in the summers, rude and crowded and horrifically expensive year-round. Getting five bags of groceries home from Balducci's market three blocks away required a Herculean effort. My rent rose to $1,540 a month, leaving me with no wiggle room at all. Somehow, while I was off doing media, New York had become the quintessential celebrity lover: perfect from a distance, yet maddeningly human up close.

Sometimes I'd think of that seventeen-year-old on the brownstone steps who stated "Right here!" with such clarity and conviction. I'd once thought she lacked a strong sense of self. Only now could I see she'd known exactly who she was and what she wanted. She'd had a belief in herself I now envied. She'd thought she'd be happy only if given enough opportunities to say yes. Only now did I realize that what I really needed was the strength and the discrimination to know how to say no.

"It's easy to see the beginnings of things and harder to see the ends." That's Joan Didion's well-worn saying, but it's never rung true for me. The first and last scenes of my narratives are always clear to me. The middles are the fuzzy parts. I can tell you in excruciating detail how New York began for me on the steps of a brownstone on Washington Square in 1981, and how it came to an end fifteen years later at a kitchen table on that brownstone's top floor, as I sat alone eating cold takeout noodles for dinner,

wondering, *What happened?* But none of this explains how a high school girl who once found exquisite beauty in a city's summer night became a thirty-two-year-old woman who thought palm trees and the Pacific Ocean might be a better plan.

I left New York in the spring of 1997, when a bicoastal relationship took a sharp turn toward marriage. I told the man I was ready to leave New York, which was not untrue. We bought a house high in a canyon on two acres of land. I craved the quiet it offered. I would garden. I would hike. I would, I don't know, bake bread or something. Whatever people who lived in canyons did.

What I really needed, I soon learned, was to leave New York for six months and return refreshed and renewed, but by then it was too late. But let's get back to the brownstone.

When I gave up the brownstone apartment, I wept. For two and a half years, it had been more than my home: it had been a fantasy come to life. Taking my family photos off the wall felt like a betrayal of my younger self, subjecting her to a painful but necessary breakup as she sat glaring at me in grief and incomprehension. At some point I asked a friend to help me pack. I couldn't face the guilt alone.

On my last day in New York, I sat on the brownstone's front steps with a pen and paper for an hour to catalogue everything that passed by. I wanted to capture a lasting, written snapshot of what had once felt like the center of the world and in some ways still did. I counted thirty-four taxis, ninety-four pedestrians, eighteen dogs, one scarlet macaw, two policemen, seven Hare Krishnas, one Chabad Mitzvah Mobile trumpeting Hebrew songs, and a woman I'm pretty sure was Diana Ross. Then I read through the list and said a silent goodbye.

I left certain I'd cycle back one day: it didn't seem possible for me to ever break free of New York's gravitational pull. But married life developed its own momentum. In Los Angeles we began having children and my husband started a company and I took a teaching job, and, well, there you have it. It's been fifteen years.

California has taught me this: you can take the girl out of New York, but all that accomplishes is taking the girl out of New York.

I never planted a garden. And don't get me started about baking bread. My friends call me the Woody Allen of Topanga Canyon. I'm a born apartment dweller, most comfortable in small, crowded rooms. I still have a recurring dream about returning to the brownstone apartment and staring through the keyhole, devastated to see someone else's furniture inside. I spend the rest of the dream searching for the key.

I know the truth: I'm not going back anytime soon. My daughters are children of freeways and wildfires and coyotes, not of subways and summer rain and gray winter slush. "New York" to them is honking and crowds and relatives they see once a year. But it's something entirely different to me.

To me, "New York" will always be those three months in the brownstone apartment between move-in day and book release, when it was possible for a motherless seventeen-year-old girl to believe she'd found a secret portal to her future. That wondrous, magical New York was the one I fell in love with, the one that I still pine for. It's the one that got away.

STRANGE LANDS

ROXANE GAY

Recently, after years of avoiding New York City—or, more accurately, not being able to afford it—I traveled there from the small middle-of-nowhere Midwestern town where I teach writing. I was going to give a few readings, meet my new agent, and hang out with friends. I was terrified. I knew I wouldn't be chic enough or thin enough. In the car on the way to the hotel, we were stuck in traffic. Radios blared and exhaust filled the air. Certain things about the city never change. My driver was on the phone having a heated conversation in a language I couldn't recognize. He was clearly on the losing end of the argument. I called my mother to tell her I had arrived safely.

In the 1970s, she and my father came from Haiti to New York separately, my father by way of Montreal. They met at a wedding in New York. They fell in love in New York. They married in New York. I was even baptized in New York, though I've never lived in the city. Back in the day, my parents lived in the Bronx, when the borough still bore the evidence of how it had been ravaged by fire. I remember this detail because they remember this detail, quite vividly. They had little nice to say about the borough, but when they first came here, they were overwhelmed—new place, new language, so much cold and concrete.

My mom asked me how things were going and I said, "Well, the traffic is interesting." She laughed. She said, "Your father can no longer tolerate that city for long periods of time. He doesn't understand why people would live on top of each other like that."

For a moment, I felt this pang of . . . envy, or maybe wistfulness, because so many of the important moments in their lives happened in New York, because some part of me very much understood why people would live like that.

Throughout my childhood, even though we sometimes visited family in New York, the city seemed more like an idea than a real place—an idea I very much wanted to be a part of—bright lights, big city.

Because of my father's job, we moved often and always lived in suburbs or rural places that bore little resemblance to the sights and sounds of the city. We were in Nebraska or in the suburbs of Chicago or on the outskirts of Denver. We were in the land of sprawling malls and new construction and chain restaurants that advertised with catchy slogans. There was more: we were always the only people who looked like us in our neighborhoods, at school. Not only were we of a different race, but we were of an entirely different culture—Haitians in the middle of America, strangers in a strange world.

My mother has a sprawling family, nine brothers and sisters. My father has four brothers and sisters. When their families immigrated to the United States, most of them settled in New York City, in close proximity to one another. They were determined not to be strangers in a strange land, alone. We'd fly to the city on holidays and cram into my maternal grandmother's apartment, so many of us, my grandmother at the stove cooking Haitian food, making fried plantains in a manner no one else can replicate (the secret is to soak them in salt water before frying), and clucking over her children and grandchildren with great fondness.

Her couches, covered in plastic, the air in her apartment thick with life, us kids always being shushed so we wouldn't disturb the neighbors as if it were possible not to disturb the neighbors when there were twenty or thirty people in a small apartment. New York was my cousins, who all seemed so sophisticated, who knew the latest slang and wore the latest fashions—Girbaud jeans and leather high-tops and baseball caps. They had sharp haircuts and talked fast, so fast, my brothers and I could barely hold on to anything they said.

New York, then, was Flushing, Queens. It was the 7 train when graffiti flourished—spray-painted bubble words and images stretching from one end of a subway car to another. New York was the Busy Bee market, which was little more than a chaotic swap meet—bright, loud people with thick New York accents selling knockoff bags and shoes, hideous costume jewelry, off-brand toys, cheap electronics—things I had absolutely no use for but considered treasures and embraced, arms wide open. New York was eating real Szechuan food for the first time and understanding that Chinese food prepared anywhere but in New York was not really Chinese food. New York was Times Square, on the cusp of being cleaned up by an ambitious mayor, still dirty enough to be terribly interesting to a young girl.

Men on corners thrusting squares of glossy paper into my hands, bright shining lights, throngs of people as far as the eye could see. Filthy sidewalks and overflowing trash cans, homeless people asking for money and breaking my tender heart. Broadway, the marquees, the names of amazing performers in shining lights, *The Phantom of the Opera,* a boat floating across a stage filled with illuminated candles, voices soaring through the theater and right into me because tragic, somewhat unrequited love is the best kind of love. There was *Starlight Express* and actors roller-skating onstage.

More than anything, New York was seeing people, so many different people, so many beautiful shades of brown, so many different voices, a place where my brothers and I could actually see reflections of ourselves in others, where we didn't feel so strange in the

strange land. New York was everything, and the time we spent in the city was never enough.

In high school, I became determined to attend college there. It was something of an obsession. If I went to school in New York, surely all my problems would be solved. I would learn how to be chic and glamorous. I would learn how to walk fast and wear all black without looking like I was attending a funeral. In adolescence, I was becoming a different kind of stranger in a strange land. I was a theater geek and troubled and angry and hell-bent on forgetting the worst parts of myself. In New York, I told myself, I would no longer be the only freak in the room because the city was full of freaks.

I applied to six or so universities, and one of them was New York University, NYU, the only three letters that existed for me for a time. I was going to go to NYU and major in technical theater and pre-med. It made no sense, but that was the plan. When I was accepted to NYU, with a merit scholarship no less, I was thrilled. My perfect future was within my grasp. Soon I was going to be in the city. I was going to be part of it all. I was going to find my people.

Alas. My parents had other plans for me. They worried that in the city, I would be distracted from my studies, and the point of college, in their minds, was to study. They were worried about safety. They were just plain worried. I remained in a very deep state of denial even after they made me agree to attend a different university, a fancy one even, that I was damn lucky to attend—a state of denial so deep I still haven't recovered from their denying me the choice to attend college in the city. I feel a pang of . . . something, whenever I see an NYU T-shirt or read about the school. I wonder what would have been, though I am fully aware that nothing in my life would be measurably better. The school is my mythical beast, my unicorn. The city is the *one that got away.*

In college, New York was just a couple of hours away by train, Metro North, New Haven to Penn Station. New York was spending the weekend at my roommate's family's apartment and eating bagels from H&H and gourmet delights from Zabar's and reading *The*

New York Times (in New York!) and men shouting "DIANETICS" and thrusting the books of L. Ron Hubbard into my hands and a Haitian woman mistaking me for a well-known voodoo priestess on a sidewalk while my American friend looked on, bewildered, and Limelight and dancing all night and hungover breakfast at the Time Café and walking through Greenwich Village wide-eyed and Broadway, the performers so glamorous, glittering from the stage, their voices clear and bold, and me, always watching, always wanting desperately to be part of it all, always feeling like "it all" was still just beyond my grasp, wanting so desperately to feel a little less strange.

I wrote my first story when I was four, on a napkin, and eventually advanced to using paper like a normal person, and as my writing ambitions grew so did my fantasies of living in the city, in a lovely apartment with brick walls, lined with books. I'd spend my days in cafés and coffee shops, with a well-worn notebook and my laptop and the latest important book. I would attend readings and rub elbows with the writers I admired most. I'd have cocktails with the editor of *The New Yorker,* and he would be so besotted, he'd ask to see some of my work and I would finally catch my big break. Then I was an adult, or so I was told. I was a writer and finally reached the point where other people knew I was a writer. I was finally more comfortable in my own skin, had finally learned how to feel less strange in a strange land. I had learned the difference between being a writer, which can happen anywhere, and performing the role of Writer, which in my very specific and detailed fantasies could only happen in New York.

New York City is the center of the writing world, or so we're told. New York is where all the action happens because the city is where the most important publishers and agents and writers are. New York is where the fancy book parties happen and where the literati rub elbows and everyone knows (or pretends to know) everything about everyone else's writing career. At some point, New York stopped being the city of my dreams because it stopped being merely an idea I longed to be a part of. New York was very real and very complicated. New York had become an intimidating giant of a place, but still I worried. If I wasn't there as a writer, was I a writer anywhere?

During my most recent visit, I stayed at a hipster hotel, the Ace, because it was the most affordable, which is to say it was not very affordable at all. There appeared to be an unspoken requirement for all staff to look impeccable in expensive jeans and adorn their bodies in tattoos. The lobby was like a nightclub at all hours of the day, loud music, expensive but delicious drinks, a place to see and be seen, whether you wanted to or not.

Somewhere in New York was my agent's very chic office. It looked like a set for an agent's office on a television show or in a movie. The chairs were modern and fancy and it seemed complicated to even sit. I felt very out of place, though I had a good reason to be there. My agent was as chic as her office. I couldn't stop staring because she is very pretty, magazine pretty, and I hadn't realized. I felt that way almost every moment of every day in New York, the writer from the middle of nowhere, surrounded by glamorous and well-dressed people with interesting eyewear.

My agent and I talked for more than an hour, as if we were old friends. I left feeling I was a Writer For Real. I felt fancy. And then, I was walking around trying to find a certain street and it started raining, and I was lost and miserable and confused and no cabs would stop for me. The fancy feeling quickly wore off.

That's what New York was becoming now that I could choose to be in the city or not. There were teaching jobs and other opportunities in New York. I had, just before the visit, turned down an editorial position at a magazine because I couldn't fathom living in the city on the offered salary. In my thirties, I've found that I am not as interested in struggling or suffering as I once was, at least not from one day to the next. During that recent trip, I realized I need at least one part of my life to be easy. I may hate living in the middle of nowhere, but there's a lot of wide open space for that hate to thrive in. For every lovely moment with lovely people in New York, there was a deeply humbling moment—getting lost, trying to hail a cab in the rain, dealing with the constant crush of people, feeling desperately out of place among so many sophisticated, beautiful people. These moments revealed just how big and overwhelming the city was. They showed me how New York was always more than an idea, even if I wasn't able to see that. New York was a strange land, and I was still a stranger and would always be one. Overall, that visit was fun. The city was good to me and I looked forward to returning and soon. But. There was nothing for me to say goodbye to in New York because I never truly said hello. I became a writer without all the glamorous or anti-glamorous trappings of New York life I thought I needed.

When my plane took off and I knew I was returning to the middle of nowhere, a different kind of strange land, I realized with startling clarity that my small town in Illinois felt less strange than the city. I was relieved. I was going home.

HOME

MELISSA FEBOS

I.

My first New York apartment was a 9-by-5-foot room on 20th Street between Seventh and Eighth Avenues. It was an all-female boarding house, or SRO (single room occupancy) as they were called before my time. The eight women on my floor all lived in cell-like rooms and shared the two tiny bathrooms in the hallway, one with nothing but a toilet, the other with a moldy shower.

My room was the smallest on the floor: just big enough for a twin bed, a mini-fridge, a small sink, and a few hundred books I'd lugged from Boston. I kept my clothes in garbage bags under the bed. If I'd gained ten pounds, I wouldn't have been able to walk the narrow aisle that ran the length of the room. Luckily, that never happened; as a depressed nineteen-year-old heroin addict, food was not my first priority.

During the day, I attended college. After classes, I'd loiter around Tompkins Square Park until I found a junkie I could trust enough to buy for me, since I was too new to the city to have my own dealer. In the evenings I got high and wept into the phone to my best friend Ariel from back home, who hadn't come with me.

I was miserable. And toward the end of my six months in that place, borderline suicidal. Still, I never thought of leaving. New York was the only place I had ever wanted to live. I'd finally made it here, and I wasn't leaving except on a stretcher or in a straitjacket. Thankfully, those possibilities receded with each year I stayed.

Twelve years later, I couldn't believe I was in perfect health, packing those same books, getting ready to say goodbye to the place I'd loved longer than anything else in my life.

When we were kids, Ariel and I would lie in the grass of her backyard in worn T-shirts, the cool earth pressed against our backs. We spent hours fantasizing about the future—a glittering mirage that was always changing but always better than the familiar world of rural Massachusetts. I imagined New York then as a blur of lights and sound. The only thing in perfect focus was the two of us together, grown tall and invincible.

In the late summer of 1987, I took my first trip to New York alone to visit my father's mother. Technically, my abuela lived in New Jersey, where my father grew up, but she was a New Yorker to the bone—all 4 foot 10 of her. In 1924, her parents had moved from Puerto Rico to Harlem, where she was born and raised. She met me at Penn Station, and as soon as we reached the sidewalk, I saw that she was different here; even her walk had changed, become faster, more confident.

On that first afternoon, we emerged into a rippling current of bodies. I froze, struck dumb by the summer heat, the smells of garbage, cigarette smoke, and roasting nuts. I looked up at the sliver of sky and ahead at the sea of faces, and experienced the only kind of love at first sight that I believe in. Abuela tugged me to the curb, and showed me how to tuck my money in my shoe.

I n the fall of 2011, when I started applying for jobs outside New York, the idea was so abstract as to be unbelievable. Sure, I might leave the city someday, the same way I might become an astronaut or a lion tamer. But in the bedrock of my consciousness, formed back on that Massachusetts lawn, I'd settled on one future: I would live here, and I would be a writer.

And yet, New York City had never been this expensive before, and writing had never paid so badly. I had imagined my dreams coming true, but not what happened after that.

I first realized at twenty that an artist in New York needs two careers to stay afloat. By the time I was twenty-five, I'd exhausted the professions that only a brave and stupid twenty-year-old can sustain. Then I started teaching. To my great delight and relief, I found I loved it. All through graduate school and the publication of my first book, I watched my students grow more alive in telling their own stories. I kept pinching myself. How lucky, to get paid to talk about the thing I love most in the world! For years I didn't care about how little I was getting paid.

Until I started trying to write another book, and realized it was going to be pretty hard to get anything done while shuttling among four different campuses, teaching six classes a semester, and sleeping five hours a night. So, in February 2011, in those melancholy doldrums of late winter, when it seems like nothing will ever change—for better or for worse—I rode a train into the deep middle of the state, and spent sixteen hours in interviews for a job I wasn't sure I wanted.

It didn't seem like it had anything to do with me—the scenery rushing past the train, the unfamiliar college town—so it didn't quite seem real. The city, on the other hand, had everything to do with me. By 2005, every neighborhood in Manhattan and many in Brooklyn, too, had been engraved with one personal memory or another. I couldn't use the bathroom in a certain diner on Sixth Avenue after having gotten violently sick there once. I couldn't eat at a favorite vegan restaurant without reliving a Valentine's Day breakup fight. For years I couldn't really handle Herald Square because the neighborhood made me remember my time working as a dominatrix there. The city was haunted in a way I hated and cherished at the same time.

But it had changed, too. The city I lived in was not the same one to which I'd come. No one smoked in bars anymore. Favorite cafés had been shuttered, and new condos had sprung up in the unlikeliest neighborhoods.

My abuela—who went alone to a Julio Iglesias concert at Madison Square Garden when she was seventy and once told me, "This is my city. I'll never be too old for it"—became too ill with cancer to leave her New Jersey home and visit the city. She left this planet soon after.

Not long before that, Ariel died of an overdose. Our childhood fantasies died with her.

A few days after the interview upstate, the college called to offer me the job. My girlfriend and I drove up to look at places to live.

Then spring arrived. Overnight, it seemed, the trees burst into blossom, and I could smell that dirty, sweet perfume of the city stretching awake. On the first afternoon warm enough for bare arms, I was walking down East 10th Street. I'd just run into a friend I hadn't seen in years and was on my way to meet another. The stack of papers to grade in my bag was heavy, but made lighter by the sunshine.

I reached the corner of Avenue A, and in front of me sprawled Tompkins Square Park. Its trees hung heavy with new growth, pollen sifting dreamily over the benches and grass, the dogs and playing children. Buzzing with laughter and motion and birdsong, it seemed more alive than anything I'd ever seen. Smelling the spring that day, and in it my own unearthed history, I wanted to lift my face to the sky and howl.

Leaving things you love is easier when you're younger. You make stupid decisions about the wrong people. You slam the apart-

ment door, throw your lover's clothes out the window onto the side-walk. Leaving gets harder as you age. You don't leave out of anger or from coming to your senses, but because your love is not as strong as your reasons for going.

II.

When we pulled up behind the moving truck in front of our new home, my girlfriend and I looked at each other and grinned. I jumped out of the car and led our seventy-pound pit bull out of his nest in the backseat. For a moment, Red stood dazed in the brilliant light, ears lopsided, watching a bumblebee hover over the overgrown lawn.

Next door, our neighbor weeded her garden.

"Hi there!" I called out.

"Hi!" she called back, pulling off her gardening gloves. "I'm Patti."

Patti introduced herself as a college professor and area native. I mentioned my new position and that we'd arrived from Brooklyn. I didn't tell her that before joining the professorial ranks, I'd been a professional dominatrix and drug addict, or that I'd recently published a memoir about my days of spanking and shooting heroin. I wasn't in the habit of hiding my recent success, but it just seemed impolite to mention.

But I had experience with hiding. In my early twenties, I had juggled the life of a junkie dominatrix with that of a successful college student. It almost killed me, so good was I at keeping that secret, at maintaining my manners and appearance. For my first three years of teaching college, I hid all my tattoos. I had been dating my then-boyfriend for three years, but in the months leading up to my book's publication, I never even told his parents what it was about. Concealing parts of me that might upset other people was a way of life.

But the year before I moved upstate marked an end to all that. The book came out, exposing me completely. I broke up with my boyfriend. I stopped wearing long sleeves to class in the middle of summer. And I fell in love with someone who gently reminded me that I had nothing to hide. It was the most terrifying and liberating year of my life. After five minutes in the country, however, I remembered how much easier it is being the person you think other people want you to be.

That night, I lay in bed listening to the crickets outside the open window. No sirens, no yelling, no car alarms, no footsteps on the floor above. The breeze drifting in the open window was sweet, but it took me a long time to fall asleep.

My new dean had described the area around the college as a "red county in a blue state," but it hadn't sunk in until we were driving around looking for a home. In some of these towns, I didn't want to get out of the car to pump gas. The people looked angry, and I spotted a Confederate flag flapping from one porch. It was difficult not to judge people based on superficialities, even as I was afraid of being judged myself.

Driving through Clinton, we knew it was the obvious choice. Clinton is "quaint." It has bed-and-breakfasts, a health food store, a population of under two thousand, and the highest median income of the surrounding towns. It is the Park Slope of its county, minus any people of color and minus the (visible) lesbians. Until us.

We were pleased to find almond milk in the supermarket, but I started to feel the subtle double takes people made in the produce aisle. I wasn't embarrassed, but something else. Something I hadn't felt in a long time. The instinctive urge to hide myself, streaked with a defiant preening—*let them stare.*

On the way home, Sini and I saw a middle-aged man and woman strolling across the village green. "Can we hold hands here?" she asked.

"I *think* it's safe," I said hopefully.

At Home Depot, where I went, alone, to get materials for a back-yard fence for Red, people still stared, but only because I was one of few women in sight, and certainly the only one cruising post-drivers in three-inch wedges and mascara. I made a mental note to ditch my city heels, to avoid looking like an off-duty stripper.

Later that week, our dryer was leaking gas, so I called a local plumber, which turned out to be two men with the same name.

"We tried replacing the tubes," I said, leading them to the basement door, "but it's still not working." They were friendly, but I found myself faintly hoping Sini wouldn't emerge from her office. Being stared at in the supermarket was one thing, but having to witness that moment of recognition in our own house made me feel too exposed, too vulnerable. That snarl of contradictory feelings emerged again, protective and defiant at the same time. I wanted to spare Sini any discomfort, any regret in moving here for me, but I knew the answer was not to let people assume that the "we" I referred to included a husband somewhere out of sight.

In mid-June, I drove Sini to the city to work for a few weeks. As I crossed the George Washington Bridge, and sped down the FDR Drive, I felt strangely heartbreaky. Seeing the East River beside us, so gorgeous and contaminated, was like bumping into an ex you're still in love with. The city wasn't mine anymore, and it hurt to see it looking so beautiful, and so familiar. Driving down Second Avenue, we saw the usuals: skater kids and college students, queens and models and junkies. My heart hurt more and more. The landmarks of my most troubled memories now tugged at my heart and filled it with longing. I even missed my ghosts.

To distract myself from my growing anxiety, I began obsessing over the fence. I pulled over on country roads to inspect strangers' pickets, their welded wire and split-rails. I Googled and watched

YouTube videos. I convinced my handy younger brother to drive out from Amherst to help me build it.

A few days before he arrived, I drove into town. Strolling around, reusable shopping bag dangling from my arm, I felt such a powerful surge of loneliness that it almost knocked me over. I fled back to my car and drove up and down the rolling hills outside town, smelling the lush twilit perfume of summer, the smell of my childhood. All of it: the beauty, the chirrup of crickets, even the homesickness was reminiscent of some past self. Change does that. The uncertainty of moving forward jostles the sleeping lions of childhood fears: that I am alone, that I am not seen or seen wrongly. That I have made some terrible mistake. That the loneliness will last forever. "I want to go home," I whispered, not sure what that meant.

The next day, I invited our neighbor Patti over for dinner. At first it was awkward, as I'd feared. But Patti was funny and kind, and we bonded over our mutual love of Middle Eastern food and dictionaries.

"I make a pretty mean baba ghanoush," she offered. "I'll save you some next time."

As I walked her out, she paused by the refrigerator.

"Is this the cover of your book?" she asked. Indeed it was, an early copy of the paperback cover, magnetized to the fridge.

"Um, yeah," I said. I took a deep breath. "Why don't I give you a copy?"

I regretted it almost immediately, and worried about it all the next day as my brother and I struggled and failed to build a fence. Had I ruined the only alliance I had in town?

That night I sat alone in my home office and watched the live New York Senate hearing on gay marriage. As it passed 33 to 29, a cheer rose up in the hushed Senate chamber, but our neighborhood was dark and silent. I imagined the celebration on the city streets. I picked up the phone.

"The gay marriage bill just passed," I told Sini, wiping my nose with my sweatshirt sleeve.

"That's amazing!" she said. "Why do you sound so upset?"

"What if we did the wrong thing?" I asked, and felt something crack in me. I'd wanted to say that for so long. "I'm so afraid I dragged us up here, so far away—" I deteriorated into sobs.

"You're just scared," she said. "Change is scary, but it doesn't mean it's wrong."

T he next day, as my brother and I came back from our last trip to the hardware store, Patti came running across her lawn, holding a Tupperware container. I pulled over and rolled down the window.

"Baba ghanoush!" she said. "I made it yesterday."

"Thank you so much," I said, accepting the Tupperware.

"I read your book," she said.

"You did?" I fought to maintain eye contact.

"I loved it," she said. "Will you stop by and sign it for me later?"

All I could do was nod.

M y brother finished the fence that afternoon. Excited, I led Red out the back door, and unclipped his leash.

"You're free!" I said, waiting for him to race around, commencing his freedom. Instead, he just lumbered to a sunny patch of grass a few yards away, and rolled onto his side, happily panting. I had to laugh. Sometimes, it's enough just to know that we're safe. We don't necessarily have to do anything differently or be anyone but the person we've always been.

People who don't love the city talk about the freedom of the country and its wide open spaces; they marvel at how one could live in so cramped and crowded a space. But I always felt free in

Brooklyn. I found safety in its enclosures. The city let me relax into being myself. Being who I am in New York didn't feel like an action I took—it just felt like living.

III.

When the pollen-soaked weeks of summer dwindled, however, so did my certainty that we had made the right decision. First, Sini got sick. Or rather, sicker. She'd been ill before we left the city, but things worsened that fall. With no diagnosis and a debilitating list of over sixty-five symptoms, a current of panic rushed beneath our daily life together, which grew increasingly unmanageable. Her diagnosis of late-stage Lyme disease came with some relief, until we realized that insurance would only cover a tiny portion of the extravagantly priced treatments.

In the cooling months of the fall semester, we settled into a routine. Red paced in the yard, Sini trembled on the couch, and I wept in the parking lot before class, panic and loneliness tearing through me in ragged gasps as I looked out at the balding lawn of the college. "I want to go home," I whispered to myself, mantra-like. "I want to go home."

We didn't fight. Instead, I fought myself, and took comfort in knowing that I would never leave her in such a condition. There were tendernesses—many nights curled in our upstate-sized bed, the dog between us as we stroked his velvet ears and fantasized about the future. But I flinched under her hands and flung myself to the far edge of that great bed in sleep.

She needed me, and that terrified me. I needed help, too, but could not accept it. If I gave in to my own choking fear and loneliness, I feared it might crush me, as our life seemed to be crushing our love. I could not afford to fall apart.

After classes and interminable faculty meetings, I jogged for hours through the farmland, then sifted through bills and claim forms. On better weeks, Sini commuted back to the city to work. The

house seemed vast without her, myself a swirling mote, carried by twin winds of relief at her absence and bitter loneliness.

A month later, I was on anti-depressants. Did it help? I couldn't tell. My hands were drier, and I suddenly became a person who napped. But I still didn't want to be touched. I still felt a caving pit in my chest when I thought about Sini's health, about New York, and the possibility of going on as we were for an indeterminate future. Though my eyes stayed dry, I still found myself whispering under my breath when alone, "I want to go home."

When, after a grueling series of treatments and astronomical costs, Sini's health took a turn for the better at the end of the spring semester, I tendered my resignation, and we began looking for an apartment back in Brooklyn.

The new apartment was over our budget, and Sini balked at the size, but I insisted, preferring location over square footage, desperately needing to be close by the people I had missed upstate, to feel close to the pulse of my old life.

On moving day, Sini drove the truck while I led in the car full of plants and medical supplies, my new prescription rattling in my purse. For a few moments, crossing the Manhattan Bridge, the river preening below in the dazzling spring sunlight, I felt free again. It felt like coming home.

But before we'd finished unloading boxes, my purse was stolen out of the car. My wallet and medication were gone. My dismay felt tinged with some deeper hysteria. Throat dry and palms damp, I called the bank and canceled my credit cards, the cave in my chest yawning hungrily.

It was a Friday, and my doctor's office was closed. For the next two days, I waited for some sign of breakage, for a panic greater than that I already felt to seep into my hands and heart. Nothing. Just the same old ache in my chest, the same aversion to my beloved's touch. I waited a week, then two, and saw no difference in my mood. Again, relief and disappointment. Whatever my condition, it would not be cured with a pill. Perhaps it could still be cured by coming home.

For the next month, our apartment remained crammed with boxes and the walls bare. Something in me resisted opening those boxes, as if the muted despair of our upstate life might rise in fumes, poisoning our new home. I raced around the city with work and social engagements, breathing in my city, but then went numb when I arrived home.

"What is going on with you?" she finally demanded one afternoon, and I could barely meet her gaze.

"Nothing," I said.

"What the hell are you feeling inside, Melissa?"

I didn't know what I felt inside, only that I couldn't stop moving, couldn't stop trying to outrun the caving feeling inside me.

The next day, a cop pulled me over on Houston Street. When the officer walked away with my license and registration, I stared at the dirty windshield, the ceaseless flow of traffic heading toward the Manhattan Bridge, and burst into tears. Something opened in me, and from that cave came a scorching flood of tears. Once I started, I couldn't stop. My body rocking with sobs, I leaned my forehead on the steering wheel and yielded to the surging waves of grief. I didn't even raise my head when the police officer returned, and he flung the ticket through my open window and fled. Hands gripping my thighs, the steering wheel slick with tears, I wailed for the lost hope that we would emerge from our troubles closer and stronger. I sobbed for my beloved, who had had to suffer alone in so many ways, and I wept for myself, for all the ways I wanted to be more than I was.

There was more between that day and the day Sini moved out of our home. I wish I could say that I recognized the moment when it was over, when I had reached the limit of my love, and that I faced it with some dignity. But I didn't. I could not face the decision to leave while we still loved each other. And we did. But sometimes, love needs more than love to survive. Were we still *in* love? I don't know. I know that I had stepped far enough outside our love that, a few weeks after I got that ticket, I touched someone else's mouth with mine. I know that the day she moved out, when I walked back into the empty apartment and surveyed the pile of dusty wires where her desk had been, the lone fork and mug she'd left me, my chest filled with a terrible sadness, and with relief.

This morning, I woke feeling lighter. Red lazed in a patch of sunlight near my desk chair as I sipped my coffee and wrote a little. I've got a new desk, new plants, and a few knives and spoons to accompany my fork. In the kitchen, light streams in, and through the cracked window I can smell autumn coming. There is more space in here, now, and I am beginning to fill it with words, with forgiveness, with a future that's only beginning to sharpen into focus.

Though my heart is in pieces, I have not found myself whispering for home. Because home is here. Not only New York, but this heart that I'm learning to trust, however much it hurts. In these emptier days, I have come to know that my sadness is not a problem to be solved. It is simply my humanity. Sometimes pain is the call of a wound that needs tending, and sometimes it is the sting of its healing. And sometimes you have to break your own heart to be true, and you have to go home to do it.

TRANSPORT

EMILY CARTER ROIPHE

I left New York, my twenties, and the 1980s behind at the same time. I was perfectly glad to do so since I had never wanted to be provincial, living my whole life in the same place I was born. New York City was the only thing I had ever felt excitement or affection for, but I refused to believe that the world ended at the Hudson River to the west and the Brooklyn Queens Expressway to the east. The famous Saul Steinberg cartoon in which the world did just that was only funny because it was accurate. In my eyes, this view was not much different from the village idiot's in *Mayberry RFD* who, when asked what lay to the east, replied, "Old Man Johnson's woods, then Kelly's Gas and Go, then . . . th'Atlantic Ocean." I knew that New York, specifically the New York of my family, was in many ways a fine and interesting place, but it was not the only place. Added to this was the fact that in New York there was no place for me, and to continue to throw the jagged shape of myself into a three-generation-deep round hole would only result in the kind of splintering that would leave me yelling tired homilies about yuppies and space aliens outside whatever outerborough group home next to a parking garage I'd be lucky enough to find myself in. I wouldn't miss the culture;

New York winnows out a lot of mediocrity, but I was only interested in heroin at that moment in time, of which, I admit, New York did have the very best, and it was cheap, too, its price being only ten dollars a unit and my integrity. It probably cost quite a bit of my future as well, but that was something I was clearly not constitutionally capable of taking into consideration. I did not, however, want to be associated with the horrid troops of well-off Caucasian poseurs who were using heroin as an expression of fashionable, expensive anomie while thousands of hardworking people had to deal with it as a blight on their neighborhoods and families. I didn't particularly care if I died at that point since I was clinically depressed, but the thought of being associated with the whole heroin-chic thing made me wish I had never existed in the first place. That being the case, I got my wealthy Caucasian family to send me to a fashionable, expensive treatment center in Minnesota. The only thing I would miss, and I missed it for twenty years and still do every day, was the New York City subway system. Keep your dawn-splashed canyons and soaring cathedrals; keep your pyramids, your temples, your gold-domed pagodas rising above ancient capitals. The Metro Underground Transit system is the wonder of the world and I was in love with it and still am, even though it's going through a "respectable" phase.

I knew right away that I was going to have to deal with transit nostalgia when I was picked up at the Minneapolis airport by a friendly young man who looked like the guitar player at the church I'd gone to once when I was ten, with my friend Eleanor out in Scarsdale. He played Cat Stevens songs and invited us to a "rap group" after the service. The Minnesota counselor sported the same dark blond receding hair pulled back in a ponytail, the same wide-wale, dune-colored corduroys, the same aviator-frame glasses. The guitar player had been transferred for what Eleanor said her parents called "overly fluid boundaries," which meant—she told me in the objective tone kids adopt when trying to scare another kid with a piece of evil news—that the stories of his putting his finger into Nancy Spencer's vagina were true. In New York, when I grew up, there were mashers and molesters all over the 6 train I took to school. You could be assured of running into one at least three or four times a year. They were no threat, however. You learned how to dodge them in a moment, and if it was crowded and you were smushed up against one, you could loudly declare, "Take your hand off my leg" and watch their faces crumple in terror. It's true I was frozen with fear the one time during a morning crush that I felt someone's hand scrabbling around my underpants. This was nothing, though, compared to the thrilling infusion of self-reliance I got from discovering he was more frightened of what I could say than I was of what he could do; one word from me and he'd be assaulted by a hailstorm of name calling:

"Fucking perv."

"Swear to God . . ."

"Quit touching the little kids, douche-wad!"

The Upper East Side professionals in the car would remain silent, not willing to abandon their class status to become involved in public theater, but they would look at us. Meanwhile, somebody would use the distraction to pick someone's pocket and he'd be likely to get accused of that as well. It happened faster than calling 911 on a cell phone, the current method of citizen action.

If I didn't feel like making a scene I just moved and they disappeared back into the cluttered background of human flesh and faces that every subway rider learns to take for granted and ignore, like a dirty but comfortable blanket.

But in Minneapolis, in the car with this odd man, whose strange pre-sexual aura reminded me of Mr. Rogers—who had always looked to me like a gentle, delicate cloud of pedophilia—there were no witnesses. Later I learned he was quite a decent sort, but I actually thought, after we headed north on I-35 and turned down a wooded road, of jumping out of the car. Even though it was January, I considered running across the flat white expanse to one of the little homeless encampments dotting what appeared to be a snow-covered field just behind the ragged black tree line. It took me a while to discover that it was not the wind-blasted prairie but one of

Minnesota's ten thousand lakes, and what I assumed were squatters' shacks were ice-fishing huts, which is only one example of how growing up in New York makes you ridiculous everywhere else.

The first place I lived when I got out of treatment was a "developing" neighborhood in St. Paul. I shared an apartment right off Selby Avenue in the Cathedral Hill neighborhood and took two buses to my job at an airport gift shop. First I took one bus down the hill past the dome of the Cathedral of Saint Paul and the capitol building and then transferred to another down on Kellogg Avenue in an area we called the flats. I didn't think about it much on the first day until I got to the transfer spot and wound up waiting twenty minutes on a windswept, vacant street in front of an auto parts distributor, a closed-up body shop, and the empty acre of a construction site. The wind was so strong that it had ripped the green-and-red soot-spattered plastic pennants around the lot into strips of dirty ribbon. When my shift ended, the last number 4 had already left, and I waited forty minutes for the 7, which connected to another bus in Minneapolis that dropped me off in front of a White Castle on Lake Street—empty streets, nail salons, occasional propositions from passing cars, because who else would be standing on a street in public but someone who was "working"—just after the last 21 had left and three-quarters of an hour before the next one. It dropped me off back on Selby and Dale, where I staggered in my first wet, now frozen, work shoes back to my apartment and fell asleep with my coat on as soon as the insistent pain in my feet turned to numbness. Later on the airport employees petitioned the Minneapolis Department of Transportation for an extra number 7, but until they did the manager would say "Must be nice" as I clocked out five minutes early and ran through the terminal to get there before it left. The trip home, if nothing went wrong, would take two hours and fifteen minutes. When I mentioned this, people looked confused. Why didn't I just drive?

The idea of someone living without a car didn't come up any more than the idea of someone walking around without a head. If you lived, you drove, was the assumption anywhere but the small island where I was born. The only people who took the bus were disabled, like me: by poor eyesight, by Parkinson's or schizophrenia, by deafness, by poverty. Those of us who rode the bus didn't merely look resigned; we looked defiant, staring straight ahead in the kind of square-shouldered so-what attitude most often used to conceal shame about our cheap snow boots and the huge sums of subtraction that showed in our faces.

I hit up my mother for driving lesson money. "Only marginal people take the bus here," I said.

"Well, Sweetie, you *are* marginal."

But she gave me the money, figuring it was but a drop in the bucket of the money I had cost her throughout my life of private schools, privilege, and psychiatrists, all of which had done me no particular good, so much so that it was no longer even a matter of throwing good money after bad but simple harm reduction. The crosstown boulevards and freeway entrances were standing between me and my last chance at a life lived outside an institution.

That being the case, I learned to drive. But I never liked it. Every day for twenty years, I wished that the buses in the Twin Cities would run a little faster.

For green spaces and civic decency, the Twin Cities beat out a great many metropolitan areas on the planet. Like the rest of America, however, they were designed for driving, not walking, and that has made quite a few of its people fatter and more suspicious than they need to be. It was there that I first wondered what really made New York different from the rest of America and why I was finding it hard to navigate. If I hadn't left the city of my birth, I would never have discovered Jane Jacobs, whose books explained to me exactly what I was missing and what made the good parts of a city good. Neighborhoods one can walk in are important, of course, but you need a way to get from one to the other without putting yourself outside space and time, without detaching yourself completely from the communities through which you move. What makes a city a real city? Number one, in my opinion, is a subway system.

When I returned to New York on family visits, I had the usual sense of melancholy. I felt like a foreigner; all the stimuli that had melded into a humming backdrop now distracted and overwhelmed. I had to get my blinders back and build up my audiovisual stamina for a day or so before I could travel reflexively again, but if I took the 2 train out to the Nevins stop to visit my sisters, it would put the spring back into my step twice as fast. It's not the neighborhoods themselves I crave; it's the commute: to go into a cool, dark tunnel and emerge twenty minutes later in a different world that is also, in the most fundamental and invisible way—the same.

Today when I walk around my hometown I see the obvious changes that money and power have wrought and I think the obvious sorrowful, angry thoughts of any person made a financial exile from the place of her birth. I'm no longer young, and of course that colors my view of the East Village and Williamsburg, where I lived in 1986, in all the expected ways. If, however, I take the train to any of these neighborhoods, or to Rockaway, or to Dyckman Street in Washington Heights, my heart still starts to beat a little faster. If the train goes elevated I still get a sting of excitement when it bursts out of the tunnel into the air three floors up, girded on either side with millions of windows topped with water towers, the iron lacework of fire escapes, and glimpses of glittering, steel blue river.

I don't like rush hour any more than anyone else, but sometimes I have to laugh, standing there surrounded by the pressing flesh and odorous breath, at the amazing, manic fact of it all. Look at us, twelve million little corpuscles pulsing at superhuman speed through the circulatory system of this grungy, grandiose giant. Someone told me, "Ah, New York isn't diverse. People just get thrown together on the subway and at work; then they all scatter home to their separate enclaves." Maybe so, but there are enough exceptions to that rule that the last time I was on the L, I overheard the conversation of a family whose smallest members, twins, were wearing identical Puerto Rican flag T-shirts. They were on their way to a bris, about which they were unnerved—you could tell by the bad jokes—but were nonetheless attending because their son's study partner and friend at CUNY was the father and he'd come to the son's wedding, so they had to reciprocate. Peace on Earth it wasn't, but you have to start somewhere. Rome wasn't built in a day and the first time anyone tried to build an underground train in New York, Tammany Hall thugs shut it down for lack of kickbacks. Now look: it was an 85-degree day and I was enjoying an air-conditioned ride, traveling in relative comfort, underground, while people hurtled from one microcosm to another at forty-five miles an hour. It would be something to write home about, if people still wrote home, and if I weren't, in fact, home already.

OUT OF SEASON

RUTH CURRY

L ike a lot of non-native New Yorkers, I have an origin story—bookish kid, bad at sports, clever and capable but not, to my mind,
sufficiently acknowledged for either and thus bitter and sensitive, friendless and constantly teased. The town I come from has
1,800 people and no stoplights. I was an outsider and felt it keenly;
my appetite for recognition was dwarfed only by my desire for new
experience, any experience, all experiences, and I desperately
wanted to ditch the lonely and provincial trappings of my life so far.
The trigger for my transformation (no lightning bolt, no cauldron of
radioactive liquid, no blinding realization) was a phone call from an
acquaintance who was en route to New York City and looking for a
roommate. I was twenty-two, and in a classic youthful misstep had
finished college with no plans beyond continuing to work at a sandwich shop with the love of my life, who promptly broke up with me
the day after I graduated. Our daily shifts together were a melo-
dramatic nightmare, and when given the chance to do something,
anything else, I took it. The fact that I didn't know anyone in New
York and had spent a total of thirty-six hours there to date seemed
irrelevant and easily overcome. I was terrified by the prospect of

mediocrity in myself or my surroundings, and whatever happened, whatever I did, if it happened in New York, my thinking went, it would not be mediocre.

Things delighted me then that I can hardly stand now—the subway, for example, and the strip of Smith Street in Brooklyn that was just starting to sprout bistros and specialty cheesemongers and boutiques selling very expensive children's goods. It was 2003; New York was engulfed in a frenzy of post-9/11–pre-2008 energy and excess. The city lent itself especially well to a mental configuration in which you were an extra in an artsy, high-budget movie and saw everything as if through a camera on a set. I imagined a helicopter's-eye view of the sidewalks, my sidewalks, pulsing with the synchronized strides of all these black-clad strangers, cocooned in their headphones and sunglasses and murmuring their own private conversations into their own personal phones, yet still unmistakably part of the same huge organism. Amid the truly astounding amounts of trash I noticed the scent of almonds roasting, sugary and delicious. In the single-minded vicious press to exit the subway as quickly as possible, someone stopped to help a mother carry her stroller up the stairs—someone who had just thirty seconds ago been testing the seemingly infinite limits of rudeness. I noticed that you could cry in public and people carefully ignored you—not maliciously, but because it's understood that privacy is in short supply.

alling in love, I think, is marked by the subconscious accumulation of a list of cherished qualities—*her hair, that laugh, brilliant, great taste in music*—and it is perhaps the realization such a list exists that marks the transition from "falling" to "fell." This is what was happening to me. The Time Warner Center then was recently finished but not inhabited. The electricity hadn't been turned on yet; for just a few days, the murky black glass offered back an unblemished reflection of the opposite skyline. I saw it, alone, trudging home from a late night at work. I breathed into my hands against the cold and stood and stared and fell.

A few years passed, and I put together a full and mostly happy life piece by sweat-soaked solitary piece: a promising career in the semi-glamorous field of book publishing; an apartment in Fort Greene, which *The New York Times* had just declared Brooklyn's most desirable neighborhood; and a group of similarly clever and capable friends. And I met Russell at a house party near the Brooklyn Museum.

I fell in love again, this time with someone who loved me back and also wanted me to leave the career and the apartment and the friends and move with him to a small town in New Zealand 9,000 miles away. As I write this, it's hard to reconstruct how much I loved him then. His good qualities read like a bloodless description of a generically attractive person—good-looking, smart, polite, funny. He was six years older than I was, with an Ivy League education and a great job, so of course I wanted to impress him, and he was duly impressed. That was what initially interested me when we met: I liked that he liked me, and I liked that he seemed to know what he was doing, in New York and in life. It was he who introduced me to all the places in New York that eventually became my regular spots, who showed me the best places to read in Prospect Park, the secretly affordable wine bar in the West Village, and Great Lakes, the Midwestern-themed bar in Park Slope. A huge mural of them all— Huron, Ontario, Michigan, Erie, Superior—hung behind the bar, and Russell and I used to hang out there, criticizing one another's jukebox selections and talking about home and our respective lake affiliations—Minnesota and Superior for him, Illinois and Michigan for me. "We got along really well" is what I usually say when I have to describe our relationship, which doesn't convey much unless you've had that kind of relaxed, thoughtless rapport with someone you're also sleeping with.

But Russell had wanted to move away for years, and he was

stubborn. He missed fresh air and open space, so much so that he issued what was essentially an ultimatum: I'm going, with or without you, preferably with you, but I'm going. It meant giving up everything I had worked so hard for, the toehold I had carved out in my career, the identity I had assembled, and everyone else I loved, so of course I said yes.

Even in the cab on my way to JFK, my adult life condensed to four suitcases bouncing around in the trunk, I felt, fleetingly, in some pre-sentient way, that this was not going to end well. A few days before I had hesitated to store any of my things with Russell's sister because I knew subconsciously how hard it would be to get them back later, after it was all over. But the morning was clear and bright—nearly summer but not yet hot—traffic was light and the cab navigated the parkways of Brooklyn with ease. I couldn't remember traveling through New York so quickly. Attributing this premonition to some other unrelated worry or insecurity was easy; there were plenty to choose from. I left a few things with his sister anyway (my kitchen supplies and some books, the things that meant the most to me), and yeah, getting them back later really sucked.

I had a layover in Auckland during the earliest hours of what is technically morning. I bought a cup of coffee from the one open shop and huddled at my gate near a bank of floor-to-ceiling windows. I had traveled from summer to winter in fourteen hours, and the chill penetrated through the glass as I watched the sky slowly shoot through with streaks of gray.

It snowed the day I arrived. Russell brought Gerbera daisies and a heavy jacket for me, and there are pictures of me wearing it at the Christchurch airport. It's his so it's a little big, and I look tired and shocked and pleased, but also out of place and like I'm wearing someone else's clothes. We got in the car (a car!) and he drove us through the city out to our house (a house!) in the suburbs (yes). Christchurch is not populous—about 300,000 people—but it is large and sprawls out like a spreading stain. A handful of buildings in the city center top out around ten stories and the downtown

area seemed exclusively populated by fifteen-year-old goths, rolling cigarettes and waiting for the bus. Everyone else I saw looked to be around forty-five and sunburnt. There were a lot of parking lots.

The house was nice, though—a three-bedroom bungalow tucked into an alcove at the top of a hill that you could reach only by driving very slowly and carefully up a windy, narrow lane that accommodated exactly one car. If you encountered someone going the opposite direction, the ensuing choreography was intense. The other way to get there was via 187 slippery and uneven stone steps that switchbacked up the side of the hill, around other people's flower gardens and cottages and car parks. I say "hill," but it was actually the remains of an extinct volcano. The former crater had collapsed and filled with water from the ocean on the other side, and dolphins would sometimes swim in it, alongside the huge freighters and tankers that came to port at the harbor. The colors of the water and the green hills around it and the sky, which, because of the thin ozone, was like the ideal of sky magnified to the power of one hundred, were surreally vivid. Every sunset was a purple-streaked glory and the stars were dazzling in their unfamiliar constellations. Russell spent every day in manic wonder and could not imagine how I found this remarkable, yes, but nothing more. Some people need to be in the presence of truth, I think, others beauty, and we were each discovering on which side the other one fell. It seemed I had good things to say about dark empty buildings and trash.

I couldn't get a job, so I cooked a lot. I planned elaborate meals that I had to start shopping for around 3 PM, and as I didn't get out of bed much before noon this created the illusion I was doing something like living. After I ran out of money, Russell left me some on the kitchen table every Monday morning for groceries. I read *The Feminine Mystique* and wallowed in the irony. I didn't make any friends—Christchurch really was exclusively populated by angsty teenagers and the middle-aged, and none of them were particularly interested in a disgruntled New Yorker. Later I would joke, meanly, that the only options for arts, culture, and entertainment were respectively rugby, rugby, and rugby.

Russell worked constantly. When he had time off, it was just the two of us, going hiking, which I hated, and trying to find reasonable similes of the foods we missed from home. We sat at restaurants, staring at pizza with corn and shrimp on it or pushing unspeakably foul "enchiladas" around on our plates. I missed bagels the most and there weren't even bad substitutes to be found, so I tried to make them from scratch. Russell came home after the first attempt and looked over the wreckage in the kitchen: every pot we owned filled with scummy cooling water, scraps of dough sticking to the faucet, the doorknob, the refrigerator handle, a junkyard of dishes in the sink. On the table was a tray of nine or so wizened rings of slightly burnt dough. "I ate two," I said. "They're actually not that bad."

"Oh, Ruthie," he said. He picked one up and held it.

"The recipe said the malt syrup is optional, but that must be wrong. I'm going to try again next week. I think I can do it."

He looked skeptical.

"Do you want to bet?" I joked, sort of. We bet: successful bagels or a naked run through the main street of our town. I am not some-one who invokes nudity casually, but it was toward the beginning, when I was still cocky and confident, and we were still flirting with each other.

The second attempt failed and Russell teased me. The third failed even more miserably. I tried to eat one, but the batch was so burnt on the bottom I couldn't manage to bite through it. I threw them away and hauled the garbage to the curb and cleaned the kitchen and didn't mention it to Russell. He continued to try to get me to hold up my end of the deal, but whatever light spirit had been with me when I proposed it had disappeared, and the fact that he hadn't noticed its absence made me sadder.

I remember reading in bed until late at night while he slept be-side me, peaceful and happy, glancing over at him from time to time, at the little stocking cap he wore because our bedroom was so cold and wondering what was wrong with me. I knew he wondered what was wrong with me too, since we had started to fight a lot about it.

He thought I should accept the circumstances and put a good face on them. "Just grow the fuck up!" he said, during one nasty argument, but I found this impossible. I had always relished new situations, never feared the unfamiliar, never failed when I put my whole weight behind something, so I did not anticipate having trouble adjusting to another first world, English-speaking country. The tricky thing was that the differences were not so much differences as they were inversions or transpositions, just similar enough to fool you into thinking nothing had changed. Orion is there in the night sky, just upside down. Christmas is a summer holiday and people spend it on the beach. The climate is mild, but houses aren't insulated or heated, so it's completely normal to wear a hat and scarf and two sweaters inside and then take them all off when you go out into the sun. For a long time I would automatically get into the car and sit there until Russell rapped on my window—I had gotten in the wrong side. Again. A cart is a trolley and a pepper is a capsicum and trash (rubbish) goes in a bin. Sheep, which outnumber people four to one, regularly join U.S. news in the headlines. Bars are open twenty-four hours a day, and people are reserved and unflappably polite except for the ones who are very drunk.

But that politeness is not a temporary shield, not a shell, not a surface: that reserve is bottomless. As a foreigner you will never reach the end of it. I understood the language, but communication was impossible. How could I justify a desire to stand out, to make something of myself in the context of a complicated culture that values fitting in over individualism? How could I even begin to describe this to someone who desperately and rightfully wanted me to follow their clear social cues and talk about the weather? "That's quite a change," people would reply, when I said where I was from, and the right response—the only response—was "It is, a bit." I had failed to plan for this, and the failure was like a pesky sprain that just would not heal. There was nowhere to go to lick my wounds, no crowd to disappear into, no ocean of work to throw myself at. There was nothing in my life before that I hadn't been able to fix by being smart or working hard (how American, to even think that for a moment), and that, I was beginning to realize, would not always be the case. This was the first thing that I would not be able to fix.

I kept going to job interviews in Christchurch, although it was obvious—so obvious I wondered, then resented, why Russell hadn't mentioned it in his Christchurch pitch—that there were no jobs in the media or in any related field for an American with three to five years of experience. After one of these pointless interviews, I picked up a tuna roll in a food court and sat down to eat it in front of a TV that was playing American football. I wasn't a football fan, but hearing the accent was comforting and familiar and I allowed myself to stare at the TV. I loaded up my chopsticks and examined the tuna roll more closely. It was made with canned tuna, gray and flaky. The food court was oppressive in a particularly dull 1970s burnt orange way and redolent with the dueling grease smells of five or six cultures. The only other people there were a group of thickly eyelined teenagers slumped nearly to the floor. I tried to identify something in my surroundings that wasn't obviously mediocre and failed. I thought about what my friends in New York might be doing at that moment, what it might feel like to be in a crowd, to hurry somewhere, to have a conversation that wasn't about rain or sports. I realized that the fabled "four seasons in a day" weather was making me sweat through my interview suit and regretted that I was incapable of thinking about anything other than the weather as well.

Finally, I landed a job waiting tables at a breakfast diner. I left the house while it was still dark, rode the empty 6:15 bus into town, and served plate after plate of waffles alongside a bunch of good-natured teenagers who couldn't quite figure me out. *Join the club,* I thought. The money wasn't enough, so I got another job working nights and weekends at a wine bar. Now Russell and I really never saw each other, I was as bitter and sensitive as I ever had been, and I had unlimited access to free booze. I had six months left on my visa. There was nothing to do but drink and fight with Russell, who still thought I should be enjoying myself.

It wasn't all miserable. When Russell took time off, we went on long backcountry hikes together, and with time, I could sense although not really understand what made a certain part of him—the part that was so different from me—operate. Somewhere in a hiker's shelter near the Cass Saddle our initials are carved together in the bottom of a bunk bed. I remember sitting in the back of our local pub, which was really cool, actually, decorated with Christmas lights and bits of kitsch straight from someone's granny's basement. A hand-painted portrait of John Travolta circa *Saturday Night Fever* hung next to the bathroom, the overhead lights were made of dolls' heads, and you could peek through the slit-like windows over the booths and see people shopping in the grocery store directly below, unaware they were being watched. The same folk singer played there every Wednesday night. He was great, but the crowd was never more than us and a few other couples. He always wrapped up his set with one or two covers, and the night he played "Atlantic City," Russell reached over and grabbed my hand. I didn't want to look at him at first because I was already crying, but when I did, I saw he was too.

Everything dies, baby, that's a fact.

I had kept a list about him once. Generous, good cook. Hazel eyes with a darker fleck in the right one matching the one in mine, just like the lyrics in a pop song we both loved. He almost never got annoyed, but when he did he made a very discreet face that he probably thought no one noticed, and it was unconsciously adorable. Wore funny T-shirts, Midwestern. Nice hands, etc. From the beginning he brought me flowers all the time, nearly every week, but the first time he blindly chose my favorite purple wildflowers, and I took them in my hands and wondered how he knew. He still brought me flowers, usually proteas from the farmer's market on Saturdays, and it was starting to feel like an empty gesture but I appreciated that he made it anyway.

Not long before I was supposed to move back to the United States, I got into a car accident. I never really had gotten the hang of driving on the left side of the road and was distracted for a moment by, of all things, the sunset. I drifted into the wrong ("right") lane, rounded a very sharp blind curve, and ran into an SUV. The road dropped off straight into the ocean on one side and I was profoundly lucky not to be hurt or worse. I also was very upset that my attempts to appreciate the natural beauty of New Zealand had resulted in this. The car was totaled. "I'm so sorry," I said through tears, as Russell held me. "I'll pay for it; don't worry."

"*You* don't worry. It's our problem; we'll figure it out together."

It was the right thing to say, but my knee-jerk response shocked me even as I knew it was true: *I'm not sure "our" exists anymore.* I kept quiet. The end dragged out for six more months, but that was the day it was over.

It's been five years, and I'm still paying for that car.

I moved to San Francisco shortly after the car accident. Russell was supposed to join me a few months later, but that never happened. We broke up almost immediately, and I spent those months drifting around the city in a haze of grief, confusion, and Vicodin. There was a whiskey bar around the corner from the apartment I shared with two college friends, and the bartender liked one of them so he let all three of us drink for free, monopolize the stereo, and stay after hours at will. We stumbled the thirty or forty feet home and I got up the next morning to temp or to wait tables. Or I didn't get up at all and just lay in bed, listening to the unbelievable din of homeless men pushing carts ("trolleys") full of bottles up and down Shrader Street and getting into fights. I was sick a lot, and I caught pinkeye three or four times in as many months. My friends said that it was from riding the bus. They were joking, but they were also right, I later realized—I cried almost every day, so I also rubbed my eyes all the time with my filthy, Muni-infected hands. I became very familiar with the schedule of the 33 Stanyan,

which went from my apartment in the Upper Haight to the free clinic in the Mission. My life was full in its own wretched way, and I had no clue what to do next.

My best friend all but physically carried me back to New York. She lined up a job interview for me at a literary agency and when I got the job, she let me stay with her until I became once again a responsible, self-sufficient person. The transition was not smooth, but I can definitively say moving to New York is easier the second time around. The subway, grocery shopping, how to talk, where to walk, what to eat—*I know how to do this*, I thought, and the thought filled me with relief. I worked hard and went out a lot, and every so often at the end of a late night I would treat myself to a cab ride home. My favorite part was—still is—going over the Manhattan Bridge, feeling the little jerk of vertigo in my stomach, and looking at the lights of all the bridges draped over the East River like jewelry.

Your experiences change you, your personality, your expectations, your beliefs, your desires. This is self-evident, but not at the moment when you're working late at a job you should have outgrown years ago, or crying unexpectedly in public, or listening to your ex-boyfriend say he's marrying someone else. At that moment you're just wondering what happened to the person who used to have your name and how you can be that person again, how to get back that freedom, or innocence, or whatever significance that old body contained for you. She's gone for good, that girl, the girl who could give herself completely to a person or an idea, who believed she could handle anything and plunged forward into the unknown as easily and thoughtlessly as she tied her shoes.

The city had changed too; New York always does. In a way, it's like that "four seasons in a day" cliché that annoyed me so much in New

Zealand—if you don't like something, just wait a little while. All the places I used to frequent during my first tenure here closed one by one, without fanfare. The last time I walked down Fifth Avenue in Park Slope, even Great Lakes had closed. In its place was a blank steel security gate and a hand-scrawled sign: THANKS FOR EVERYTHING.

HOMECOMING

MIRA PTACIN

I t's late November and my husband and I are walking down a
plain gravel path headed toward the Atlantic Ocean. We pass a
tall compost heap, a wobbly wooden tree fort, a nervous clus-
ter of chickens pretending to ignore us, and a baseball diamond
where, to no one's surprise, a beige miniature horse is roped to a
bench and contentedly mowing the lawn with her mouth.

We live in Maine now, the Pine Tree State. The only state in the
country with just one syllable. The state whose motto is *Dirigo* ("I
lead") and state slogan is "The Way Life Should Be," which, to me,
after living in New York City for just over half a decade, Maine is.

It wasn't easy getting here. One day about four months ago, after the air conditioner in our fourth-floor Brooklyn walk-up broke yet
again, after our dogs had met the police twice (once for nipping at
a Hasidic man's *tzitzit* and once more for attacking a soda can collector's garbage bags), after we'd drained our bank accounts and
accumulated a severe amount of debt, spent more time with strangers on the subway than we did together at our own kitchen table,
and finally had enough of New York, Andrew and I quit our day jobs,
gathered the dogs and our belongings, rented a U-Haul, and said

goodbye to all that and hello to more peace, more quiet, and less distraction.

I had moved to New York six years earlier because I wanted to be a famous writer. I was twenty-five and determined, but without a road map. I'd been living a blissful life in Portland, Maine, but felt, like so many young people, I needed a "New York Chapter." So I uprooted myself. My very first night in New York, my car windows got smashed and then the car was towed (I didn't realize I'd parked illegally), and at midnight that same night, my license plate expired. I spent my entire first week in New York trying to find and retrieve my car; each day, the impound lot was charging me fifty dollars. I spent my first six months in New York subletting a room above a sushi restaurant in Carroll Gardens, Brooklyn, with a putty-faced girl my age who happened to be the assistant to a famous and important and powerful magazine editor and who behaved as if, by association or osmosis, she was just as famous and important and powerful. She was rich and intimidating and well dressed and had attended Columbia University. I owned three pairs of shoes and had gone to a public college in Michigan. I was broke and sensitive and naïve and knew no one fancy in Manhattan; I could barely navigate the subway. I felt sorry for the mice in our apartment building that our landlord was trying to poison—*they were just trying to survive*—and I found it painfully unnatural and difficult not to look the people sitting across from me on the train in the eye. I thought that in order to be a writer in New York, all one had to do was live in New York and write, and write well. My putty-faced roommate introduced me to the notion that, to be a successful writer in New York, one must dress the part, act the part, know all the players, and sleep with a good bit of them. It was a game that I just didn't want to play. Within a year, I'd become drearily drained of hope and money, I was walking dogs profession-ally during the day while moonlighting as a data entry clerk, and, to boot, I lost the few belongings I had to bedbugs. But the worse things got, the more determined I became to beat New York at whatever game we were playing: it would place obstacles in front of me, and

I'd hurdle over them until I reached the finish line. I refused to give up, no matter what, no matter how hard New York got, until I felt I'd achieved what I thought was success.

Within time, my career started picking up speed. The literary circle opened itself up to me (or maybe the barrier eventually toppled after I'd thrown myself against it enough times), and I started getting published frequently. Then, out of nowhere, I met a man. I hadn't planned on dating anyone, let alone ever getting hitched, but after I reluctantly agreed to go on a blind date with him, Andrew and I hit it off. We both were eyeball-deep in our career goals, but we fell in love and soon after got married. The Monday morning following our wedding, we jumped right back into our manic work routines.

With financial security and some material comfort, we thought we had it pretty good, but in reality, we were unhealthy newlyweds. We lived right next to Prospect Park but fought over whose turn it was to walk the dogs and who got to stay home and work. Unless we were sleeping, we rarely spent more than two hours a day together. Andrew would get home from work at night and I'd be heading out the door to show my face at a colleague's reading. Weekend days were spent getting chores out of the way (Andrew: laundry; Mira: clean apartment) so that we could spend our precious evenings tending to work projects. We saw a marriage counselor, who suggested we pencil in date nights, but by the time date night rolled around, we were always too tired to follow through. We fought all the time, and in time, the threat of divorce slipped into our arguments.

Nothing was irrevocable. Everything was within reach. Joan Didion's words rang true, but what we hadn't considered was that once we reached one rung in the ladder, there was always the next rung above it, and another, and another. Our spirits became comatose because our lives revolved around our careers; even our marriage felt like a business arrangement. The day our dog bit that soda can collector in the park (who eventually sued us) and a policeman came to our apartment to file a report—the day we had to defend our pet—was the first time my husband and I had worked as a team

in months. That's when we realized it was time to leave New York and save our marriage.

One of the first things Andrew and I did after we left the city was go to a funeral. Brent, the father of one of Andrew's childhood friends, had been diagnosed with liver cancer a couple of weeks earlier. Days before he passed, Andrew and I brought cookies to Brent's wife Rosemary, who'd been keeping vigil at her ailing husband's bedside in a nursing home. I remember it was the Fourth of July and nearly 110 degrees outside. In a shared room, Rosemary sat beside Brent, who was reclined in a bed and sedated with morphine. She'd been barely eating or sleeping and was still coping with her husband's fate. "It feels like a dream," she'd told us. "It feels like just yesterday we even found the cancer." Once diagnosed, her husband had been given about a month to live. As she stroked Brent's arm, Rosemary told us how the doctor had told her husband his fate and left them alone in the exam room; then the couple, who'd been married for thirty-five years, had raised two grown kids, and had three grandchildren, suddenly had to say goodbye.

"That was it," she said. "That's when Brent turned to me, took my hands, and said, 'Well, Rosemary, we've had a good run.'"

The day after we visited him, Brent was gone.

Brent's funeral was held three days after he died. After the burial and as the sun was setting, we gathered at Brent and Rosemary's home. We walked there from Andrew's childhood home, too, and we stayed until nearly 2 AM, drinking on their wraparound porch, exchanging stories, eating Doritos, passing photo albums,

and handing out tissues. This went on for three nights, and kept going even after Andrew and I left town.

Here are some of the things I learned at Rosemary's that first week after leaving New York: I learned that when a widow is crying and smoking a cigarette, you let her cry, and if you speak, it's to ask if you can get her another Diet Coke. I learned that no one cares that much what you do for a living, but they will be grateful if you stay up with a six-year-old and watch *Dennis the Menace* because his grandfather is dead and he cannot sleep. Rather than get into a political debate about the war, you thank an Iraqi veteran for his service. You do not check your BlackBerry in the middle of a toast, and when someone hands you a crying baby, you hold it. I learned that ice cream cakes make grandpas feel really special, and when a neighbor invites you to swing by the food pantry during her volunteer shift so that she can take a look at that nasty poison oak on your shin, you go, and you wait patiently until she can get free to see you. I learned that you don't judge someone's worth based on what they can do for you and that you aren't expected to ask, "How can I help?" Instead, you just jump right in.

Here are some of the things I learned while living in New York: That you shouldn't interpret direct and efficient communication as rudeness. That a sidewalk operates by the same rules as a highway: if you walk slow, walk in the right lane, and if you have to stop, pull over. I learned that once the late June sunshine hits the streets, pretty girls in summer dresses come out of the woodwork. I also learned that summer brings with it the inescapable smell of marinating garbage and human urine. In the city, you can get weed delivered to your front door by a hipster on a bicycle or pick up a screwdriver in the dead of the night at a twenty-four-hour hardware store. I learned that the city has resilience like no other city during natural (or man-made) disasters, and that the people of New York generally coexist peacefully, which is impressive, considering there are 27,352 people per square mile. But it is a class-divided society. It's a rich cultural environment, full of galleries and incredible restaurants

and museums and shows, but unless you're wealthy, the city requires sacrifice to enjoy those things. Unless you are rich, you struggle every day. You grind. You ride the subway for two hours just to work at Starbucks. But there's also nowhere else to be for professional networking. You can access the movers and shakers. You can *be* a mover and a shaker if you work hard enough. Just plug yourself into the scene, whatever your scene is. But what ends up happening—or what ended up happening to me—is an unplugging from family life, an unplugging from the things that make you feel whole and rooted. While living in New York, I eventually came to realize that for every good thing about the city, there was also a dark side. We go to New York to make our careers, but we end up stepping over homeless people on the sidewalk on our way to work. Successful New Yorkers can ignore those dark sides, but I could not.

However, small towns have their dark sides, too. Small towns can be conservative and close-minded and tacky. People in small towns often like to be all up in your business. Yet I can get over those things. And I can still be a successful writer and not live in a big city. I couldn't be my true self while living in New York. If I had stayed, my spirit would have died. My marriage, my health, my sense of peace—all had been placed on the back burner, and they would have stayed on the back burner. It wasn't the city's fault; it was mine. I was unmoored; my ambition trumped my principles. If I had stayed in New York, my marriage to Andrew might not have survived. Our run would not have been so good.

The morning after our third night on Rosemary's porch, we left Andrew's hometown and headed to Maine. During our drive, I thought about all the hopeful lonely faces I saw when we set foot in the nursing home where Brent stayed. They were all so sad but smiling, so hopeful. They were wearing Fourth of July hats and T-shirts and big bead necklaces. I wished so hard that someone would be coming to visit them that day. We drove, and I thought about the lines in the funeral home, the unsophisticated décor and the casseroles, and how long the friendships had lasted. I thought about who cared about me like that, and I tried to remember the person I was before I arrived in New York City. Driving into Maine, I started to wonder, *Who would visit me on my deathbed? Who would take a rain check or tell me their subway line wasn't running? If I couldn't talk or walk or even go to the bathroom, who would help take care of me? If I died tomorrow, who would attend my funeral?*

We kept driving. We passed a public supper, a scarecrow contest, some steeples, and sailboats until we crossed Commercial Street and drove our car onto Casco Bay Lines ferry and drifted along Portland Harbor until we reached our little sanctuary on Peaks Island, Maine. Population: 800.

We walk through a pine tree forest, step across a homemade bridge, and there, strong like a mother, is the Atlantic. Ahead of us, the tide is coming in. I breathe in the moist air; I remember how desperately, when living in New York, I wanted to inhale such things: saltwater, sand, isolation. I didn't want to smell smog or hear so many signs of life, millions of them, all at once. I was too soft for New York, too easily saddened or distracted. I didn't want to be callous. I just wanted to remain the sensitive creature I was, to write, love, and be a little hidden. Now, here on this small island in Maine, I'm beginning to feel alive again, and unafraid, as if something in the air has taken over me, as if the water is breathing out the secret to something I'd been looking for, something I'd been looking for so long that I'd nearly forgotten what it was. The answer. I'm home now. This is where I'm supposed to be.

LEAVING MY GROOVY LIFESTYLE

CHLOE CALDWELL

Although it was only two hours away from Hudson, my small town upstate, New York City seemed like a fictional place until I moved there. My older brother was living in Brooklyn and working at the Strand. When I spoke with him on the phone, it was noisy in the background and there was something new to his voice—my shy, introverted brother sounded almost *joyful*, if not a little manic. I've always been the type of person who sees something she likes and then sets about getting it in her own life. I liked New York. So when there was an open "room" (a couple of feet on the creaky wooden floor without a door for $600 a month) in my brother's railroad apartment on North 6th Street in Williamsburg, I dropped out of college and moved in a week later.

Like Joan Didion, I moved to New York in summer, when I was twenty years old. I slept with the sun on my face while my mother drove. But in late afternoon, the sun became too yellow and too hard to ignore, awakening me on the Williamsburg Bridge. I opened my eyes just in time to read "Brooklyn—Like No Other Place in the World," and the juxtaposition of the filthy water and brick apartment buildings and plants on fire escapes and men on construction sites and clear broad sky exhilarated me, made my body tingle. A skittish feeling struck me at my core, alerting me that I was really *going*. This skittish feeling lingered inside me for months. My mother says it was exactly like when she dropped me off on my first day of preschool—I was so amped up that I didn't turn to wave and watch her car drive off. My brother and I skipped off to thrift stores, and he helped me pick out a flowered curtain to hang up as the door to my new bedroom. I thought my room was beautiful.

That first summer—the summer of 2006—I lived on the streets of the city. By that I mean I was only at home for my four hours of sleep. I moved in on June 2, and one night in early August, my brother said to me, "This is the first night we're not out doing something since you got here." Everyone I met during my first three years in New York seemed exceptionally exotic and exciting. The cokehead bartenders, cute baristas, and hipster girls. The guys with long hair and borderline personality disorder. I fell in love with almost anyone who looked my way.

When a friend who was not living in New York City visited me, she watched me get dressed one morning, smirked, and said, "Who are you, Johnny Cash?" Black jeans, black boots, black sweater, black leather jacket. My best New York friends and I wore each other's leather jackets. We were always accidentally wearing the wrong one home. Leather jackets in dark bars tend to get mixed up. We shared our black jeans and lace-up Doc Martens and black riding boots too. The subway in the wintertime always cracked me up: fifty shades of black. My brother left New York for Berlin, and when he came back he was against the all-black fashion statements that he once adhered to. "Color is . . . nice," he said to me on a subway platform after surveying the scene. "It's okay to wear color." But black was slimming, black was enigmatic and ninja-like.

We ran around the city like street rats. A lover once told me not to get in his bed with my "street clothes" on. "You get in here in your jeans and boots and track dog shit and who knows what the fuck else," he said.

I'm not saying we were dirty, exactly, but grooming wasn't too important. We were never home straightening our hair. Grooming was trading leather jackets and jeans. Grooming was going to Sephora and using and stealing their lipsticks that claimed to be the color of "Brooklyn." Grooming was cutting each other's bangs in dark bars. Grooming was stealing the eye cream of a lover's girlfriend. Grooming was buying leggings at that trashy, cheap chain, Strawberry. Grooming was buying a thong at Forever 21 while coked up out of our skulls because we had plans to have anal sex that night. Plus, how clean could you really be when you lived in apartments where you never knew when the hot water, heat, and plumbing would be out?

If I wanted a metaphor for my life in New York in my early twenties, it would be this: In 2008, the opportunity had arrived for me to finally go to the dentist. I worked as the manager of a jewelry store and I now had dental insurance. My boss was on my back about going to the dentist. Not that I had fucked-up teeth—she just always worried about me, pushed me, and mothered me. So she made me this dentist appointment way in advance and she talked about it every day. I had the day off from selling ass-loads of jewelry to the women of the West Village. I never had days off, not even Christmas. I woke up that morning where I was living, on Audubon Avenue in Washington Heights, put on my Johnny Cash clothes, and marched to the 181st Street station. Hopped on the A train. I was a bit early, so I went to the Strand to see my friend Skye on her break. We went to this hole-in-the-wall bar (that's all people did on their breaks at the Strand—drank—seriously—they called it "liquid lunch") and sat outside in the courtyard. I told Skye about my dentist appointment. But instead of going to the dentist I ordered another whiskey and soda. And when Skye went back to the Strand I ordered yet another and kept writing in my journal and texting and decided that it was too late to go to the dentist. I left the bar and walked around the East Village. The Lowes Village multiplex on Third Avenue caught my eye. The first *Sex and the City* movie was playing. Next thing I knew I walked into the theater, buying not one pack of candy, but *two* (Milk Duds and Whoppers) I munched as I watched the movie. I lied to my boss when she asked how my dentist appointment went. "No cavities!" I told her.

I had this thing for strangers—the stranger the better—for train wrecks, and for grit. I liked the dirty parts of cities, though I didn't realize that then. I wanted to be as out of my element as I could be. I wanted to talk to everyone and anyone. I sat on bar stools for hours.

My friends from upstate were off at college while I was living in New York, but I was learning too, just different things. Plumbing, for example. I learned that there is a website called Fix a Toilet. I learned how to be away from home, how to read maps, how to be lost and find my way home. I learned how to make lattes and how to waitress. I learned what I liked in bed, how to come. How to feed myself, how to pay bills, how to cope with unrequited love, how to work for micromanaging bosses. How to ride a bike in traffic and how to live on thirty cents a day (buy bagels on Grand Street, at the bakery with moldy wedding cakes in the window.) I learned that coffee is your friend and cocaine that looks like baby formula is not. I learned how to cope when a lover commits suicide. New York City during my college years was like being enrolled in Heartbreak, Sex, and Death 101.

I was unlearning things, too. Unlearning how to drive, unlearning what was acceptable and unacceptable behavior. Forgetting to look for doors on my bedrooms before signing leases. Forgetting how to keep my voice down. Forgetting how to relax. Forgetting that bathtubs were a real thing. Forgetting what moderation was. Forgetting that I wasn't stuck there, that there were actually other places to live. I moved and moved. I thought I'd stay everywhere forever. I lived on North 6th Street for one year, moving next to India Street in Greenpoint. After I came home one night to cops and a crumbling fire escape, that apartment was condemned, and I was left homeless for one week. I moved in with a friend in Washington Heights and ended up in Inwood, the very last stop on the A train. "The girl that never wanted to leave North 6th Street lives in *Inwood*!" my friends laughed.

New York pushes you and moves you along, testing your endurance, daring you to quit at any time. I moved the same things over and over: My three-pound purple weights and my eight-pound lime green ones. My sunflower mirror. My pink and white polka-dot sheets.

Eventually, I did remember there were other places to live. I was getting tired and I was only twenty-three. The sun was too harsh, yet I became even paler each year. I grew uncomfortable looking people in the eye. I felt paranoid around people, and whenever someone closed their eyes on the subway I assumed they were insane. I wanted to leave because even after dozens and dozens of times walking into a store and telling myself I would *not* come out with something black, I always walked out of the store with at least fifty dollars' worth of black clothes. When my father visited, he'd look at me and say, "Because black's how you feel on the inside, right?" I remember being at a café in Greenpoint, listening to a Belle and Sebastian song: "The city was losing it's ap-pea-ea-eal . . ."

I was terrified that I would come to hate New York. I never wanted to be like any of the buzz-killing, jaded people I met who hated it. They'd been there too long. I'd thought of Didion's essay "Goodbye to All That" as a how-to. Like *New York City for Dummies* or something. I read into it that Didion advised leaving New York before turning twenty-eight. I was going to learn from her mistake; I wasn't going to be like her and "stay too long at the Fair." I wouldn't be like the guys at the Strand who didn't know how to smile anymore. No way. I was going to get out alive at twenty-three and go experience other fairs.

Part of it was that I couldn't sustain my "groovy lifestyle," to borrow a term Lena Dunham's parents use in the first episode of HBO's television show *Girls*. My lifestyle was definitely groovy, and at some points felt unhealthy. Though I'd grown up playing beauty parlor in the woods with berries and playing in the stream behind our house,

I'd forgotten about all that. I rarely went upstate anymore and was a slave to the pavement, making choices that sometimes scared me.

"Totally unbalanced groovy lifestyle" is probably a more precise term for how I began to feel in New York. There was a subtle beating, a ticktock in my chest telling me I should probably leave. I began to wonder what my life would be like if I didn't have to jiggle the handle on the constantly running toilet after I flushed. When I took the time to listen hard enough, I could hear the subtle ticking of a clock inside my body, gently telling me to leave.

But I wanted to leave New York on my own terms. So I didn't leave after my apartment was condemned or after the guy I loved hanged himself. I didn't leave when I was unemployed for three months. I left of my own volition, on my own schedule. I chose a random date in late April and moved back to Hudson. I wanted to leave New York on a high note. The night before I left, I sat at Lucy's Bar on Avenue A with my best friend. We were both wearing Indian headdresses and drinking whiskey. We were on our way to a sexual adventure— we had agreed to go have a five-some with the guy I was seeing, his best friend, and his younger brother. We'd just snorted a bag of cocaine at our friend's apartment—a forty-year-old ex-dominatrix, a British cokehead. She lived on Avenue B near 7th Street, above the Moroccan restaurant Casimir. We went over there to get cocaine and tips and confidence on how to have an orgy. What I'm getting at is this: I didn't feel safe around myself in New York. I never knew what I was going to do.

Last year I moved to Portland, Oregon. Slowly here I am growing out of my restlessness and finding balance. I'm not sure what it is, but I know I cannot live there forever the way I could live in New York.

"Time passes, that's for sure," Eileen Myles writes in *Chelsea Girls*. I remember when one of my friends informed me that the for-

mula of seven dog years to one human year is inaccurate. "What it is," he patiently clarified, while alphabetizing the dollar carts in front of the Strand, "is that one human year in *New York City* equals seven human years." I suppose that explains why having lived there three years felt like twenty-one.

There's a distinct change, an evolution, that happens between twenty and twenty-seven. In my early twenties, I felt that my life could be one big experiment, and in my mid-twenties I am coming to terms with the fact that no, my life is actually *my life.* Five years after leaving New York City for Hudson, life has taken me to Portland, Oregon. This past Election Day, as I went about babysitting and writing, meeting someone for coffee, the sky darkened and the memory of the Election Day four years prior crept in. I couldn't help but note the ways in which my life had changed. Four years before, in 2008, after work, I took the subway back to my apartment on Seaman Avenue and waited for my lover to join me. I had a large room, windows and walls I'd painted yellow myself. My lover came over. I had this tiny little bed and also a futon. We took both mattresses off and put them on the floor. We had sex off and on for a couple of hours. Then, from the streets we heard the cheering. Obama won! Obama won while we were having sex in New York. We declared it a holiday.

I was not having sex this year while Obama got reelected. I was sitting on the couch in my friend's apartment in southeast Portland.

I moved to Portland because after visiting a bunch of times, I fell in love with it. Not the same love I felt for New York: "The way you love the first person who ever touches you and you never love anyone quite that way again" (Didion). But it was love nonetheless. I moved to Portland because I can afford to work less here and write more, a very important thing for my well-being. I moved to Portland because over time it seemed I had more friends here than in New York. When I visit New York City now, I have nowhere to sleep. We've all moved on, but I don't allow myself to think about it too much because it breaks my heart. New York City gave me everything it had, and greedy as I was for experience, I took and took. I carry with me every day the gift of the lessons New York taught me.

There have been nights when I've clutched the pillow in tears, grief-stricken for New York. The other day I was waiting impatiently for the bus and found myself walking into the street and leaning the top half of my body out even farther to look for the bus. The movement felt so familiar, and then I realized it was what I would do while waiting on a subway platform. I feel New York inside me when I talk too loudly, when I'm in line for coffee and feel rageful and restless, when I ask inappropriate and personal questions of strangers. When I say, "Oh, I walked," and people look at me quizzically and say, "That's a *long* walk."

I can't say if I'll stay in Portland because I'm in my mid-twenties and still floundering around. When you tell people you're going to leave New York, they like to tell you, "New York will always be here." But it won't always be there. My insides ache when I think, "I will never be twenty again and moving to Williamsburg with the sun on my face." So I don't let myself think it.

I wear a bright red winter coat this year and I feel that if I had a dentist appointment, I could make it there. On Friday and Saturday nights I've traded binge drinking for yoga teacher training. I work at Powell's City of Books, and sometimes I pretend I'm at the Strand because somewhere deep in my gut, I long for my Johnny Cash clothes, my irreverent best friends, the whiskey I could keep down, the hellish sun, and the debilitating snow—the groovy lifestyle that I could once sustain. Now I decline cocaine when it's offered (though I'm tempted) and I wear colorful clothes (but it's a challenge) and I rent apartments that have working locks and doors, but none of them charm me the way my New York City squalors did.

I used to think that every eventful thing that happened in my life would feel as good as moving to New York City did, that my life would be like moving to New York, over and over and over again. I know now that as with falling in love, you're lucky if it happens to you even once.

MISFITS FIT HERE

MARIE MYUNG-OK LEE

ven before I'd ever set foot on its teeming streets, New York City represented to me the perfect place. As in perfectly opposite of the place I was: I was nine and growing up in Hibbing, Minnesota, a rural mining town where, in winter, snowdrifts could easily engulf cars. I was bookish, introverted, the daughter of Korean immigrants. Everyone else seemed tall, blond, athletic. The center of town was the indoor hockey arena that seated hundreds. *My* favorite place was the tiny public library. My love of reading and solitude did not make me a particularly sought-after playmate.

The billboard that welcomes you to Hibbing boasts WORLD'S LARGEST OPEN PIT MINE!! There is little preserved to indicate Bob Dylan ever lived here, confounding the pilgrims who've driven 200 miles straight north from the Minneapolis airport. Any and all locals of a certain age will instead cheerily recount how he was laughed off the stage at the high school talent show or suggest that he hadn't written his own songs. To the town, he wasn't a cause for celebration, but a long-haired countercultural freak. My introduction to him as a child was when we sang "Blowin' in the Wind" in music class—with no adults ever mentioning that *the man who wrote it* was from our town.

If you're a misfit, either you acquiesce to having your rough edges pummeled to fit the groove of conformity or you leave. Dylan left Hibbing almost immediately after that disastrous performance at the high school and headed for—where else?—New York.

For me, I'd similarly marked New York as my future destination—I'd already decided to become a writer, and that's where the writers went. Logical.

Taking William Saroyan's advice about how to become a writer—"You write, man, you write"—I wrote. In my senior year of high school, my essay "Volunteer Workers Are Not Schmucks!" was accepted by *Seventeen*. "Schmuck" was a word I picked up from *MAD* magazine, unaware of its origins in the word "penis." The lack of Jews in our town (again, Robert Zimmerman's family was one of the few) left me unacquainted with Yiddish, yet here I was already speaking like a New Yorker. My editor gently changed the title to "Volunteer Work Does Pay Off!"

It is strange to think you can have a spiritual home even before you have ever been there. But some places are so iconic—the Taj Mahal, Paris, the moon—it is possible to know them from afar. That was New York for me. When I arrived, everything was instantly familiar. What people are most apt to complain about—the bustle and chaos—both excited and soothed me. I didn't like the urine smells, the near-suffocation by crowds, the unbearably hot subway cars covered with lurid graffiti. But that was also a symptom that the place was chockablock with *people*. What it was, I realized, was the teeming number of human stories being pushed right into my face—a cornucopia from the muse, the freedom to observe unobserved. This environment doesn't exist in a small town, where you never escape surveillance.

When I was out and about in Hibbing, curtains would swish aside, Vincent Price eyes peering out. Was it small-town snoopiness or the dreaded invisible letter "A" (being Asian in a white town)? Once, when my sister and I went to play at the house of a little girl we knew from church, she started closing the electric garage door on top of us when she saw us, saying: "My mother told me I'm not supposed to play with you!" *Asian*, I could only conclude.

In New York, being Korean American would be just part of who I was, along with single female writer, recent college grad, cat owner. Ironically, being among such diversity allowed me to seek out others of my various tribes: writers and Asian Americans. I even ended up cofounding the Asian American Writers' Workshop, many of us also former Midwesterners. Hating being singled out for being Asian elsewhere, we could choose to identify as such in New York. And, ironically, with Korean groceries starting to dot the Upper West Side, the owners would sometimes chide me for not speaking Korean; in New York, sometimes, I wasn't Korean *enough*. A former premed student who majored in economics, I had a day job at an investment bank. Therefore, I didn't live in a garret or with tons of roommates. A Wall Street salary allowed me one of those 1970s cookie-cutter high-rises, across the street from the Merkin Concert Hall, the name I secretly smiled at every day (look up "merkin" if you haven't read *Valley of the Dolls*). The apartment was a studio sloppily bisected by a fake wall to make it into a one-bedroom. It made the space smaller, but I liked having another room to go into. The "view" was a close-up of the Chinese consulate, a similarly featureless brick building. Tower Records (now defunct) blocked out any aspirational sun, so that even on the brightest days, the best I'd get was a pencil-thin shaft of light moving through the interstice between the buildings, not enough to sustain even an air plant. Instead, I got a cat, who spent all day snoring on the printer.

On weekends, I wrote, often straight through the day. I found I longed to look into the distance while writing. The longest view I had was straight down, six stories into the Chinese consulate's courtyard, where people would be walking in endless circles as if they were in prison.

Something about having that first New York City apartment made suffering fun. Maybe not fun, but novel, a sacrificial rite of passage, the way medical residents have to stay up all night for days

at a time. It had been almost comical, the logistics of containing the necessities of daily life in two shallow closets, then trying to make the only-in-New-York decisions such as determining which cleaning supplies were attractive enough to remain out (vacuum) and which needed to be hidden (bucket, mop, and rubber gloves).

I had moved to New York with an inchoate sense that writers went there and then stuff happened. Writing-wise, the straightforward transaction—write, get paid, make a living—that I'd envisioned given my early *Seventeen* success turned out to be more complicated. The alumni contacts at magazines that I'd been given by the college career office all rebuffed me. At the investment bank, I earned ample money with handsome benefits, but the work left me so exhausted, I understood the logic of seeking a no-think job like waitressing. I was waking up at 4:30 AM just to get in a solid hour of writing before heading off to my job where a misplaced decimal point could mean disaster. I was a terrible employee but also a stunted writer. While my e-banking peers were applying to Harvard Business School, I continued to write. But on a practical level, while I occasionally did a small nonfiction piece for *Seventeen*, for which I received twenty-five dollars, I couldn't even get journals that didn't pay to take my fiction. During those early years, the highest-paying gig I scored was a free dinner for winning a writing contest at *West Side Weekly*, describing my travails at the DMV. My first short story publication was still a decade away; by then I was so accustomed to rejection, I reflexively threw away the acceptance letter, only later to dig it out of the trash— *Wait, did it really say, "We would be happy to publish—"?*

I still wrote. I even finished a novel. And what had begun as mild distaste for my job at the august Goldman Sachs became full-bore loathing. But it brought in the money and allowed me to stay in New York, where I still held out hope that proximity to the literary world might engender its affection for me. I acquired an unexpected "in" when my boyfriend (now husband) followed me to New York one year later and won a job as an editorial assistant at a venerable publishing house. To make up for the poverty-line salary ($13,000), assistants often received invitations to literary events. One of my favorites was a book party at the now-defunct Mars bar in the East Village for a literary journal called *Between C and D*, where we sat in the semi-dark as an author read, accompanied by a screeching flute.

At a more sedate PEN event, I was standing in line to get a book signed by two authors I loved. The signing broke up before they got to me, and Author number 1 said the equivalent of "Fuck off, kid," while number 2 actually took a minute to chat with me. When I tremulously mentioned that I'd written a novel, she said I should send her twenty pages.

As improbable as it seems, that is how I found my first agent. Not only that, Author number 2 has become a good friend, thus confirming that the daily slog of living in New York—the crowds, my long commute to Wall Street, the lack of space, the heaviness of bags of kitty litter—could pay off.

In your twenties, you always secretly think you're the one person who's never going to grow old, your evidence being that the next day you're not old, or the next or the next—ta-dah! But one day, you're thirty, and no matter how well preserved you look, chronological limitations begin to become apparent. At thirty I was a published novelist, had sold an op-ed to the *The New York Times*, had done a few teaching gigs—and I was also very tired.

Goldman Sachs had to plunder the U.S. economy without me. I'd quit to write full-time and found my new life still kept me on a frantic treadmill: paying for rent, food, utilities *plus* my own social security taxes. And no more luxury medical insurance where I actually *made* money every time I went to see the dentist, no more free Wall Street travel clinic where you could get your shots for dengue fever and prophylactic antibiotics for your trip to Cozumel. Now, I had a high-deductible "catastrophic" plan paid out of pocket that dissuaded me from ever seeking medical help for anything short of losing an extremity. To make up for the inevitable shortfalls, I established a small word-processing and editing business from my apartment, as well as a job reading submissions for *Ladies' Home Journal*'s "Helpful Hints" column. Even income from three sources wasn't enough; I returned to work part-time for another investment bank.

My personal life was also starting to shift. The idea I'd had at age nine of life in New York—cat, tiny apartment, lots and lots of writing—turned out to be eerily accurate. But its sustainability came into question. Because my building was a singleton's warehouse—almost all studios and one-bedrooms—as soon as people had children, they moved out, most of them directly to Westchester or Jersey, leaving the child-free to age alone. Given the building's proximity to Lincoln Center and Juilliard, there were musicians and actors who, you could tell, had begun full of youth and potential and were now bittering past the ingenue parts and prodigy stages, realizing that after they had sacrificed space, sanity, fertility, and whatnot in pursuit of their art, New York was not going to keep up its half of the Faustian bargain.

I knew I would always write, but I wasn't sure I wanted to end up like my neighbor, an older man named Vincent, who slowly went batty as his aging brain oxidized: Yelling at me for allegedly not saying hi to him moments after I did. Leaving his door open at all hours, which also meant I could see he often didn't leave the apartment for weeks. He seemed to have no discernible relatives or friends or outside activities besides procuring the minimum for biological survival. Sun, rain, snow: the days marched on by, his relentless routine—and mine. One day, the clock ran out for Vincent. Nothing violent, just whatever battery that had been animating him ran out.

After a dozen years, I had a hankering, if not for open spaces, then for something new. The exigencies of my current novel, which was set in Korea, drove me to apply for a Fulbright to do research.

I won the Fulbright and believed my leaving New York to be temporary. My plan was to spend the next academic year in Korea, come back, and resume writing and life as it was before. Life,

however, had other plans. My boyfriend (who selflessly agreed to take the cat) was now my fiancé. I was just as adamant about my writing career, but becoming less rigid about where to conduct it. We wedged our wedding in between my leaving for Seoul and Karl's first job as a professor at a college in Ohio. Somehow, in this short time, my mother-in-law was diagnosed with pancreatic cancer. I hadn't even fully unpacked in Seoul before I flew back from Korea to take care of her until she died, a few weeks later. Then my new husband had two cats to take care of and no wife. It was a long year, at the end of which we received the wonderful news that he'd been chosen for a job at our alma mater, Brown.

We inherited one of Karl's family cars, an aged but sturdy Jetta, and I remember an odd sense of relief as we drove my stuff from the Upper West Side north to Providence. No more ridiculous humidity in summer! A yard! Being by the ocean! And because we'd both gone to Brown, the place was already familiar, and manageable. It was a wonder, the small stuff, like driving to the grocery store and stocking up heedlessly, instead of mentally calculating how much one could stand to carry.

We bought a house. It was a modest four-square, but our New York friends marveled at the size. There was a single-car garage for the Jetta, and even a pizza-slice of a yard. This was the early 2000s, when most of our friends had also left New York, either priced out by the beginning of the hedge funders' era or smoked out by the devastation of 9/11. Even our most stalwart friend, Gordon, who lived in a tiny apartment not far from mine, a place so small he slept in a loft and kept books in his unused stove, gave up and went to graduate school in, of all places, Indiana.

It was an end of an era, of my twenties, of my youth, but also of much of my searching anxiety: What would the future hold? Would I succeed as a writer? Would I get married? As I headed into my fourth decade, I finally realized what would happen would happen, whether I worried about it or not. I enjoyed my new outlook in the easy yet circumscribed life of a college town. I began to associate

anxious or harried feelings with New York, where anything could and would happen at any time—but in a bad way—as opposed to Providence, where nothing much seemed to ever happen at all.

I didn't miss New York. We had a child with medical issues, and treatments and driving him from doctor to doctor consumed a decade. When he was stable enough that I could travel, I could go into New York for the day on the train and be back in the early evening. One year, I judged a literary contest whose gala celebration was held at the Marriott Marquis in Times Square. The crowds were so thick, I got stuck in them like quicksand. Once I staggered into my room, there was still no peace: the crazy blinking NIKON CAMERA sign still invaded the space with its red neon light, even through the blackout curtains. This was all way too fast, annoying, unsustainable, right?

Actually, as with the addict who still dreams of the lingering taste of the forbidden, that upswelling feeling—of happiness, of unobserved observation, of the strangest kind of normalcy—came back with a rush, even staying in the tourist trap that is Times Square. Yes, I had quit New York, but it hadn't quit me. I still carried around those feelings like a magnet that became reactivated every time I returned. But I had a child now, a teaching job, a house, and a community. New York was for the dreamers, the unattached, mobile types.

Act II: an opportunity for jobs in New York, for both my husband and me, came seemingly out of the blue. At first, we categorically dismissed it. It was going to be too hard on our son, now twelve. To prove it to ourselves, we brought him down for an interview at one of the specialized schools for the disabled and waited for the stress and endless tantrums. To our surprise, he didn't tantrum, not once. In his own unique way, he found the chaos oddly soothing. He lost his phobia of dogs in a day. He has severe cognitive impairments, so I know he didn't pine for New York or even know what it was. But he wasn't unhappy, and that's something, because he often seems very, very unhappy. Could it be that New York might be a destination for him, the way it was for me?

Reader, we moved back.

MANHATTAN, ALWAYS OUT OF REACH

ANN HOOD

"You can go anywhere you want," my father told me, "except New York City."

It was 1973. I was sixteen years old and had my life savings—eight hundred dollars earned from modeling for our local department store—burning a hole in my bank account. Summer loomed. I'd ditched my boyfriend of two years, and now I was ready for an adventure.

When I approached my father with my cockeyed plan of taking my money and beginning what I hoped would be a lifetime of globe-trotting, New York City hadn't even occurred to me. I had palm trees on my mind. Sandy beaches. Sailboats and balmy nights. Boys. To me then, New York City existed in Doris Day–Rock Hudson movies. Women wore pillbox hats, cute pajamas, bobbed hair. Everyone worked in a skyscraper. Men acted goofy; women whipped them into shape.

"Go to New York City, and you'll be grounded for life," my father continued. "People get murdered there. Or worse."

"Worse than murdered?" I said, unable to imagine what that might mean.

"That's right. And young girls are especially vulnerable."

I nodded, suddenly very interested in New York City.

"Do you understand me?" my father said with his *I mean business* glare.

I slid a brochure I'd picked up from the travel agency at the mall across the table to him.

"How about here?" I asked him.

The pink sand beaches of Bermuda glistened on the glossy cover.

My father smiled. "Perfect," he said.

For the next several years, I saved my money for those summer trips. Nassau? Okay with my father, who somehow missed that they'd just had a violent civil war. Rio? Sounded great to my father, who had no idea that crime there was higher than in New York City. Off I went, navigating pickpockets, street curfews, poverty. What, I wondered, could possibly be going on in New York City that was more dangerous, more threatening, than all this? And, of course, like anyone who is told no often enough, I went to find out.

M y first trip to New York City, when I was seven, was a whirlwind of Macy's, the Empire State Building, and club sandwiches at a diner. On a whim, my parents took us there for the day, and my strongest memory is of revolving doors. It seemed to me then that to enter anywhere in Manhattan, you had to step into one and spin. One night in college, my friends and I decided to drive to New York City. None of us had ever really been there, and so we drove into Times Square and, terrified by the porn shops and hooded drug dealers, turned around and drove home. Another college trip by bus took me to MOMA and then safely back to Rhode Island. That was it.

Until the November morning in 1982 when I boarded a flight in San Francisco and met the guy in 47F who was moving to New York

that very day. I was a flight attendant, and even though I flew out of JFK, I lived in Boston, commuting by airplane to work. When I got stuck or had an early morning check-in, I crashed on my cousin's couch in his fifth-floor walk-up in Greenwich Village. Nothing I saw there enticed me to move to Manhattan. But that guy in 47F changed my mind. On our first date, we walked from his East Village apartment to the Café Riviera across town, the November wind making us cold enough to have to hold hands to stay warm.

I could see what my father didn't like. We had to sidestep homeless people who lined the sidewalks. The graffiti-covered subways smelled like urine and unwashed bodies. Panhandlers, drug dealers, drug addicts, scam artists, and muggers crowded the streets. There was noise—traffic, shouting, horns, boom boxes. What surprised me was how my father had known that I would be seduced by the city and all it offered up to me.

On the walk back to 47F's apartment, I turned to him and, surprising both of us, announced: "I'm moving here."

"When?" he said, his brown eyes twinkling.

"Next week."

Always impulsive, always someone who leapt before she looked, the next week I found myself squatting in a half-empty apartment in my cousin's building on West 4th Street. Some of my friends thought I'd moved for a guy. And they were partially right, I suppose. But what I realized that afternoon I spent walking in the cold, dirty city was that I had outgrown my life so far: the pretty seaside town where I'd lived with my Springer Spaniel, sailing and drinking oversized Cape Codders; the neat brownstone-lined streets of Boston, crowded with people in Izod shirts the colors of sherbet; the familiar roads of my hometown, with its sad empty mills and triple-decker houses.

But Manhattan seemed to open its filthy arms to me that day and beckon. I could not tell the Empire State Building from the Chrysler Building or uptown from downtown. I didn't know east from west or streets from avenues. I only knew that, despite my father's warnings and fears, I had finally found the place I belonged.

My first apartment was at 228 Sullivan Street, in a former convent painted pink, its Caribbean exterior a sharp contrast to all the grimy black around it. The day I moved in, I boldly left my 300-square-foot studio and walked the maze of Greenwich Village. The guy from 47F was going to show up that night, so the entire day stretched out before me without obligation or purpose. I wandered into Three Lives Bookstore to browse, into Café Reggio for a cappuccino, into the Third Street Bazaar and the Grand Union and every tiny store that sold earrings or posters or fruit or magazines. At some point on that journey, it felt as if all my cells settled into place, as if my body had shifted, rearranged itself, and I became exactly who I was supposed to be.

I will never leave here, I thought that June afternoon. That thought repeated itself almost daily as my first summer moved along. It was a very hot summer, relentlessly so. I would go to the Grand Union supermarket on Bleecker Street and stand in the frozen food section to cool off. Or I would ride the Staten Island ferry for a nickel round-trip and stand at the front each way to catch a breeze thick with East River stench. On the Fourth of July, I joined the throngs on the closed FDR Drive to watch fireworks. *I will never leave here*, I thought as the neon colors exploded over the river.

That fall, I left Sullivan Street for another sublet at 320 West 23rd Street. I got a cat I named Daphne, and as I sat on my futon writing stories in a notebook, she perched on the windowsill and watched the pigeons through the iron grate there. One day she jumped down and landed with an odd thud. As soon as I glanced up, I saw what I should have noticed sooner: Daphne was pregnant, had come to me already pregnant. Within a week, she gave birth to a litter of six kittens in my only closet. That same week I bought a co-op at 77 Bleecker Street, and as soon as I could move them I took a taxi there with a box of kittens, Daphne, and my trash bag of clothes. A U-Haul met us there, filled with my belongings from my former life.

I had only lived in New York City for a little over a year, but it felt like a lifetime already. When I opened the boxes I had carefully packed and labeled, what I found inside seemed to belong to a stranger. The blue-flowered couch I'd saved for years earlier looked out of place now; the brass bed with its red-and-blue sheets and matching comforter made me cringe. How could I have changed so much so quickly? My clothes, bought at a vintage store called Cheap Jack's, hung only briefly beside the winter coat I'd worn in Boston and Polo sweaters I used to collect, before I packed up everything from my old life and put it all out on the sidewalk. That winter, I didn't have a coat. Instead, I bought a black motorcycle jacket and a scarf from a street vendor. My uniform. *Me.*

I *will never leave here*, I thought every day.

Yet all I did was leave. Again and again, my heart breaking each time I watched Manhattan recede.

The first time I moved away, I decided to follow my heart to live with a man in Washington, D.C. He rented us a house with a screened-in back porch in a nondescript neighborhood near Georgetown. From the minute I stepped inside, I knew I had made a mistake. But I'd given up everything to try this, so try I did. I got a car after years of subways and walking. I searched for the kinds of places I'd grown to love back in New York, the perfect bookstore and café and restaurant, the vintage stores and one-of-a-kind shops. Surely they were out there. I was in a big city, wasn't I? But everything I found fell short. The entire city felt off somehow. *I* felt off. I would spend entire afternoons flopped on the bed, a pillow over my face, trying to figure out how I could find my way back to where I belonged. Finally, my father convinced me to just do it. Leave, he told me.

On a walk that night with the man I had followed there, I announced that I was going back to New York. "Well then," he said, "let's get married." Confused, I told him I was leaving, moving away. He nodded. "Okay," he said, "but let's get married." And just like that I found myself back in Manhattan, in a sublet apartment in the Ansonia on the Upper West Side, with a husband.

A husband who hated New York.

As soon as I'd happily settled in, he was looking for a way out. Every night he offered me a new city or town. Portland, Maine. Nyack, New York. Montclair, New Jersey. Boston. Or Boxborough, Massachusetts. Westport, Connecticut. No, I'd say. No, no, no. When the sublet fell through, we found ourselves homeless and at an impasse. I was touring lofts in Tribeca; he was house hunting in Westchester County. "Can't we just give someplace else a try?" he asked as we stood in front of a white house a few blocks from the main street in Katonah, a suburb just an hour's train ride from the city.

"If I hate it," I said, hating it already, "we move back to Manhattan."

The deal struck, I found myself lost again. I took that train into the city as often as I could, wandering the streets of the East Village, crying. Meeting friends for lunch and crying. Sitting on the train back to Katonah, crying. There, I'd drive the beautiful country roads wondering what was wrong with me. Why couldn't I love it out here? In no time, I was back on the bed with a pillow over my face, making an escape plan. "Just leave," my father said again.

"I'm moving back to the city," I announced over dinner. "I hate it here."

The man I'd married looked upset. But then he brightened and offered me yet another option. "How about Brooklyn?"

I took it.

B ack then, no one really wanted to live in Brooklyn. Now, when I see twenty-somethings eagerly leaving Manhattan for Brooklyn, I can't help but remember how our Manhattan friends wouldn't even come out to Park Slope for dinner. We moved into the third floor of a brownstone on Montgomery Place, and although I wasn't completely happy with my latest compromise, I wasn't miserable either. Now that I was near enough to Manhattan to feel at home, now that my cells could settle into place again, I realized that although our geographic preferences differed, it was actually the marriage that wasn't making me happy.

I didn't need my father to tell me what to do this time. I was going to leave my marriage, and when I did, I was going back to Manhattan. We carefully divided everything in half, and with my half I moved into a skinny duplex on Leroy Street. Just as quickly as those other places felt wrong, this one felt right. I would lie in bed on Sunday mornings with my fat *New York Times* and NPR playing, my cats on my feet, and the sounds of the city outside my window, content.

I will never leave here, I'd think.

And then, yet again, I left.

"Y ou are going to move to Providence and marry me and have a baby," the handsome man told me.

I laughed. "You're crazy. I'm never leaving New York."

Six months later, his prophecy came true.

This time, with a baby on the way, I didn't have time to feel miserable. I was too busy being terrified, excited, confused. When that baby was born, my crying began. I didn't know anybody except my handsome husband, who went off to work every day. So I strapped Sam into his carseat and went to New York. All the time. We slept on friends' sofas. We ate at Benny's Burritos and the Cowgirl Hall of Fame. I agreed to teach writing workshops at NYU and lived a half-

life in Manhattan and a half-life in Providence. Whenever my hand-some husband and I fought, I reminded him how much I missed New York. But this time, there was no going back. Not really.

I had a baby, and then another baby. Even spending half my time there became difficult. Eventually I stopped teaching at NYU. I made friends in Providence. I built a life. A nice life. A happy one.

Until the day my five-year-old daughter died suddenly from a virulent form of strep, and in that instant nothing was the same. The young woman who had moved to New York City, and who had spent so much time trying to get back there, seemed distant and foreign to me. My world became the walls of my bedroom. Beyond it lay too many painful memories. Sparkles from Grace's art projects still littered the floor. Her laundered clothes waited to be put away. The contents of her backpack—a perfectly filled-in *Weekly Reader,* a Ra-mona Quimby book, a paper on which she'd counted by tens all the way to five hundred—and her shoes tossed by the door and her ballet bag and her lunchbox, all of it was out there. New York didn't matter. Nothing mattered.

I locked myself in my bedroom and thought, *I will never leave here.*

Time passes. It does. The fog of grief lifts, unbelievably. And when it did, I found that I needed to redefine myself. Or at least, to try to remember who I had been and who I would be from now on.

When I was invited to teach in New York, I asked my hus-band and son what they thought. Maybe they knew me then better than I knew myself. Do it, they told me. I rented an apartment on Barrow Street, and two nights a week I stayed there. I did it partially for convenience, but also to reclaim that piece of myself. It didn't feel like a half-life this time. Instead, New York reminded me who I was.

I was a woman who liked to walk the streets of New York City, fast and for hours.

I liked to eat Vietnamese sandwiches standing up or to walk across town to try a new dive restaurant. I liked to spend hours in the Strand bookstore or in a museum or even waiting in line for half-price theater tickets. All those years ago, my cells had settled into place that first time I left my Sullivan Street apartment. Now I was getting in touch with that girl I was—optimistic, open to anything, wide-eyed and willing. Grief had taken that part of me. It had turned me fearful and sad. But that winter in New York, that fear began to crumble. I understood that it would never leave me entirely. Nor would the grief. But somehow, I could open my heart again.

Even though I've kept an apartment in the city ever since that sublet on Barrow Street, my heart still breaks a little every time I leave. And it lifts every time I go back. My New York, no longer filthy or crime-ridden, still opens its arms to me and takes me in when I need it. Even though my father believed it was a dangerous place, what I know now is that to me it is a place of comfort. It is a place of discovery. It is the place where I found my own true self, again and again and again.

THINK OF THIS AS A WINDOW

MAGGIE ESTEP

I fell in love with New York City one day in 1971, when I saw dozens of people blithely stepping over a dead body on a sidewalk. I was seven years old, walking in Midtown with my grandfather. It was summer. The air smelled like rotting fruit. Steam rose from food vendor carts. There were snarls of traffic, bleating horns, women in cheap knee-length skirts. And that dead body. On the sidewalk. It was probably a drunk, very much alive, just unconscious, but I didn't know that then. I thought that this city was a place where people lay rotting in the street and no one noticed.

I looked to my grandfather's face, then to the faces of the other passersby. Everyone was completely ignoring that dead body. I gave my grandfather's sleeve a tug, but he didn't feel it or maybe didn't want to explain what that body was doing there. Even though it would have been excellent evidence in the case he was constantly building against the city that, to him, was a dirty, dangerous place filled with thieves, hippies, runaways, con men, and hookers. He only lived there because my grandmother was ill and needed to be close to good hospitals.

I lived elsewhere, with my nomadic horse trainer parents. We moved a lot. I was always the new kid in town, the one that favored black clothes and smelled like horses.

As I watched people stepping over that body, I felt relief. If the people of New York didn't bother looking at a dead body, then they weren't going to bother looking at me. I had found the only place where I was not out of place, where looking vaguely Mediterranean wasn't a cause for staring.

I moved to Lower Manhattan ten years later, when I was seventeen. The only things I cared about were books and music. I got a job as a receptionist at a record company on West 57th Street and rented the only apartment anyone would rent me, a slanted-floor two-room hovel on Ludlow Street. I knew nothing of the neighborhood's venerable past as the overcrowded home to thousands of immigrants, gang members, shysters, corrupt politicians, and would-be presidential assassins. It was just a cheap place to live. The building superintendent, a Haitian man named Mike who wore talisman necklaces and had a lot of facial scarring, gladly took my security deposit and handed me the key. "You call if you need anything," he said, "anything at all." He failed to give me his phone number, and anyway, I didn't get a phone installed.

There was a pay phone at the corner of Ludlow and Stanton. Every month or so, I'd get a fistful of change and call my mother to tell her I was alive. She was suspicious about the song of the Mister Softee truck in the background. It didn't matter what time of day it was, or even which season. The Mister Softee truck was always around, and its insane circus song always playing. One day, I saw a guy with a sawed-off shotgun inside the Mister Softee truck. Probably a lookout for the heroin trade that was the chief industry of the Lower East Side in the early 1980s. The guy saw me staring at him and smiled. That was the thing: I was like a rat or a pigeon, blending in perfectly in this neighborhood. No one bothered me or was bothered by me.

Down the hall lived a man named Jody who was very beautiful. He often shot heroin and sometimes wore women's clothing. He told me that Taylor Mead, the writer and performer of Warhol fame, lived

on the top floor of our building, across from She-Bear, the woman with a hundred cats. Jody said if you stood in the hall at certain times of day, you'd hear Taylor Mead clanging around up there, recording himself talking. But I didn't like standing in the hall. I had moved to New York to be near lots of people without actually having to interact with them.

Sometimes, I went to nightclubs with my lone friend, Bliss, a big-breasted blonde. We would dance all night with beautiful men. Most of these men were gay, but that was fine; we were more interested in dancing and getting drunk than in having sex. One night, at the Mudd Club, we were dancing so violently to James Chance and his band that a man who had been staring at us all night came over and asked if we were being paid by the band.

When the clubs closed, I'd walk home through a silence so deep I could hear packs of rats moving through garbage bags. Many of the buildings were vacant, holes in their sides where windows had been. Over a bricked-in window someone had spray-painted THINK OF THIS AS A WINDOW.

When the end of the world came, this is what it would be like. And I'd be ready.

I was a loner, but there were people I saw so often that talking to them was unavoidable. There was the pasty guy with dyed black hair who waited for the F train in the same spot I did every morning. I went on a date with him and, a few days later, moved in with him over on Suffolk Street. Two doors down was an empty building with a thriving heroin trade, its entrance guarded by Tina, a tiny Puerto Rican girl. Tina sat on a milk crate in front of the building, tugging at the hem of her miniskirt, speaking in rapid-fire Spanglish to customers and loudly calling out "Agua, agua," or some equally arbitrary word, when a police cruiser drifted by, as if the cops would have no idea what the touts were doing when they suddenly started crying out "Water!" at the top of their lungs.

Tina usually had a brown paper bag in her lap. I always figured she had a sandwich in there. One day, she opened the bag and

showed me a tiny black pistol. "Is that real?" I asked. Tina grinned. She was missing a tooth.

Tina vanished at some point, and eventually, the wide-open drug emporium did too, pushed from the Lower East Side over into Brooklyn and up into Harlem before eventually disappearing entirely as beepers took the place of people like Tina, and investors bought up all the abandoned buildings.

I broke up with the guy from the subway, got fired from my record company job, and then left the Lower East Side for a few years, living in Colorado and belatedly going to college. When I came back to the city, it was different. Avenue A was dotted with boutiques. There were new restaurants that were not Polish diners.

I moved into a room in a rent-controlled apartment on Avenue C. There were rats. I would hear them at night, knocking things over. I'd put boots on, walk into the kitchen, flick the lights on, and find the rats nonchalantly snacking on dry goods, like a bunch of old people at an early-bird buffet. They wouldn't budge until I swung a broom at them. Sometimes, they rose onto their haunches and hissed at me.

This was exactly the New York my grandfather had railed against when I was a little kid. It was squalid. Probably more squalid than anything he'd seen in his years living there. He was now in Princeton, New Jersey, in a clean, contemporary house that I was afraid to visit for fear I'd dirty anything I touched. It wasn't just the city that was squalid now. I was too. I lived in the margins, as did most of the people I knew. I wore outfits cobbled together from hand-me-downs from my friend Tom, a struggling filmmaker who stocked up on clothing from dumpsters and thrift shops in Ohio. I lived on very little money. Which isn't to say I felt deprived in any way. If I wanted to partake of that alternate New York, the one above 14th Street, the New York of dinner parties and polite society and elegant cocktail dresses, I could clean up pretty good. But the New York I loved was down here. The New York I loved was a lawless, exhilarating place where anything was possible.

My fortunes improved by the early 1990s, when I graduated

from a long succession of odd jobs to earning money as a writer and performer. I rented a vermin-free garden-facing apartment on East 5th Street. It was by no means luxurious, but it was clean, and very quiet for a New York apartment. Except sometimes at 3 AM. I had an upstairs neighbor who woke in the middle of the night to play his keyboard and croon in an eerie low voice that wasn't without beauty. The songs he played over and over were so unusual that I didn't really mind being woken.

One day, my kitchen ceiling started leaking. Water poured from the apartment above, where the Crooner lived. I went up and knocked. I could hear him in there running water, but it took my knocking several times before a small nervous man in a bath towel opened the door a few inches and peered out at me. I explained that something from his apartment was leaking and pouring down into my kitchen.

"Sorry," he mumbled before shutting the door. That was my lone interaction with him until one day, when I opened the *Village Voice* to the music section and found a picture of the Crooner. He was, it turned out, Stephin Merritt of the Magnetic Fields. In the same issue of the *Voice* was a review of one of my books, and apparently he saw it: a few days later, I passed him in the hall and we both stopped short and, for the first time, said hello. That was it. Just eye contact and a hello. An acknowledgment. *Oh, so you're that person.*

By the late 1990s my beloved Lower East Side wasn't squalid anymore. The once-vacant buildings had been scrubbed, the people selling books and bicycle parts from blankets spread on the sidewalk were replaced by sandwich boards hawking gourmet foods. The Key Foods on Avenue A no longer required the full-time services of rent-a-cops to stop the shoplifting junkies. There were no junkies. They had all died or moved, migrating to the outer boroughs or to cities that were still sordid, like Baltimore or Philadelphia. Tompkins Square Park was now a clean, safe place where white women with small children gathered and purebred dogs frolicked in the dog park.

I hated it.

I decamped to Brooklyn, to an apartment in the tiny cobble-stoned Vinegar Hill neighborhood just north of Dumbo, where brothels had once thrived in the still-intact storefronts along Hudson Avenue. Two blocks away from my new digs were the Farragut Houses, a housing project that, for a while at least, deterred developers. After moving to Vinegar Hill, I learned that my novelist friend Donald Antrim had lived in that very apartment a few years earlier. The city had a way of entwining us around one another, throwing us all together, stacking us one on top of the other, shuffling us, making us begin friendships or collaborations or romances. Or sometimes we just noticed each other, nodded once in recognition, moved on.

From the window of my home office, I could see one of the towers of the World Trade Center. That morning, my then-boyfriend John and I heard a sort of muffled boom. A few minutes later, a neighbor came and told us the World Trade Center was on fire. We walked to the nearby Brooklyn Bridge, went up onto the walkway, and saw hundreds of people pouring across the bridge, fleeing Lower Manhattan. Some were covered in ash. Everyone kept looking back, eyes wide, at the burning towers. Then the first tower collapsed. A wail rose from the crowd. People started screaming prayers up to the smoke-filled sky.

That night, Lower Manhattan, blanketed in debris, smoky, silent, lightless, looked like a disaster movie set. John and I had ridden our bikes over the Manhattan Bridge. It was so soon after the collapse that barricades had not yet been erected. I didn't even know that a firefighter friend was dead, that another had survived, that my friend Judy had been ten minutes late for work at Morgan Stanley and thus not in the building when it was hit.

The streets surrounding the giant pile of death were empty and quieter than any quiet I had ever heard in New York. People in hazmat suits were tromping around in a daze. The air was smoky, and there was a thick coating of ash over everything. It didn't occur to us that we were breathing in dead people, including some that we knew and cared about.

In the ensuing weeks, I imagined that New York would go wild again, that the rich would flee, infrastructure would crumble, the populace would grow restless, manic, and inspired. Graffiti would come back; punk would be born all over again. Quite the opposite happened. For the few tired souls who did leave after 9/11, replacements arrived, buying real estate, spreading the gentrification so that soon much of Brooklyn was overcrowded and expensive and large parts of Queens too.

Around this time, I started taking longer and longer bike rides, pushing into the far reaches of the outerboroughs, looking for still-untamed pockets of my city. I was location scouting. For books I was writing or would write. For images of the city to burn into my heart. I didn't know it yet, but I was starting the long process of breaking up with New York.

Luc Sante, inspired chronicler of New York's underbelly, wrote, "The more I felt I was losing my city the more preoccupied I became with it."

That was it exactly.

I came to know every crevice of New York. I rode to the northernmost tip of Manhattan, to the then-end of the bike path, past the George Washington Bridge, and then across town to the Triboro Bridge where I rode over crack pipe shards and bird shit, down into Randall's Island.

I rode my bike to Aqueduct Racetrack, where I would lose myself in the grandstands. Just a few thousand souls wandered the cavernous, faded facility that had been built to hold many more. Almost all these characters, of wildly varied economic and ethnic backgrounds, were men. I was a novelty. No one bothered me, but they noticed me. A man named Mohammed, who was allegedly a diplomat, thought that by virtue of my gender and relative youth I must be in possession of secret insights into the outcome of races. Sometimes I was. Once when Mohammed asked, "Who do you like in the finale?" I shrugged and indicated a fit, happy-looking gray horse named Napoleon Solo, whose odds were 60 to 1. The horse

won. I was, for a day, the queen of Aqueduct Racetrack. At least as far as Mohammed was concerned.

I rode to Coney Island often, especially in winter. I loved the slumbering rides, their metal limbs sticking up from the earth like the skeletons of large birds. Fortune-teller stalls and balloon shooting games were shuttered, the only signs of life coming from nearby trailers encircled by chain-link fencing. Dogs, mostly pit bulls, roamed the small yards. I would stand staring at these beautiful muscular creatures, who didn't bother with gratuitous barking, who simply looked at me, read my face, found no mal intent there, then looked away.

I rode to the home of the Federation of Black Cowboys, out at the edge of east New York, where Brooklyn butts up against Howard Beach, Queens. These cowboys (and some cowgirls) have a stable spread over a few acres on South Conduit Avenue, just before JFK airport. For a time, the overflow from the main stable found refuge across Conduit Avenue, in a cul-de-sac at the end of Dumont Avenue known as the "Hole." There were a few ramshackle homes and, there, stretched along bumpy, ill-paved streets named for gemstones, row upon row of makeshift stables and miniature paddocks, horses poking their silky, benign noses over fences. My friend Cornelius, a member of the federation who kept his paint horse, Dalton, at the Hole, would find someone willing to loan me a horse and we'd go horseback riding, crossing Linden Boulevard, snaking our way through tracts of modest vinyl-clad houses. Crossing the Belt Parkway, we'd see the seriously startled faces of drivers as we made our way into Gateway National Park to ride along Jamaica Bay.

Sometimes I'd ride the bike out to Rockaway, across the Marine Parkway Bridge and to the water's edge. The beach was exquisite, pristine even, and I seldom saw another human being. I could have been anywhere. But I was in New York. No matter how far I went, to the very end of the land, when I turned back, I was still in New York City.

As I rode toward home after these jaunts, everything crowded in on me: cars, people, garbage, noise. The whirring of humanity.

I started dreading the crowded subway, so I stopped taking it.

If I had to travel from Brooklyn to Manhattan, I rode my bike. If the weather was too extreme for that, I stayed home. I mapped out a special route to walk my dog to the park, a route where there was some likelihood I would not encounter a single human being.

My world got very small. I barely ventured to concerts, hardly went to the Met to visit the paintings I loved. My city had become so crowded and bright I couldn't think in it anymore, almost couldn't see it anymore.

I'd been going upstate to the Woodstock area for years, and one day, on a whim, I called up a realtor friend and went to look at houses. I found a strange, fairy-tale-looking house made of brown wood with purple trim. It only had half an acre, but to me it was a universe, a lush world for my dog to explore, a place that I could study and figure out the way I had studied and figured out New York. The kind of enchantment I yearned for now was in learning the basics of human existence, living near forest creatures, stacking firewood, and growing vegetables. I wanted to write about people who could tell time just by looking at the position of the sun in the sky.

I had never imagined living anywhere but New York City until, one day, I did imagine it, and almost immediately I left the only home I'd known.

It was time to leave the noise and the bodies behind. Time for the kind of quiet that only happens deep in the woods, lost, craning my neck up to the sky to find my way.

RUSSIA, WITH LOVE

EMILY GOULD

During the first half of 2009, I left Brooklyn to spend three months in Moscow. The city was cold, smelly, and uncomfortable, and despite some effortful hours spent shouting into the headset provided with the Rosetta Stone software I impulse-bought on the day I applied for my visa, I didn't speak the language. I had no idea what I was supposed to be doing there. One of my most vivid memories from that first trip is of eating tainted Uzbek veal-tongue salad and, as a result, coming the closest I've ever come to shitting myself in public. I managed to make it to a squat toilet outside a train station that I had to pay—god, figuring out that transaction!—an elderly woman for the privilege of using. I had a lot of bougie Brooklyn-born expectations about how things should work and how things should smell and how people should act, and I felt guilty for feeling peeved when those expectations weren't met. I felt my foreignness emphatically all the time. I never really came around to the food. It was probably the happiest I've ever been in my life.

Of course, if you'd asked me how I was feeling at the time I would have said that I was confused and scared, insecure and angry, worried about who I'd been and who I might become. I had come there to stay with a man I loved but still didn't know very well, and some of the time we got along and other times there was a heartbreakingly vast gulf between us, exacerbated by his being comfortable in Russia, and in Russian, and fundamentally unable to imagine how it might feel not to be comfortable there at all. I was working on a book at the time, my first real book, which I'd sold based on a very brief and frankly terrible proposal, and I had no idea whether I'd be able to actually write it. My Russian boyfriend was an established writer, and I compared myself with him a lot. It was not a flattering comparison.

So I felt like a phony who might be found out at any time. I wasn't the kind of person who jetted off to Moscow for no real reason besides that there was nothing preventing me from doing so. I'd never been anywhere before: my twenties up until that point had been spent working a series of all-consuming jobs in Manhattan; my longest vacation from the city since graduating from college there had been a week spent in Delaware. I wasn't on vacation in Moscow, exactly, but I wasn't exactly working, either. I was wandering around the city and procrastinating about my book for many hours every day. I was still coasting on the burst of editorial goodwill that had floated me into the book deal, and there were a couple of easy-peasy freelance assignments that had helped me to pay for my plane ticket. One was a roundup of Hollywood types' favorite onscreen moments from the previous year, and it was easy to do the interviews because the time difference worked in my favor—I could procrastinate until late in the evening and people would be just getting to work on the West Coast. Other than this goofy assignment and my book, I was supposed to be writing something about my impressions of Moscow for an oligarch-funded English-language Russian magazine; my impressions of Moscow were so stupid that even that fluffy publication politely declined to publish them.

Nearly four years later, my impressions are still a bit confused and confusing. After much more experience of Russia and Russians, including the Russian who brought me there in the first place, I almost feel as though I understand the culture even less. It took me a long time to realize, for example, that Russian people aren't mean and cold; they're just not fake. They don't pretend to love the strangers they encounter in shops and restaurants the way Americans do. Russians save their warmth for friends and family and dispense it mostly in the privacy of their own homes. This meant that no one humored me when I tried to bluff and joke and apologize through customer service interactions. When I ordered tea in Russian, the person taking my order would dispassionately ask me, in English, what size I wanted: "Smol or lahj?" "Small," I would say, feeling cheated of an opportunity to say one of the twenty or so words I knew off the top of my head. (I would have gotten the case ending wrong, anyway, though.)

I was mostly alone in these wanderings, which was terrifying at first; navigating the Metro with only vague hunches about how the station names being announced corresponded to the Cyrillic characters on the subway map made me constantly hyper-vigilant lest I end up inadvertently traveling to the Moscow equivalent of the South Bronx. My arrival coincided with the closing of an issue of the literary magazine where my boyfriend works, and he didn't have time to do anything but point me toward various attractions. I spent my first few days in a haze of jet lag, visiting tourist attractions because I felt I had to: the Tretyakov gallery; the impressive, forbiddingly too-perfect mall near Red Square; onion-domed churches galore. I don't remember any of these places very well, only the palm-sweaty interactions I had with ticket takers at their entrances.

My first vivid memories are of grocery shopping, which really was too complicated for me to undertake on my own because, except in the fanciest Western-style overpriced supermarkets, the various foods were kept behind counters and you have to go around asking the meat guy, the canned goods lady, the egg person, the produce mistress, et cetera, to get you what you want. In one basement-level food market near the apartment where we were staying, there was a honey counter (Russian people love honey and take it very seriously) staffed by a man in a white lab coat whom we called "the honey doctor." I wanted very badly to cook for Keith's little grandmother, Baba Ruzya; I thought she would appreciate a night off from the laborious production of the borscht, fried meatballs, and mashed potatoes that constituted our un-changing diet. Of course, when I finally did undertake a meal, produc-ing a salty chicken soup flavored with garlic and ginger that was a highlight of my repertoire at the time, she sweetly refused to eat it, as I should have known she would. She was charmed by my efforts, which I for some reason continued to make during the remainder of my stay, but she simply did not recognize what they produced as food. In ret-rospect, I understand why someone who has managed to become a nonagenarian by eating nothing but borscht and meatballs would be hesitant to change her diet. Well, that's an exaggeration: she also loved pastries, candy, and the extraordinarily unappealing Russian take on ham, which is a creepy pale pinkish gray. "No, thank you. I'm not very hungry," she would say in Russian when I offered her food I'd made, and then eat an impressive pile of gray ham.

When I imagine myself during this time, I see someone who spent a lot of time blithely trying to feed the world an unappeal-ing experimental soup despite overwhelming evidence that no one found it quite as delicious as I did. In many ways this hiatus from my life in New York, with its many competing distractions, marked the end of my oblivious youthful obnoxiousness. No one was really buy-ing my shtick there. No one was impressed when I took yoga classes in Russian and couldn't understand anything the teacher was saying. No one indulgently smiled when I sat on the wrong bench or bagged my own produce at the grocery store; they yelled at me loudly and I had no idea what they were saying and I just stood there with a stupid American expression on my bizarrely, aberrantly un-made-up face and then made my way back to the apartment and cried about it later on in the (low-pressure) shower. No one was sympathetic to my feel-ings of lostness and loneliness and homesickness and pointlessness and confusion, except my boyfriend, who assured me that feeling lonely was important; loneliness would help me to write my book.

Loneliness did help me to write my book, loneliness and having no Internet access in Baba Ruzya's apartment. (Well, there was one corner of the window ledge that you could occasionally get a whiff of WiFi in, especially if you stood on the ledge and held your laptop aloft to get the signal, which I often did.) After a few weeks of aimless wandering into Internet cafés, I woke up one morning and, without knowing exactly how or why, became a slightly different person.

Something had shifted in my brain while I slept, breathing the acrid smell of Moscow that drifted in through the always cracked window of the overheated apartment: diesel exhaust, cigarette smoke, snow and garbage and perfume. Keith made us breakfast: instant coffee made tolerable with condensed milk, buckwheat kasha fried with eggs. I did a few yoga poses in the living room while Baba Ruzya peeked in occasionally to murmur something admiring; occasionally she would walk by and give me a friendly swat on the behind. And then I sat down at my laptop, facing the window with a view of the courtyard behind the building with its dingy old playground equipment and parking lot, and I wrote "World of Blues."

I realize this doesn't sound very important or impressive. More disciplined and productive writers probably have days like this several days a week, but sadly, that was the only time in my life that I've sat down in the morning, started writing, and then stood up seven hours later feeling confident about having finished something, something real. It was Moscow, or kasha, or new love, or loneliness, or not being in New York, or it was just something that happened. That essay isn't the "best" one in my book. It might not even be in the top three. But it's an important one to me because, though I didn't think about it in these terms during that perfect, trance-like day, writing that essay—which is about a brief stint spent serving cocktails in a very bad blues bar on Bleecker Street—was the first time I realized how important it is to illuminate the subjectivity of the character who's usually hanging out at the periphery of men's stories: the waitress, the girlfriend, the living prop that male narrators project their fantasies onto. I would tell her story, which happened to be my story. The course of the rest of my life was set.

MY CITY

DANI SHAPIRO

1. The city, was what people from New Jersey called it. The city, as if there were no other. If you were a suburban Jewish girl in the late 1970s, aching to burst out of the tepid swamp of your adolescence (synagogue! field hockey! cigarettes!), the magnetic pull of the city from across the water was irresistible. Between you and the city were the smokestacks of Newark, the stench of oil refineries, the soaring Budweiser eagle, its lit-up wings flapping high above the manufacturing plant. That eagle—if you were a certain kind of girl, you wanted to leap on its neon back and be carried away. On weekend trips into the city, you'd watch from the backseat of your parents' car for the line in the Lincoln Tunnel that divided New Jersey from New York, because you felt dead on one side, and alive on the other.

2. At least once or twice a month, when I was in high school, I'd slip out of third-period algebra. No one noticed. I'd walk a mile to the train station in Elizabeth and board the 11:33 to Penn Station. The windows were gray with the film of cigarette smoke. You could write your name on them. The train car, largely empty. The men who worked downtown had long since commuted, and the women tended to drive or stay home. Some of my friends' mothers had never even been to the city. It was the end of the 1970s. I was fifteen, and not a soul knew my whereabouts. I disembarked in Penn Station and made my way through its urine-stained halls in my corduroys and Fair Isle sweater, trudging along in my Wallabees. North up Eighth Avenue, past strip joints, neon xxx signs, bodegas. I stopped when I reached Lincoln Center and took a moment by the fountain in the plaza, looking at the Chagalls framed by the arched windows of the Metropolitan Opera. Hungry, I continued north to 72nd Street, where I spent my allowance on a turkey, tongue, and coleslaw sandwich and a Dr. Brown's Cel-Ray soda at the Fine & Schapiro delicatessen. I imagined that I was already a woman, that I had shed Jersey, my extreme youth, like a layer of baby fat. By the end of the school day, I'd be back home, delivering monosyllabic answers to the question, "How was your day?" But secretly, I was high on the knowledge that I had done it. I had been *there*.

3. In a popular TV commercial of that era, for Charlie perfume, an actress named Shelley Hack strode across the screen in her pantsuit, blonde mane flying. She was the Charlie girl—tall, urban, glamorous, on her way to important places—someone who was "kind of now, kind of wow, Charlie," as the jingle went. She had it all—and why not? With the hubris of the very young, I planted both feet in my fantasy. I was the Charlie girl. My life in New York was going to involve some sort of career in which I could wear pantsuits like that.

4. I moved to New York at nineteen, into the West 75th Street walk-up apartment of a boyfriend. The boyfriend owned a small shop on Columbus that sold South American artifacts and the peasant clothes popular with a certain urban-bohemian crowd. My father—an Orthodox Jew—threatened to disown me if I shacked up (his words) with my boyfriend. So I married him. It seemed like a fine solution. We divorced a year later. But in between—as a college student—I threw dinner parties in that brownstone apartment, making the one

98   GOODBYE TO ALL THAT

dish I knew how: Chicken Marbella from *The Silver Palate Cookbook*, with olives, prunes, and cinnamon, flavors I haven't liked in combination since. In photos from that time I see a round-faced girl with feathered hair (hello, Farrah), dimples, and a ring that had no business being on her finger. Our block was home to several dancers from the New York City corps de ballet whom I'd see heading to rehearsal early in the mornings, their heads small and neat, their long necks wrapped in soft scarves. I made the mistake of thinking that we were alike, these dancers and I, because we were the same age. But in fact, they were moving toward life, and I—masquerading as a happy homemaker—was drifting away from it.

5. "Kind of now, kind of wow, Charlie." Another one of the Charlie girls was an actress named Cheryl Ladd, who went on to be one of Charlie's Angels (no relation). And then there was a model, Shelley Smith, whom I would meet many years later—in another life, a future I couldn't possibly imagine—after she had opened an egg donation agency in Beverly Hills and I was trying to have a second child. But back then, to me, she was part of a trifecta of blondes who epitomized life among skyscrapers—a burnished, free-floating glamour that seemed, in itself, a worthy goal.

6. Divorced and twenty. How many people can claim that? For years, I erased that marriage from my life story. It was just too hard to explain—to others, to myself. But now, thirty years later, I wish I could reach back through time and shake some sense into that lost little girl. I wish I could tell her to wait, to hold on. That becoming a grown-up is not something that happens overnight, or on paper. That rings and certificates and apartments and meals have nothing to do with it. That everything we do matters. *Wait,* I want to say—but she is impatient, racing ahead of me.

7. The city. It isn't possible for me to write about the city without writing about real estate and men. From the baby-marriage, I moved on to a full-blown affair with an older married man. From a walk-up on 75th, I graduated to a duplex in the West Village and finally to an apartment on the top floor of the Dakota. The Dakota apartment looked like a dollhouse, with a string of tiny rooms, slanted ceilings, walls papered with peach and lavender Laura Ashley flowers. I ate next to nothing and drank white wine and frozen margaritas. I drank champagne with my girlfriends at Petrossian, and we charged our drinks to our parents' credit cards. I had my nails done next to Madonna, my hair blown out next to the original uptown girl, Christie Brinkley. I took back-to-back aerobics classes at Bjorkman and Martin, a cultish studio run by a compact woman with powerful thighs named Lee who taught us intricate dance steps and yelled at those who couldn't follow. When the Space Shuttle Challenger exploded over Cape Canaveral, we—all of us drenched in perspiration at that studio—held hands and said a prayer.

8. There were other apartments, other men. Chance encounters, coincidence, desires, and invitations. Another brief, failed marriage. All before I was thirty. I was trying, flailing, failing, in an attempt to chisel myself into a woman who existed only as a fantasy, airbrushed, photoshopped, as lost as that high school sophomore who wandered in a fugue state past the strip joints of Times Square. I was a girl who hadn't gotten the memo about not taking candy from strangers—and New York was full of those strangers. A girl who was playing a part she was wrong for, whose own gifts were elusive and strange to her, contraband, brought home from a foreign country and best stored out of reach.

9. But still, all the while, I was becoming a writer. How to explain this—how, without conceiving myself as a split screen, one part of me blurry and undefined and the other honing skills, finding the words, becoming, in the invisibility, the solitude of these rooms, these apartments, someone with something to say. I wrote my first novel, then another. I began to teach. I interned at a literary maga-

zine on 17th, lugged home laundry bags full of manuscripts, and sat cross-legged on my bed as if mining through coals for gold. I went to book parties in clubs and smoky bars and had them thrown for me. I lunched on vertical salads with my terrifying agent at Michael's on West 54th Street, where table position determined pecking order, and no one was ever quite focused on their own dining companion. Wasn't that Barbara Walters being shown to the window table? I posed for a portrait in *Vanity Fair* in a tiny lemon yellow suit, my hair big and fluffy, a face covered in makeup, in a coffee shop on West 83rd Street. Once, late at night, as I was in bed reading manuscripts, a giant water bug flew across the bedroom and landed on my shoulder. I screamed and called the doorman, a man who must have been in his late seventies, who poked with a broom through the shoes and boots littering my closet floor until he found and disposed of it.

10. I could lecture on metaphor; I could teach graduate students; I could locate and deconstruct the animal imagery in *Madame Bovary*. But I could not squash a water bug by myself. The practicalities of life eluded me. The city—which I knew with the intimacy of a lover—made it very possible to continue like this, carried along on a stream of light, motion, energy, noise. The city was a bracing wind that never stopped blowing, and I was a lone leaf slapped up against the side of a building, a hydrant, a tree.

11. I am writing this from a small study in a house high on a hill in the Connecticut countryside, two hours north of the city. It is winter. The bare branches of wisteria that climb our roof are banging against the window. One of my dogs is curled up at my feet. I hear the sharp pitter-patter of the other as he forages through the house for crumbs left from a party we threw the other night. The walls of my study are hung with photographs: My son as a ring-bearer at a friend's wedding, tiny in his first tuxedo. My husband, from his years as a war correspondent, lighting a cigarette in his flak jacket on a rooftop in Somalia—a

reminder that he, too, had a life that he left behind when he met me. While I was drinking champagne on my parents' credit card, he was filing stories from the bloody streets of Mogadishu.

12. It has been ten years since we left the city. A decade—long enough for our friends to stop taking bets on how long it would take us to come to our senses and return to New York. *What do you do up there? Whom do you see? What's it like?* They drive up to visit us in their Zip cars or rental SUVs, bearing urban bounty: shopping bags from Citarella filled with pungent Epoisses and chorizo tortellini; boxes of linzer cookies from Sarabeth's; delicate, pastel Laduree macarons. In turn, we take our houseguests on hikes or to lakeside beaches or to quaint village streets lined with shops selling cashmere and tweed. But we aren't hearty country folk. I don't own muck boots or a Barbour coat. We don't ski or own horses or build bonfires in our backyard. I spend most of my days alone in my writing study, with a midday yoga break in the next room. My husband now writes and directs films, and the closest he gets to an outdoor activity is when he takes his chainsaw out into our woods to clear brush. Our son, like us, is an indoor dreamer. We are urban Jews, descended from the *shtetl*, pale and neurasthenic. Living in our heads.

13. Deep within my recesses there is a turntable, its needle skipping, skipping. My twenty-year-old self, straight from Jersey, watches me, hands on hips. *How could you?* she accuses me. *When we'd come so far?* I want to tell her that we were refugees, my husband, son, and I, fleeing north, heading away from a place and time that we hoped would recede, like the view from our rearview mirror, until it disappeared entirely, until it became nothing more than a memory. I want to tell her that my baby had been very sick. That my father was dead, my mother dying. That we watched as one plane, then another, crashed into the towers, debris swirling in the sky above us like a storm of blackened snow. That everything I thought I knew about living no longer applied. That the champagne and the men

and the real estate and the book parties were like the fool's gold that my now-teenage, healthy son unearths on his geology field trips. Look, I want to say. This life you think you want is a shiny apparition. Those restaurants and clubs, those bars bathed in a light pinker than sunset? Those cafes where photographers from magazines took your picture, and makeup artists dusted your pretty nose? They will be submerged, as in a shipwreck, the seas of time washing over them until something new has taken their place. The joint where you now drink those frozen margaritas will become an organic juice bar. The bistro with the best steak frites is now a T-Mobile store. The bookstore where you will eventually give your first reading sells boxes of hair dye and curling irons. It all changes—even institutions, even concrete towers, even, or perhaps most of all, our very selves—my foolish little sweetheart. That's how I could leave. Trust me. You'll thank me someday.

14. I am not yet old, but I am no longer young. My city—the one that beckoned just beyond the smokestacks and Budweiser plant—has vanished. Only glimpses of it remain, in the sandstone facade of a Fifth Avenue building, or Washington Square Park, when seen from a certain angle. My city broke its promise to me, and I to it. I fell out of love, and then I fell back in—with my small town, its winding country roads, and the ladies at the post office who know my name. I did my best to become the airbrushed girl on its billboards, but even air-brushed girls grow up. We soften over time, or maybe harden. One way or another, life will have its way with us.

15. I still drive into the city once a week or so. I see doctors, get my hair done, have lunch with my agent, have dinner with a girlfriend at a candlelit restaurant where we share a bottle of wine and order the cheese plate. I give readings from my books in crowded, East Village bars. If I can, I squeeze in a yoga class near Union Square, in a loft filled with plants and statues of the Buddha. Mostly, I watch the young people—their new designs in facial hair, piercings, and tattoos—who are in the midst of their own love affair. They're from Ohio or Nebraska. Or New Jersey. They've arrived, and they're here to stay, just as I once was. It's their city now. I have become invisible to them. I could be their mother. They laugh and whisper, lovely heads bent together. Sometimes, if it's going to be a late night—the theater, perhaps, or a boozy dinner party—my husband and I stay over at a hotel. We pull up to the entrance in our SUV with Connecticut plates, a middle-aged couple from out of town, just as my parents once were. "Can I help you folks get a taxi?" the doorman asks. "Do you need directions?" No, my husband tells him. That's okay. We're from here. We know our way around.

SOMEDAY, SOME MORNING, SOMETIME

EMMA STRAUB

Most people get to move to New York, the city's gritty seductive-
ness pulling them out of their family's clutches, sometime in
their early twenties. They get to arrive by car or airplane or
bus and see the skyline and say "Wow." They live in an apartment with four roommates somewhere in Bushwick or Murray Hill
or Windsor Terrace, and six months later, they refer to themselves
as New Yorkers. This is a story about how I want to smother those
people in their sleep, but this is also a story about how I envy those
yokels, not for their wide-eyed wonder, but for the fact that they will
be able to leave the city someday without having an existential crisis. The city isn't theirs, and they aren't its people—they're interlop-
ers, long-form tourists, around for long enough to be able to tell their
children stories about when they lived in New York, lo those many
years ago.

I grew up on the Upper West Side of Manhattan, half a block
from Central Park, two and a half blocks from Broadway, a city girl
from the start. My parents weren't native-born, but they both loved
New York unequivocally. The people were more interesting in the

city, more open-minded, smarter, cooler—these were things I understood as facts. New York was the center of the world—not just my world, the entire world. My parents had friends from other countries and other cities, and they would all wind up in New York eventually, at our dining room table. This did not seem like a coincidence. All the time, every single day, people came to New York City because they couldn't get what it had to offer anywhere else.

I went to Saint Ann's for high school, all the way in Brooklyn Heights. The subway ride was forty-five minutes each way, but it could have been twice as long and I wouldn't have minded. The school was not what it sounded like—not a prim Catholic school but a progressive one started by lunatic visionaries in the basement of a church, with no knee-length kilts unless they were ironic. No grades were offered. The school had a reputation for producing brilliant drug addicts, though it was only true of one section of the population—the other half were brilliant mathematicians, brilliant painters, brilliant actors, brilliant talkers, plus a handful of dummies with very rich parents. There was poetry hanging in the stairwells, the students looked like fashion models, and I was in heaven. My friends and I ran wild all over Manhattan and Brooklyn, our drunken little bodies falling in and out of taxicabs and each other's houses, each of us mad with love for the Brooklyn Bridge, for the way the pavement glittered in the moonlight, for our own youth, which by its very existence seemed made of pixie dust and dreams. Until then, New York City had only mattered to me because the Macy's Thanksgiving Day Parade lined up on my corner, and I could eat H&H bagels warm out of the bin, but once I was able to traverse the city without my parents in tow, New York became my jungle gym and playmate all at once.

This is the trait I have come to loathe in others, this rhapsodic reverence, though I'm much better at controlling myself than I used to be. When I came home from college in Ohio (because where else would I go but home), I was horrified to discover that my entire graduating class seemed to be following me back. Worse yet, they were excited about it! They all moved to Williamsburg and rented practice spaces for their bands. I would get email invitations to their shows, their house parties, and their art openings and feel sick to my stomach. It was like watching someone—an entire fleet of someones—fall in love simultaneously, all the goofy grins and public declarations of affection.

I don't like to talk about this in public because I know it paints me in a very specific light—overly precious about my youth, selfish, spoiled. These things are all true. But still, even at thirty-two years old, I refuse to admit that I'm in the wrong. It might be uncharitable or close-minded, but there aren't very many places in the country that people revere the way they do New York. I do have friends who grew up in Los Angeles who feel this way, and maybe this is the way everyone feels about their hometown. *This is my place. I was here first. You don't get to say what's good or cool because it's mine.* But because my hometown is New York City, everyone else thinks it belongs to them, too.

Don't get the wrong impression—I want everyone I know to love New York, just as I want everyone I know to love my parents, because they're as much a part of me as my limbs. I want strangers to love New York, as long as they're not walking slowly in front of me, their faces turned skyward in amazement. I love giving directions to tourists and scribbling down embarrassingly long lists of recommendations for recent transplants: Sahadi's for hummus, labne, and dried fruit; BookCourt, Word, and Three Lives for books; Mary's Fish Camp for lobster rolls; the Shake Shack for hamburgers; the Film Forum for both the movies and the popcorn. I cover the backs of envelopes with illegible penmanship, imploring the visitor to eat six meals a day, if they have to, to absorb as much as possible.

When I went to college in Ohio, I saw the whole thing as temporary, like boarding school or prison—you don't move there, you just sleep there for a little while. Most of my college friends were from New York, if not from my high school, then from another one nearby. We'd gone to each other's parties and had all the same reference points. It was like making cake from a box— all the ingredients were already inside. I was miserable and lonely there, in a town with only a handful of traffic lights and a smaller handful of restaurants. By my senior year, I'd made some progress, but not much. I was a horse with blinders on, thinking the whole world was one long, narrow street.

When I was twenty-four, I moved in with my boyfriend. We lived in Carroll Gardens, Brooklyn, in an apartment directly over an Italian restaurant—we had to walk through the restaurant in order to get to the stairs to our door, and the hallways always smelled like tomato sauce. None of my high school or elementary school or summer camp friends left the city, and then all of my college friends arrived. I saw my parents once a week, and had jobs through which I made additional friends, and suddenly, there was never enough time. I began to imagine life outside New York City—life outside one's hometown—as empty calendar days, where someone canceling plans disappointed you rather than cheered you up, where you could take a walk and not run into every single person you'd ever known. That might seem backward to those who grew up in small towns and found them stiflingly small, but one of the greatest gifts New York City has to offer to newcomers is anonymity, and that wasn't on the table for me.

Two years later, I applied to graduate school and was accepted at the University of Wisconsin–Madison. My boyfriend and I went to visit and took long walks by the two lakes at the center of town (Madison's capitol building is on an isthmus, the rarest and most delightful of land formations). We sat in a park and were nuzzled by a roaming pussycat, clearly someone's pet. To think! You could live somewhere and let your pets run free with nothing more than a collar, secure in thinking that they wouldn't get run over by a car, or stolen by some pet poacher, or eaten by a pit bull, or infected by sewer rats! When we finally moved that summer, we took everything—our own two cats, our heaviest furniture, things to hang on the walls, and the tools with which to hang them. Even so, the program was only two years long, and that was exactly as long as I thought we'd stay. In the end, we stayed for three years, but in all that time, I didn't swap my New York driver's license for a Wisconsin one.

Life in Wisconsin was quiet—our house was quiet, our street was quiet, our neighborhood was quiet. At first, I was frightened by the calm, sure that it meant an axe murderer was going to climb into my window. (That didn't happen, but for the record my house in Madison *was* robbed, something that has never happened to me in New York City.) A few months in, a sense of calm arrived, along with the cold and the snow. I knew so few people in town that I invited every single one of them to every party I had. This meant that my relationships were strong—stronger, probably, than many of the friendships I'd left behind, built as they were on long-ago memories and shared experiences we'd outgrown. In Madison, my friendships were forged out of proximity and time, as in, suddenly, I had the time! I had time to take a walk with a friend because she only lived three blocks away, and we had nothing to do otherwise. It was like living on the stage of an absurdist play, where the characters sit on a darkened set until they have another scene, or like *Sleeping with the Enemy,* the Julia Roberts movie in which she swims away from her abusive husband to start a new life. I was Julia Roberts, and New York City was my husband.

Things became clearer with distance—the way I had always deferred to my friends, the way my friends had always been kind of mean, the way New York City looked from the middle of the country, like some haughty socialite obsessed with her own reflection. When I went home to visit, I was instantly exhausted by the city's pace, and by my own insistence on seeing as many people as possible, even if it meant having a date for breakfast, a date for lunch, a date for dinner, and a date for after-dinner drinks. My boyfriend and I fought like rabid dogs on those trips, stressed from the overstimulation. One miserable trip, we met a friend and his wife and his parents at a department store the day before Christmas for a quick chat in the handbag section because that's all we could spare, tourists with shopping bags shouldering past us.

In contrast, Madison seemed like paradise. Everything that had ever bothered me about New York—the cranky postal employees, the trash-strewn sidewalks, those shopping-bag-laden tourists—was gone. My boyfriend and I walked for miles every day, only occasionally crossing paths with other people. We were hermits who weren't afraid to leave the house. The movie theater was never crowded; neither were the restaurants. Nothing was expensive. No one was trying to seem cool. We joined the food co-op and cooked our own meals. We could even find decent pizza and bagels. If it weren't for the winters, we might have stayed. If it weren't for the lack of a literary community, we might have stayed. If it weren't for the lack of family and friends, we might have stayed. If it weren't for not being New York, we might have stayed.

Why didn't we stay?

Part of our deal going into Madison was that my boyfriend would be able to choose where we went next. When it came time to leave, he wanted to move west, all the way to California. Married now, we loved to visit Los Angeles, to tool around in a rented car and suddenly find ourselves at the beach. It was lovely to be outside even in the dead of winter, a perfect contrast to Wisconsin, where we wore mittens as large as boxing gloves. Our rent would be more than it was in Madison, but less than it would be in New York. I could wear dresses without tights most of the year and bury my snow boots in the back of my closet. We had some friends there, but not too many—a proposition that seemed like a continuation of our social life in Wisconsin, where we could easily keep up with all the demands on our time.

Despite our deal, I said no. I had never thought for a second that he'd choose anywhere other than New York. My father had been having some serious health problems, and the thought of moving even farther away scared me. It was hard enough to be in Madison, which was less than a two-hour flight. I wanted to go home.

And so we moved back to New York, into a beautiful house in a neighborhood far enough away from everyone else we knew that it felt like a retreat. But even if the streets are clear of people we know (not counting our neighbors), they are still crowded with people, and the frustrations of living in the city have come back. Not a week passes that we don't talk about Madison, or Los Angeles, or that perfect fantasy place in between, cosmopolitan enough to keep us from getting bored and feeling deprived but quiet and low-key enough to maintain our normal blood pressure. Is it Chapel Hill? Rhinebeck? Montauk? Is it Albuquerque? I like the way my husband looks in a sweater and a jacket—if we moved to California, would it be all T-shirts, all the time? Would we learn to surf?

In the three years we'd been gone, things had changed. Once I was back, I met new friends, this time out of shared interest instead of just proximity, and that added a whole roster of people into the rotation for dinner dates. My schedule is worse now than it has ever been, but the busy-ness has helped ensure that the people I see are the people I love—the older I get, the less time I waste on the one-sided friendships of my youth. My father's health is better than it has been, but still goes up and down. My parents will be seventy this year, and I'm six months pregnant with our first child. I can't imagine our lives getting any simpler from now on.

When my husband and I first traveled abroad together, years before we moved to Madison, he guffawed at the sight of my passport, which clearly states that I was born in Norwalk, Connecticut. His says "New York, New York," though he was born in White Plains and lived in Mamaroneck until he was twelve, when his parents moved the family south to Jupiter, Florida. You can tell by my need to qualify the place of his birth that I remain somewhat salty about these bare, clean facts. I was born in Connecticut, forty-five miles from the house I grew up in on the Upper West Side. When I entered preschool in Manhattan, shortly after our move, no one seemed to think anything of it, but by the time I hit elementary school, several of my classmates refused to think of me as a genuine New Yorker. I'd already missed so much in those first years of life—how would I ever catch up? How many years does it take for the city to become home?

My parents, now married for almost fifty years, have lived in New York City for thirty years. Still, if you walked up to them on the sidewalk in front of their house and asked them where they were from, they would say Milwaukee and begin to check you for physical resemblances to people they knew there, friends from their childhoods. If they were somewhere else, though, traveling in this country or another, they would say, "We are from New York." And, of course, they are. Most of my friends who grew up outside the city always knew they would leave their hometowns—if they were ambitious, leaving was a given. In New York, the opposite is true. The ambitious stay, forever elbowing back the newcomers. The ones who don't like the hustle get the hell out of town, and fast.

Would it be easier for me to leave my parents behind if they lived somewhere else? Maybe. Which came first, my devotion to my family or my devotion to my city? I know several people who have moved out of the city, their former lover, to be closer to their families. These people almost always have small children, which might mean that families win out over cultural advantages, especially if the babysitting is free. I wonder how their Brooklyn Bridge tattoos fare out there in the world—what can they say? "For a few years, I lived sort of near this?" As for me, I'm forever on the fence, searching for my own Shangri-la, though I assume no such place exists. I spend a little time every day looking at real estate listings on the Internet, telling myself, *It would only be for a little while. I wouldn't stay away for the long run; how could I? Could I?*

VIEW FROM THE PENTHOUSE

VALERIE EAGLE

W hen I was little, I pretended I was a pretty white girl. I believed you had to be white to be successful. I didn't have
many successful role models in my life. My aunt Debbie went
to college, became a teacher, got married, and bought a
house. But she was light-skinned. I learned that "if you wasn't light
. . . you wasn't bright." As far as I knew, my complexion was an ugly
thing, something to be ashamed of and made fun of and ignored.
My dreams of becoming a model, dancer, or actress seemed unattainable.

Sitting in Nana's house, in Metuchen, New Jersey, my sisters and
I would watch the news and dream of life in New York City. It didn't
matter that all we saw on TV were prostitutes being arrested. Their
lives looked glamorous. They had money and power and beautiful things. And besides, I had been sold for sex starting at age six
so my mother could pay for her heroin addiction. The women on
Eighth Avenue got to keep their money! All my sisters and I ever
wanted was a way out of Nana's house—the place our mother had
left us, the place where we paid for our wrongdoings with beatings
and abuse.

So, when I was seventeen and my great-aunt Pat came to visit and decided to bring me back to Brooklyn with her, I jumped at the opportunity. She looked like me; she was dark. We called it blue-black. But somehow, she figured out how to be successful. She married a rich white man. Then she became a singer. They lived in an exclusive part of Flatbush—Avenue H between New York and 32nd.

Until I arrived, she was the only black woman in the building. Her husband died and I guess she was lonely, so I was a replacement. She said she was going to mold me into a decent girl because we lived so poorly in Metuchen.

Aunt Pat had dreams for me. And she had connections; she knew white people. She was going to help me become a dancer and an actress just as I had always dreamed. But first, she had to send me to etiquette school: "Sit up straight." "When you have guests over, put the glasses in the freezer to frost them." "Always hang up your nightgown."

Before I knew it, I got a job at A&S in Brooklyn, off Flatbush Extension on Livingston. I was hired because Aunt Pat taught me how to hold my head up and sit up straight. A&S hired me as a floor model in Ladies' and Men's Fragrances.

I was making money. Aunt Pat was proud of me. I was living the good life in New York City. You couldn't tell me that I wasn't going to reach the stars, that I was not going to make it. Everything was going better than I had ever imagined. But I could not rid myself of a gnawing curiosity about the dark side of New York. Behind every legitimate success there was a destructive whisper calling "Valerie." It had always been that way for me, but in New York, I heard the whispering everywhere.

Now the only thing I needed was some man to sweep me off my feet. That was how Aunt Pat found success. I needed some city slicker. And Phil was the one. He was Italian. He sauntered into A&S and after I smiled and we flirted a little, I sold him a bottle of Paco Rabanne. The next day he sent me flowers. My very first affair with a white man was about to begin!

Phil wined and dined me. He asked me questions, and my innocent ass would just tell him everything: "I want to be a dancer and a model and an actress!" He said he knew people. But he had a secret. He had a dark side. He had exactly what I had always been curious about.

He told me he was going to help me with my career. What he did was get me a job dancing at Boney's Bar. Exotic dancing. It was a sleazy, dumpy dive, but it didn't matter. I was going to be *seen*. I was going to make Phil proud of me. And besides, I wanted to be a dancer. I told myself, "You gotta start somewhere." And I did. I became popular fast because I wore revealing outfits that would get me the most attention and allow men to do what they wanted to me. I did whatever it took to be seen, noticed, praised, and in my sick mind, loved. But I couldn't do it without something in my system. I started with seven-fourteens, Quaaludes. They did the job back then.

I was living a double life—I was an elegant woman working at A&S during the day and a sleazy woman dancing at night. Aunt Pat had no idea what was going on, especially after she got a good deal on an apartment in Harlem, where her sister lived, and gave me the Flatbush apartment. *Gave it to me!* It was $138 a month, in 1980. I could not believe where my life was taking me.

Phil invited me to his apartment for a party. I couldn't wait to see what his place looked like. I knocked on the door. This white woman opened it, high as a kite on a windy day—topless! "C'mon innnn! C'mon innnn!"

Now, where I come from, you don't go to a party without a shirt and bra. You don't answer the door topless! At that moment I thought, *That must be some shit only white people do.* But even then, the very next thought I had was, *I'm in! I've made it! I'm here.* There were white men with suits on and beautiful women with high cheekbones. They had fancy jewelry on—diamond studs in their ears, rings with big rocks on their fingers, gold necklaces around their necks. I wondered whether it was all real. They were all made up, with big, big hair, and the most beautiful shapes I'd ever seen.

I walked in there in my black dress and heels, and it was like everything just stopped. They watched this black woman walk through the door, and the sea just parted. "Sit, sit," the white men said. So I sat down. Phil was so excited to show me off. "Baby! How ya doing?!" He kissed me in front of everyone and said, "This is the one I was telling you about." He got me some wine. In the middle of the coffee table there was a gigantic chalice with long tubes coming out—long enough that you could sit back and take a pull on them. Next to it, there was a tray of white rocks. They had a torch. They'd put the rock in the chalice and spark the fire, and everybody around the coffee table would pull. There were thousands and thousands of dollars' worth of drugs in front of me. Freebase. Wasn't nothing free about it, but that's what it was. "Crack" wasn't even a word yet.

Phil leaned over and said, "Here, take a hit. It won't hurt you a bit." I took the hit, and it was pure heaven. I had never felt anything like it in my life. It was better than any glass of wine or Quaalude. It was perfection. But for some reason I started fixating on my bag, a clutch. I started digging in it, looking for something. Phil said, "What are you looking for, Val? You're embarrassing me." I started hallucinating; I started feeling my skin crawl. He told me to get up and go into the kitchen with him. He opened the cabinet and retrieved a small crack pipe. "Calm down, calm down," he said. He handed me a pill. I didn't know what it was, but he said, "Take that, sip it down with some wine," and so I did. "Now here, take a pull," he said, and showed me how to pull on the pipe. "Just calm down; you're alright. You look great, baby." Then he hit that piece of rock and I took my mouth off the pipe and got down on my knees to get the pieces that fell. I was picking up crumbs and putting them in the clutch. I was already addicted; the first hit had me hooked.

I lost my job at A&S. I stopped dancing at Boney's. All I wanted to do was freebase, so I started working the streets. I finally got to see firsthand what it was like to be an Eighth Avenue girl.

It took a while before I got evicted from Aunt Pat's apartment. First I met Tyrone, a nice black man from a good Southern family.

He was a nice dresser, always decent and clean. I instantly fell in love with Tyrone, but I had a secret. I was a freebaser. Tyrone was innocent; he didn't know about any of that stuff. But I really adored Tyrone. And I needed him too—I needed his money. After being together a little while, I asked him if he wanted to do some coke with me. He said, "I don't really do coke, but you want some?" He took me to Church Avenue and bought an eight ball. It was a nice amount of coke. Sniffing wasn't my thing, but I had to ease Ty into knowing what I did.

By this time, the news was informing people about what freebasing was doing to people. All the comedians were making jokes about crackheads. Richard Pryor had set himself on fire. When I heard that, all I thought was, *I'm not gonna be like that stupid-ass. I'm not gonna mix the gases like he did. I know how to cook up my shit.* Eventually, I got tired of sniffing and showed Tyrone what I did with it. I did to him exactly what Phil had done to me. I said, "Don't worry, Ty; it won't hurt you a bit." It hurts my heart to think of the innocence I robbed from him. He did it and he was hooked.

In the midst of all this drug use, I got pregnant. His family noticed he was losing weight and always broke and they knew it was because of me, so they gave him an ultimatum. He stopped using and moved back in with them, but he was not allowed to be in contact with me if he wanted to stay there.

I was crushed. Now what was I going to do? I really did love Tyrone, but I couldn't help myself. I loved freebasing more. I had to smoke. I couldn't stop. Still, I pleaded with Tyrone, "I'll stop if only you'll come back to me." But he didn't; he chose his family over me. Who could blame him? His refusal to come back led to even more freebasing. I didn't care that I was pregnant.

After Tyrone left, the rent stopped getting paid. Men came to my house in a white truck and knocked on the door. I answered it, and they pushed themselves in. I was eight months pregnant. I pleaded and pleaded with them, "Please don't put me out. Please!" They said, "Miss, grab whatever you can." They put Aunt Pat's old records, dirty dishes, my clothes, whatever they could get their hands on, in plastic bags. It was the cruelest act of dismissal. I never knew that's what they did in New York City. I sat on the curb in front of the building. All the white folks looked relieved to see me there.

Aunt Pat was devastated when she found out I had lost a place that she had had for thirty-five years. Only $138 a month and I lost it.

I did drugs until the day I went into labor. Miraculously, my baby girl Brenda was born without a speck of drugs in her system. She was a gift from God. When Brenda was seven days old, I went to Odyssey House on Randall's Island, a rehab facility that housed addicted women with their babies. I stayed there for eight months.

My mother, who had been clean and sober for a while, was willing to come into my life as long as I was going to a program. And so I went from program to program to program. My mother took my child until I graduated from the last one. Then I stayed clean for eight beautiful years.

During those clean years, my daughter had anything and everything you could dream of. I was working in the art departments of different magazines and finally started to make some decent money. I started modeling again on the side. I was part of Tracy Holt and Her Stunning Models—we came on during intermission at the Apollo. I studied acting at HB Studios in the Village. I started getting small parts. I was an extra in some of Spike Lee's movies. If you look closely, you can see me three times in *Malcolm X*. I did an off-off-Broadway play called *Women in Rain*. I was working it out.

But then my mother died of cancer. The day before she passed away, I went right into a bodega, bought two Lowenbrau, walked to my apartment, and drank them. After she died the next day, I went from drinking beers straight to yelling "Taxi!" on Madison Avenue uptown so I could get an eight ball of crack. I wasted no time—it was like Brooklyn came right back to me. Like I'd never fucking stopped.

I didn't become homeless right away because my mother had insurance. But when the money ran out, things went downhill fast, and I had to move from the nice house I was renting in the suburbs

to the projects in Harlem. I smoked crack there while Brenda was at school or sleeping.

One morning I walked her to school with a bag of crack stuffed down my pants. I couldn't wait to get back home. I locked the doors, draped the windows, took the clock off the wall, turned the TV off, got buck-naked, and smoked my ass off. I got so high, I never realized my daughter never came home that afternoon. When she finally came home, I knew something had happened to her—the same thing that had happened to me when I was a young girl and my mom was using.

She was a latchkey kid. One day after school, Charles, our neighbor from the sixth floor, took her from the elevator to his apartment. I was so high, I didn't even notice she never made it home. Later that night, around 9 PM, Charles brought her home. I couldn't let them in right away, though; I made them wait because I had crack vials all over the place. I ran into the bathroom and then told her to come in. I did not realize she had Charles, whom she now referred to as her friend, with her. Later, Brenda got herself ready for bed, and finally I cleaned myself up and came out of the bathroom. I started to read her a bedtime story. The book fell out of my hands, and when I picked it up, I found her little panties beside the bed, tarnished with blood. He had violated my baby. I went berserk. I wanted to kill this creep and actually tried to. When the police arrived, they could see that I was high. They deemed me "unfit" and wanted to arrest me. That's when I knew my baby had to go.

I gave Brenda to my cousin Tracy. She was nine years old. "You're going to live with your cousin Tracy," I explained. "Mommy's sick." She looked up at me with her innocent little face and said, "Mommy, you go get yourself better. Just hurry up, and I'll be waiting for you."

It was ten years before I returned.

With Brenda gone, I was off to the races. I was in deep. And things crumbled around me at rapid speed. I became homeless. This time, they put me out and told me to grab whatever I couldn't live without. I grabbed my head shots and put them in a shopping

cart. I was a homeless crackhead about to start living out of a shopping cart on the streets of Manhattan, and my denial was still so thick, *I thought I needed my head shots.*

For ten fucking years, I lived from rooftop to rooftop. I made one rooftop on Lexington Avenue my home for five of them. In my mind, I pretended I had a marvelous apartment, just like those rich white people who lived on Fifth Avenue. I thought, what else could a city girl ask for? I lived on the very top floor, "the Penthouse," I called it. It had a magnificent view of New York City, a skylight and two entrances and two decks for sunbathing whenever I wanted to. *Hey*, I deluded myself, *this is living.*

I would go down to rich white people's neighborhoods. They would put out their furniture and their pillows. Some even put out clothes for the homeless with money in the pockets. I would bring my winnings uptown and decorate my rooftop.

I was homeless until the seventh and last time I went to jail. The cops had chased us off the roof. It was cold, but as far as I was concerned, the only thing I had to do was scrape the stem of "Scotty," my crack pipe, and it would beam me up higher than anything or anyone else I'd ever known. I went to the laundromat. I had on at least three layers of clothes. I weighed eighty pounds. I went to the bathroom, scraped the stem, pushed it, packed it, and lit it up. As soon as I inhaled, somebody knocked on the door. I held my breath, walked through the laundromat, and blew the smoke out when I got outside. That's when I got arrested.

I'll never forget how the cop looked at me, with so much sadness, so much compassion. He said, "Oh, my god, Miss, you're not being arrested; you're being rescued. Look at you; you're gonna die out here."

In jail I got healthy, gained my weight back, cleared up my complexion, and found out I was HIV-positive. And then a strange thing happened: when I found out I could possibly die, all of a sudden I wanted to live. I had never wanted to live so badly.

After I got out, I was ordered to attend rehab. Until then, through

program after program, I was half-assed about recovery. This time was different. This time those New York City streets whooped my ass. You think New York is expensive? Yeah, it almost cost me my life.

I could not get away from the city quickly enough. I had no choice but to leave anyway; drug dealers were after me. Men I had tricked with were after me, too—word got out on the street that I was HIV-positive. I couldn't stay there.

So I said goodbye to all that shit and moved upstate, to Kingston. Once I got over the culture shock of living in the boondocks, I contacted Brenda. She was living in Paterson, New Jersey. We met at Port Authority. I easily picked her out among all the people hustling and bustling about. She was standing against the wall of Cinnabon. She was all grown up now, and the tears just started to flow. I didn't know this young lady. Who was she? I'd missed it all: her first training bra, prom, boyfriend; talking to her about getting her period; teaching her how to shave her legs. I'd missed the soccer and lacrosse games. I'd missed everything. We would have to start all over again—if she would allow it. It took time—many years—before I heard the words "Mom . . . I love you" again, and they were music to my ears. God, I'd waited so long to hear those words.

There, I resumed the same relationship I'd had with New York in my childhood: the only time I saw it was on the news. And for a long time, that was as close as I wanted to get. I didn't have fantasies anymore about New York's glamorous lifestyle and its dark side. I knew where the city was capable of bringing me and where I was capable of going without it. The thought of getting on a Metro North train to ride through Harlem, get off at 125th Street, go down to Port Authority—it was too much. I couldn't do it. I wasn't ready.

Now, though, I think I am. At fifty-one, I've been clean for four years, I'm working my ass off to graduate from college, and I'm telling the story of what I've been through—in monologues onstage and at jails—in the hope that my story might help someone. And it has. Often, after performances, audience members approach to tell me how much they related to my story or how it gave them hope. But the most rewarding experience happened when I helped facilitate a storytelling workshop in a boys' juvenile detention center. I started off the workshop by telling my own story, and you could see on the boys' faces how amazed they were to hear about someone just like them eventually getting clean and pulling her life together. At the end of the workshop, one of the boys wrote these words in his own story: "I'm happy I got to meet Ms. Valerie, because now I know I'm not alone in the world all by myself. Ms. Valerie is a strong, motivated lady who has a lot to offer, to a lot of people who want to listen, and I'm willing to listen. When I look at her I just see a beautiful woman who made something of herself. She made something of me. She made me a stronger man."

After several years in Kingston, I've come to accept the fact that living in New York City isn't for me anymore, that I missed the boat for reaching my stars there, and that the city really wasn't the land of opportunity for me back then that I thought it would be. I wasn't ready. I was young and dumb. Sometimes I look back and ask myself, "Why couldn't I get it right?" God only knows where I would've been by now if I just hadn't taken that first hit. I had so many dreams of becoming successful in New York City. I thought it could only happen there.

Now I have a new set of dreams. I have friends I could never have imagined having, who love me for who I am, just the way I am. I have a place I can call my home—one I actually have a key to. I have a beautiful grown-up daughter. I am in college, and I am reaching for the stars. What more could I ask for? I am living my dreams, and I have never felt more alive.

Now, I feel free to go wherever I please. I don't ever want to live in New York City again. But I am no longer afraid to visit.

LOSING NEW YORK

LAUREN ELKIN

P eople move to New York from all over the world, drawn to what
it stands for: work, success, freedom, acceptance, glamour; give
me your tired, your poor, your ambitious, your determined. But
they are always approaching the city from somewhere else,
which amplifies its power. There are so many viewpoints on the city
that "New York"—the idea—is magnified in the imagination through
thousands of tiny windowpanes.

But it's hard to get any perspective on it when you grow up next
door. My parents are from the city, and as soon as they married they
bought a house in the suburbs, where they raised me and my sister.
(We, in turn, moved back to the city as adults.) That decision created
my particular attitude toward New York, my particular windowpane.
To those of us who grew up not *in* it but *next* to it, in its shadow, a
short train ride away on the Long Island Rail Road or the PATH or
Metro North, New York is the city. As if there are no others. And for
the rest of our lives, our relationships to cities will be defined by
New York.

Unlike Joan Didion's Sacramento, the suburbs of New York de-
rive their very identity from the city. Elizabeth Bishop describes the

city's "long long legs" stretching out into the countryside, begging it to "subside." The suburbs take shape under the weight of that pressure. They are New York but not "New York," the city. They are New York but not "New York," the state. They are somewhere in between. "Where are you from?" people ask me. "New York," I say. "The city?" they ask. Well—and then the answer depends on my mood, on whom I'm talking to, on how well they know New York. Can they be trusted not to say "Oh, Long Island. You're not from New York, then."

Am I? Am I not? When you're from New York but not from "New York," you're on shaky ground. I spent seven years in Manhattan, first for university, then for work, and then for graduate school, before I moved abroad in 2004. If I had moved to the city from somewhere else in 2004, by now I might be saying I'm from there and no one would question me. New York is one of those cities that welcomes you, takes you in, lends you its name. Instead, I moved from New York to Paris, where I'll never be able to say, "I'm from Paris," no matter how long I live there.

I n Amor Towles's recent novel *Rules of Civility*, the heroine, born and bred in Brighton Beach but trying to make her way in the upper echelons of New York society, pretends not to know someone from her past when he recognizes her at a newsstand. Observing their exchange, the newsman pronounces: "That's the problem with being born in New York . . . You've got no New York to run away to." When people ask me why I moved to Paris, I sometimes say it's because I was tired of New York, and when New Yorkers are tired of New York, there's nowhere else for them to go but Paris. But that doesn't explain why I left. I'm not sure I have an answer to that question.

I had a certain kind of clichéd, magical New York childhood, full of Broadway shows and the Met and FAO Schwarz and Tribeca

restaurants. New York in adulthood is less magical. Everything costs more than it should. It takes forever to get anywhere. Life moves so fast things are half-over before you notice they've begun. It's dirty, cramped, and smells bad. Adoptive New Yorkers will brook no criticism of it; it represents everything to which they have aspired. The smell and the grit are part of the dream. But why would you stay there when there are so many more pleasant places to live?

Of course, Parisians think I'm out of my mind. They feel exactly—*exactly*—the same way about their city as I do about mine. The French have two fantasies about the United States: a West Coast fantasy and an East Coast one. The West Coast Parisians dream of giant trees and the sun setting over the Pacific. The East Coast Parisians want to eat cupcakes in the West Village or drink with hipsters in Brooklyn. They're the ones who spend the most time asking me questions. How could I, why would I, give up my city for theirs? New York is not a city you leave. But it's a hard city to start from.

When I left New York it was well before the current economic crisis, a time when you could find headlines in *New York Magazine* like "Filthy Stinking Rich," "Growing Up Trump," "The Best Beauty Docs," "Where to Buy [small parentheses: "or rent"] Now," and, anxiously in 2003, "Will the Bubble Burst?" The cult of wealth in New York was too much for me: I couldn't ever see myself getting a foothold in it. I was working in publishing but envisioned a transition to academe and to writing. But how would I ever support myself? I would never have been able to do it on my own; I would have needed a partner with money. I found one, and he was very good to me, but I couldn't shake the sense that I was some kind of dirty mistress to him, living a life he paid for that I could never have afforded.

Although, as Didion writes, "It is often said that New York is a city for only the very rich and the very poor," it could also be said that "New York is also, at least for those of us who came from somewhere else, a city only for the very young." And yet all around me, friends were careening toward a New York adulthood. They were being hired at corporate jobs at ridiculous salaries and living in doorman buildings with gyms and private cinemas. They were moving in with their boyfriends and talking about what cut of diamond they preferred. The New York I knew then was for the very rich and young who wanted quite badly to be no longer young. My own live-in boyfriend bought a car and used it to drive out to see his parents on Long Island every weekend. He talked about buying an apartment and eventually a house in Nassau County. It made me uncomfortable, all the getting and spending and the courting of maturity. One night I was out for dinner on Long Island with him, his parents, and my parents, and I had a panic attack right there at the table. There were electric currents of energy shooting down my spine and into my legs, and I had to jump up from the table and go stand outside the restaurant. It wasn't only that I couldn't afford those things. It was that I didn't want those things, or not yet, or not the way they wanted them.

In leaving New York there's an element of failure. Why couldn't I make a go of it? "If I can make it there, I'll make it anywhere," you hear after every Yankees game, but there's a strange kind of pressure behind those lyrics, an implicit challenge for a native New Yorker. *What if I can't make it here?* you have to ask yourself. *What then?* Moving to Paris seemed like a way to make it on my own terms.

Which begs the question: Why couldn't I just rewrite my life in New York? Start over with new friends with priorities more in line with my own? I think I can't live in New York for the same reason I can't cook in my mother's kitchen. She's set it up so that it works for her, and she has her ways of doing things within that space that I feel I can't deviate from without, somehow, rejecting her. I love my family's New York, but I can't succeed by its rules, and I can't live within its limitations. The New York that I would inhabit, if I moved back there—hail, literary Brooklyn—is difficult to reach from Long Island and is as foreign a place to me as Moscow. It was easier to move to a different country and start my whole life over from scratch than it was to continue on their path. I sensed that I could make my own choices in Paris, that I could make a life for myself

on my own terms, in a context that was mine alone. I didn't know anybody when I first arrived, so there was no one looking over my shoulder, no one to attempt to enforce continuity on my life. I could reinvent myself. For the first time, I met people who were like me: writers, thinkers, adventurers. I knew writers and thinkers in New York, of course, but in the circle of friends I formed in Paris, we all had that in common: at a given moment, we had all chosen not to stay where we were from, but to leave home and move to Paris. We were all high on that, though what we felt there was different for each of us.

When it comes to place, there are two kinds of writers: those who more or less stay where they're put and look around themselves, and those who need to go somewhere else to look around themselves there.

I've never been a writer content to look at the world I come from. Unlike John Cheever, or A. M. Homes, I don't find the suburbs flint the creative spark. I'm more interested in what happens when people go other places, in the profound exchange that can occur between person and place when the two are foreign to each other. Maybe this, too, is my legacy as a New Yorker. My grandparents and great-grandparents came to New York from Italy, Latvia, Lithuania, Ireland, Germany, and the Deep South. That makes at least six places to which I am connected by blood, six places of origin, six places that have a claim on me. Perhaps lacking any kind of local personal history, I'm bound to need to go digging elsewhere.

In Paris, I have all I need to write. History, atmosphere, and the physical remnants of the modern city that so inspired the writers whose vision of the world has so shaped mine: the Surrealists, the Situationists, Benjamin, Beauvoir, Barthes. The slight differences in everyday life make even the crushing drone of popular culture more interesting: the crap songs on the radio, the gushing commercials on the television. Whatever inspiration needs to thrive, Paris has it in spades; whatever conditions facilitate discipline and hard work, Paris supplies as well.

C ities are many different people to us. I never felt the way Didion felt about New York, didn't love it "the way you love the first person who ever touches you and never love anyone quite that way again." Maybe you have to meet it as a stranger to love it that way. New York was always destined for me, as if I were betrothed to it when I was a baby. Paris was the *coup de foudre* who stole me away from my betrothed. I wanted to move to Paris after I graduated, but then I got involved with another Long Islander, and we eventually moved in together, living first in Gramercy and then on the Upper East Side. I told myself that I belonged in New York, even though I was unhappy. "Has anyone ever been so young?" Didion wonders at her twenty-three-year-old self, unable to call and ask for the air-conditioning to be turned down because she didn't know how much to tip the person they would send. I was twenty-five and I thought, with the moral resolution (or perhaps the affected maturity) of the very young, that because we lived together I had to stay. Finally I couldn't take it anymore; it felt like my choices were narrowing more and more every day. I moved to Paris like I was coming up for air.

Not that Paris is so terribly different from New York. The Cartesian rationality that prevails in France has always prioritized the straight logic of the mathematically predictable. Look at a French garden: order and geometry imposed on nature. The Lettrist International (the precursors of the Situationists) complained of the authoritarian control these values exerted over the population, citing a sign in Paris's Jardin des Plantes (my neighborhood park) as an example: "One can discover at a single glance the Cartesian organization of the so-called 'labyrinth' of the Jardin des Plantes and the inscription that announces it: GAMES ARE FORBIDDEN IN THE LABYRINTH. One could not seek a clearer summary of the spirit of a whole civilization."

The same holds true in French life. For the wellborn French child, the road from *crèche* to *prépa* to *grande école* is well traced, and beyond that to marriage, country homes, *vacances scolaires*, and the repetition of the process with the next generation of wellborn French children. This is the status quo for the French 1 percent, and they will fight to maintain it. As Will Hutton commented in 2006 in *The Guardian*, the French are the only people on the planet who will take to the barricades to defend the status quo. In principle it's similar to the narrative of success in America that I was raised with, but the difference is that you are set on your track much earlier in France, and if you deviate, you'll be off the track for the rest of your life. You might claw your way onto certain aspects of the track—you might get a good job, you might get a country home—but you'll always feel like an impostor. As a naïve young academic, I thought I could slip into my corresponding rung on the social and professional ladder. But it's clear—they have made it clear—that I'll always be on the outside here.

I think of that scene in Sofia Coppola's *Marie Antoinette*, the one in which the young archduchess Maria Antonia crosses the border from Austria to France by shedding every vestige of her old life— her clothes, her jewelry, even her little dog—to become Marie Antoinette. *It is the custom that the bride bring nothing belonging to a foreign court,* she is told. The French demand total assimilation, even as they remind you of your essential, immutable difference.

Yet I still feel more comfortable there than anywhere else. Probably because the French assume I'll never do anything their way, so they'll tolerate me—unlike Marie Antoinette—doing it my own way.

Revisiting New York in the first years after I left felt a bit like catching up with an ex: comfortable at first, familiar, but then you remember why it didn't work out and all the things that drove you crazy. Why are the sirens so loud? Why does the subway smell like piss? Why is it so exhausting to transfer from the 1/9 subway line to the N/R? Oh wait. They got rid of the 9. Is there still an R? You lose track of things. You no longer know where to eat. Is that Tuscan place on Park and 22nd still open? You lose track of people. Where are you working now? Where are you living now? You try to keep up, but it's impossible. If you lose your facility with New York, like a language once deciphered, it covers itself over again, becomes incomprehensible through disuse.

As I have built a life in Paris, I have moved ever further away from where I started. When I visit New York now, I feel at once like a native and a visitor. My home is no longer my home, but then again—yes, it is.

I haven't come to terms with leaving New York. It is hard to leave New York. Every time.

My parents drop me at Kennedy. They get on the Van Wyck Expressway. My mother's still crying, though she's trying not to. My father's wondering why I don't just come home. And I'm sitting on the tarmac, wondering the same thing.

The airfield at night, in the dark, is so beautiful, and it's like New York has the potential to transform itself into the kind of haunted place I'd need it to be in order to stay. Layers of yellow, red, and blue lights, and the horizon looks rimmed with fire and there is the blue-lighted bridge beyond. The planes hang in the sky as they approach, flashing their lights to signal their arrival. A subway train runs alongside us, miles away, a string of lights on a track. And then we're 45 degrees from the earth, and the yellow lights of home arrange themselves geometrically and become a grid, until they disappear behind the fog and clouds.

But there is Paris on the other side.

When I look at a map at the whale-shape of Long Island, I could cry. My territory. My lost home. Perhaps if Long Island had a stronger identity all its own, or if it had another connotation than vulgarity and new wealth, I would be less reticent to claim it as my place of birth. But then why does the place you happen accidentally to be born in come to define you for the rest of your life?

Leaving home does something to your sense of identity. Either you become more of that place than you ever were while you lived there, or your identity calcifies around the rejection of this place. It is challenging to inhabit the space between these two positions.

All of these perspectives on the same place. It's dizzying.

Not long ago, when Hurricane Sandy was raging and I couldn't get my parents on the phone, I passed a sleepless night checking *The New York Times*' live feed every half hour. I felt gutted not to be there. I haven't lived in New York for nearly a decade, but it's my home, and these were my people rowing themselves out of their flooded houses in Queens. The day after the storm, I went on a short trip to Champagne with my partner. This trip had been planned for weeks, and there seemed no reason to cancel it, but I felt uncomfortable the whole time. What was I doing drinking champagne while New York was underwater?

But this is normal. Since I left New York to live in Paris in 2004, guilt is more a part of my life than it ever was when I lived there— and I come from a Jewish-Catholic background. Living abroad, I miss weddings, funerals, hurricanes, and everyday life, maintaining a lifeline through my parents, sister, friends, through Skype, Facebook, Twitter. I see New York, now, through the open windows of my computer screen. I see it, like the rest of the world, from someplace else.

CURRENCY

ELISA ALBERT

1.

Maybe you'll be an actress. Maybe you'll do stand-up. Maybe you'll suck dick for money. Maybe you'll wear intense glasses and make dramatic proclamations into a swank office telephone. Maybe you'll meet your married lover for a drink on a rainy night somewhere dark wearing nothing but lingerie under a coat. Maybe you'll make art in an airy loft in a deserted part of town. Surely there'll be long ruminative walks through the park. The voice-over will be witty as hell.

You can be weird in New York; you can be strange and melancholy and buxom and tall and dark and discerning and behave generally like the exuberant dyke you believe yourself to be. Apparently they value that sort of thing there!

Ape the hell out of Didion's prose in conversing with Dear Diary and get into a decent college despite your hilariously low GPA. Damn, her sentences are cool. Mr. Bellon's English class is the only thing about which you can muster a shit to give.

"Let's go down to the East River and throw something in," Ani DiFranco growls over and over again, louder and louder over the din of your mother's tirades outside the locked bedroom door. "Something we can't live without and then let's start again." Mutter this phrase tunelessly to yourself while you ride out panic attacks in the shower. Soon you'll be there and here won't matter anymore.

It won't be Didion's New York, though. Not Ani DiFranco's. Not Nicole Holofcener's, Nora Ephron's, Fran Lebowitz's, Jonathan Lethem's, Susan Sontag's, Andy Warhol's, or Patti Smith's either. Silly, though tempting, to pretend otherwise.

You're neither spoiled nor truly reckless enough to fully inhabit the extremes of the experience, but do what you can. Get regularly shit-faced with a gaggle of girls more or less exactly like you. Give spike heels a try. Take strangers home from bars. (Fucking dork: keep a list of their first names, the names of every man with whom you ever so much as make out.) Rarely turn down an invitation or a narcotic. Wind up in strange/desperate/squalid/exorbitant apartments, clubs, bars, restaurants. Forget how you got there. Guzzle jack-and-cokes until everyone seems like a dear friend you'll meet again in another lifetime. Bring the house down at Marie's Crisis with your off-key "Adelaide's Lament."

The Second Avenue Deli, Veniero's, Tompkins Square on the verge of sanity. Grey Dog Coffee, where your first husband gets himself banned for general orneriness. City Bakery. The community garden on Avenue D. St. Mark's Bookshop. Flatiron office job, Midtown office job, Gramercy office job, Chelsea freelance job. Forever late to work. One boss gives you an embroidered robe from ABC made of wool and silk, which almost a decade and a half later turns out to still be one of the nicer things you own. LifeThyme Natural Foods, Cobble Hill Theater, Yoga Lab, the Victory, Flying Saucer, Blue Sky Bakery. Read *The New York Post* and *The New York Daily News* cover to cover over lunch.

There are so many people, other people, always more people. Don't bother to remember the bars; bars are interchangeable.

Dress in costume. The weirder the better. Going to the laundromat is a treat. Anytime you can walk the streets. Not as in L.A., where life unfolded in the car or at home or in the car or at school or in the car or in the locked bedroom or in the car or at the mall or in the car. Barf, L.A., where girls competed to see who could stand out the *least*, who could literally almost disappear. Your whole childhood boiled down to eating a surreptitious ice cream cone slumped behind a book in the backseat of a car driven by a raving lunatic. Ice cream and books got you through. The books all pointed in the general direction of New York.

Orthodox girls in doorman rental on West 96th. Railroad shithole with appalling broker's fee on East 11th. Nesting pigeons cooing in the air shaft day and night. Boyfriend's squat on Carmine. Transient girlfriend in a garret down on the Hudson. A garret! Amazing below-market brownstone floor-through on Washington Place. Your favorite college professor comes to crash. You host parties. Neighbors complain about noise.

Warren Street sublet. State Street gem. Fifth-floor walk-up with super in VFW cap forever smoking on the stoop. F train, A train, 2 train, 6 train. Bodega, bodega, bodega. Amazing consignment on Atlantic. Brooklyn promenade.

At Lil' Frankie's Friday nights, Matt the hot waiter picks up the tab and shares the last bottle with you and your bestie. She thinks he wants her, but you are pretty sure he wants you. It's a flirt-off! He wants you both, obviously, but you have zero desire for her, which is probably why you've been friends for so long. Some other girl eventually sleeps with him and years later informs you gleefully, as if she won something.

On a rooftop in Brooklyn at one in the morning, P.J. Harvey sings about being on a rooftop in Brooklyn at one in the morning, and someone says something you've never forgotten. Your story's not seldom told, sweetheart.

Spend a summer stoned, Dean Wareham flooding the headphones. Cry constantly. Become a student of yoga. Lose friends. Write your way out. Write your way in. Filthy cliché. Fall in love and out and back in. Let a love or two pass you by, so you have something to think about wistfully in old age. Stop drinking, mostly. Have

a baby in the bathtub of a condo on the fourth floor of the old Board of Education building on Livingston. Gather up your fledgling family and flee.

2.

The question is: where do you belong?

"Where do you feel taller?" asks a tarot queen in the Berkshires on a perfect October afternoon. Excellent question. Up here, you guess.

"There's your answer," she says.

Growing up, you loathed being tall. Girls were not supposed to be tall. Girls were supposed to be as small as possible in every way.

What happened was a wildly great guy. No idea where Albany was, but you were game. Then the baby, and the living-in-two-places thing got old immediately. You could've fought to stay in the city. But you didn't have a whole lot of fight in you just then, and it was easy to say fuck the city. Felt pretty good, actually. Fuck Brooklyn. Fuck the scene and all who flock to it.

But then the harsh reality of Albany. There was some idea that it'd be a friendly place, an insta-community kind of place, because people have to stick together, even more so in a post-industrial wasteland kind of place, right? No.

A town designed (rather, corrupted; see William Kennedy's "Everything Everybody Ever Wanted" in the definitive *O Albany!*) to discourage human contact, communal life, organic gathering places. Your basic urban-planning nightmare American state capital. Pathetic monument to the personal automobile. The highway blocks direct human access to the river. To reinvent Sinatra: if you can love it here, you can love it anywhere.

At first you get off on going to the mall. After a decade in the Center of the Universe, a cheese-ball exurban mall seems the height of exoticism and delight. Classic beige sterile trying-too-hard fifteen plants in an atrium under a skylight of which some third-rate ar-

chitect was very proud. State-of-the-art-twenty-years-ago multiplex with arcade. Escalators, Muzak, teenagers up to no good. Israelis accost you with samples of Dead Sea shit from a cart. The hideous seasonal store: Halloween crap, Christmas crap, Valentine's crap, St. Patrick's Day crap, Easter crap, Fourth of July crap, back-to-school crap, around again.

People in the city cock their heads and say, "How *is* it up there? Is it, like, really, really *cold* up there?" Don't blame them; you couldn't find it on a map two years ago, either.

A film buff tells you lots of early noir films were set in Albany, which adds a nice new dimension. We live on an Olmsted-inspired park in a grand, creaky house built around the time your great-great-grandmother was keeping house in some muddy *shtetl*. Fireplaces, oak moldings, 1950s tile, original tub. A stoop with pale pink columns. Wild, mature perennial garden. When people visit from the city, their jaws hang open. "Albany consolation prize," you explain.

Once you and the kid get caught in a surprise summer downpour on your way home from the park and a lady on her stoop sees you from across the street and calls you into her house, where she makes you tea and gives the kid toys and insists you stay for dinner. The struggling local businesses on bedraggled yet faintly charming Lark Street, forever On the Verge. At Lark Fest, drunk dudes urinate and puke on everyone's stoop and neighbors commiserate and it's almost cute. *Metroland,* the highly lovable alternative news weekly. Perpetual fryer smell from Bombers, where you eat once and vow never to eat again. Pristine haven of Crisan Bakery, treats made from scratch by Iggy and Claudia. Dove and Hudson: walk in and breathe books and something you've been thinking about—say, Mircea Eliade, or Paula Fox, or a guide to Ayurveda—appears on a shelf at eye level. They keep your honey's book in the window, next to the Robert Caro doorstop about Robert Moses, proud of the neighborhood guy who done good. Ben & Jerry's on the corner, across from the enormously fat cats at the bodega.

"Hi, kitty cats," waves your boy as he strollers then trikes then scooters on by.

A spring then summer then fall then winter.

"Little guy's growing too fast," says the pockmarked guy who stands out front smoking and keeping watch. A couple open an organic café and bakery on Delaware, down from the Spectrum and New World Bistro. She was crying once when you went in and you understand that their undertaking is unimaginably difficult; traveling to Phish shows in the yellow VW van used to be way more fun than convincing this struggling, shit-balls community to rally around its local organic café.

Takes time, but you find wonderful people. No worries about where the kid will "get in" to preschool. A shaggy collection of earthy midwifery-supportive fellow families. No one gives a flying fucking shit what you're wearing. There's always room for you and your laptop at the okay coffee roaster.

From your kitchen window watch the sun rise on Empire Plaza, Rockefeller's misguided monument to his prick, with its impressive collection of modern art, reflecting pool, neofascist concrete expanse, bizarre underground city, wintertime skating rink. The way those four capital buildings stand sentinel on the horizon. The aptly named Egg, where Rickie Lee Jones opens with "Satellites" in the hundred-seat theater.

The drive on I-90 to preschool, past Nipper the dog, the hills and the river and the skies you would not believe. The river walk, the pedestrian walkway. Miles and miles of bike path. The U-Haul truck rotating slowly on top of a storage facility on the river.

At the Shitty Bagel Chain surrounded by Real People (meaning: not living meta-lives on top of actual lives, not trained in matters of ultimate coolness, not wealthy, not angling for notoriety), notice how it's a bit less noisy in the superego sense. You can relax. You have nothing to prove.

A Manhattan-reared artist who now lives in western Massachusetts shakes her head in disgust at the thought that anyone still wants

to live there. "Take your art where it matters," she says. Think about an inward-focused life. Where can you best lead one? Do your thing, stand tall. Life's a turning inward, you're convinced lately, a getting quiet, learning to observe and be still. Some call it meditation, but you get scared off when it has a name.

Within a forty-five-minute radius: Troy and its vibrant art community, too many kick-ass farmer's markets to name, Saratoga, Hudson, Berkshires, Catskills, Ghent, Chatham, Great Barrington, Saugerties, MassMoca, Tanglewood, Kripalu. You actually love it here, turns out. Look closely: it's a promising place. There's work to be done. There's potential here. Put your money and effort and energy *here*, where it's possible to make a dent.

And god, how about those creepy birdcalls in the train station garage? They sound like rhesus monkeys. What the fuck are they? No one seems to know. Detailed conversations between those animals, day and night. It's so weird and uncool here that it turns out to be pretty cool. But the question remains, only partially because of the mindfuck of having recently become someone's mother: who the hell are you and what are you doing here?

"Where upstate do you live?" wonders a cool girl behind the counter of a cool north Brooklyn café.

"Hudson," you say, because you can't deal with this chick writing you off as some irrelevant bumblefuck mom. Hudson has name recognition, artists and art and currency. You need this random chick to understand that You Are Culturally Relevant. Shame, rage. You're ridiculous. Why this need? Are you *twelve*?

"Oh, my god, I love it up there!" she says. "Sooooo cool."

You nod. You matter. You are an arbiter, goddamn it! AN ARBITER.

3.

To talk about New York—living there, aspiring to live there, having lived there—is to talk about currency. Not privilege and not money, mind you; money is simple. Money is straightforward. Money can

give you choices, options. Privilege skews how you see yourself and others, fucks with your head. Currency is something else. Currency is terrifically complex. Money and privilege can make you comfortable, but only currency gives you real power. You can't buy currency; it eludes plenty of rich, entitled people. Beauty, originality, fearlessness: these are some of the currencies of New York.

Papa Irwin, small-time shyster genius youngest son of an alcoholic Montreal policeman, bought a parcel of land in Los Angeles on the corner of what is now Sunset and La Brea in 1950 and moved his family west. Rumor has it he and his uncle, traveling salesmen, sold condoms to whorehouses. Papa called New York City "that cesspool," aghast at your living there. Alone, no less.

Your parents got married at the hotel from *Pretty Woman*. Big Brentwood Spanish-style homes, Bullocks Wilshire, I. Magnin, Sweet Sixteen at Louise's. Birds of paradise, magnolias, palms. The flats of Beverly Hills before the Persians. Bat mitzvah a few blocks from Santa Monica beach. Fancy private school. At sixteen Maggie Gyllenhaal had sumptuously hairy armpits, a most incredible vintage wardrobe, the confidence of a legend. (Currency, friends.)

It's not until you're long gone that you begin to understand: it's unusual to be "from" a place that comprises a lot of fantasy lives. But from there you are, and what an education you got, man. The culture of name-dropping and status anxiety, the whiff of desperation inherent in any attempt to assert oneself that way: it was in your microwaved baby formula.

"You don't seem like you're from L.A.," people always say.

"Thank you," you reply.

New York was your escape from that bullshit, all the *yeah so we were having brunch at Balthazar when I blew this marginally famous person in the bathroom of that bar on Ludlow the night of the Williamsburg heroin orgy wearing the dress I bought at the Barney's warehouse sale to the best show ever at the venue no one's heard of yet.* Puff out your chest and prove just how connected and prescient and rooted you are. When the real currency lies in who lives in the shittiest neighborhood and cares the least? Who gets in free? Whose art is so essential it cannot be ignored?

Love letters to New York are invariably designed to make the reader feel like a loser, no? You might feel powerless in New York, but you can always make some poor schmuck who's never lived there, or, better yet, *only recently just moved there*, feel even more power-less. Fine: so maybe you remember when Alphabet City was scary and Brooklyn was cheap. Maybe you went to Elaine's, KGB, Mars Bar. Maybe you got mugged. Congratulations. If you remember its previ-ous incarnation, or the incarnation prior to that, you own New York. You came, you saw, you conquered. Here's your I HEART NYC T-shirt. You're legit. You're rooted. Now shush. An ultimately boring-ass eco-nomics, and honestly the whole marketplace can pretty much suck it.

Your identity isn't reliant on that place, on any place; it's just a construction. Magical thinking. It's as if you have Stockholm Syn-drome: the city took you captive, stole your heart, ran off with your imagination, left you broke and battered. Sure, sing it a freakin' love song. But make no mistake: the city owns you.

Still, you really miss that goddamned place, something about its weird, destructive pull. Plenty of good reasons to hop a train down: gigs, friends, family, marvelous headshrinker. Kiss your family, get on the southbound, read a silly rag, watch the river whiz by. Usually a whole row to yourself. The conductors smile. Mustachioed flattop guy and buxom grandma type are your favorites. Once in a while, the vibe's a little on the scary side. Once there were bomb-sniffing dogs and TSA agents. And compared to the train situation in, say, Western Europe, Amtrak is an overpriced disgrace.

But it's a lovely liminal space, the train. Put on headphones. More often than not a little stoned. (Only backfires when you miss your train. Once you had to drive to Poughkeepsie to catch Metro North absolutely baked and your friend stayed on the phone with you the whole way, and you said out loud to her and to yourself and to the empty highway, "Okay, this is really not okay. I'm being an asshole and I gotta cool it with the pot.")

At Penn Station, gather up your stuff. Deep breath. Sentimental souls need rituals. Go up a few escalators and emerge across from the grand steps of the post office on Eighth Avenue, where the camera would pan up in a dizzy spiral, if there were a camera.

"Paying respects to lost youth," you text people. "Drink?" You hate making plans too far in advance. You also hate alcohol but want that looseness you used to enjoy, that who-knows-where-the-night-might-take-us, lately in such short supply.

Needless to say, you love your family. You are awash in love and gratitude for your beautiful life up the river. But you cherish these field trips. Time is not linear. The old you is a fossil trapped in amber here, perfectly preserved. Stay at a friend's tiny studio. Read a good book over breakfast at the perfect tiny brasserie down the street.

Sit on your old stoop for a while. A couple of hours before the train home. The girls are all in costume. An old lady shuffles past, looking at you, amused. You're in costume, too: city drag. Way more "interesting" a look than is worth wasting on preschool pickup in Albany. Scribbling in a notebook, to boot. Two women walk by. One is pushing an infant in a stroller; the other's hugely pregnant. The pregnant one says she feels "a lot of pressure." The other one says something-something "heavy." If you're not immersed in such things they can seem repetitive and boring. But if you are immersed in them, they comprise your life, so what are you supposed to do? You too waddled these streets with friends, talking about bodies and birth and pressure and heaviness. It now seems an almost unbearably special time, but it was just life unfolding.

This lovely film guy and his actress girlfriend moved in when you left. What if they find you sitting here on their stoop? That would be kind of sad. You once ran into the actress around the corner and it was embarrassing, as if she knew you were casing her apartment. You're upset they live here, kind of. This magic gem of an apartment that used to be yours. They still get mail for you occasionally. The super died last year. Never saw him smile, but he was a good guy.

The way he sat there, smoking, vacant stare. They way he said "Yeahhhhhh" in his sandpaper voice.

You fell in love here a bunch, wrote a couple books, gave birth. How could that time not hold you in thrall? "Change is seen as something evil only by those who have lost their youth or sense of humor." That was Cookie Mueller on the East Village, 1985. The city's not the same and you're not the same and you'll never get that time back because time is a spiral, girl: a spiral. Life is elsewhere now. Live it.

All accountable, reasonably happy grown-ups are the same, but unhappy immature drama-queen wretches are all unhappy in their own way. There's something terrifically sad about growing up, which is why sometimes people refuse to do it. (Some of your very favorite people.) I mean, Jesus, it's only a place. It isn't responsible for who you've become; it could have been Tel Aviv or Berlin or San Francisco or London. Could've been rural Idaho, Sebastopol, Ireland, Texas. Anyway, how many people are lucky enough to *choose where they live* in the first place?

It's just you miss the reckless girl who lived here. Petulant funny stubborn blind unforgiving little wench, beholden to no one, blindly enacting her will on everything, everyone. She was nobody's mother. It was your youth! Now you're older and wiser and better in about a thousand ways. A halfway decent sense of self on a good day, for starters. Now you know a thing or two about where to put your energy, what it means to build up instead of tear down, what it's like to nurture valuable things so that they grow. You wouldn't trade anything for anything. All of this is true. And yet, let us not skirt the issue that something was lost. Something has been lost.

A WAR ZONE FOR ANYONE LOOKING FOR LOVE

LIZA MONROY

Bear Stearns, August 23, 2001

I stood by the pay phone outside my former fiancé's office, fresh
off a red-eye from L.A. and jet-lagged in the muggy afternoon. After
barely speaking to him during the nine months since we had broken
off our engagement, showing up unannounced to tell him I wanted
him back and was moving to New York City to prove it was the kind
of thing only stalkers, *Sex and the City* characters, or early-twenty-
somethings would do. I was at least one of those things.

My former fiancé, the boy from high school in spray-painted
jeans and earrings who would go on to become one of Wall Street's
youngest managing directors, proposed the year I turned twenty-
one, while I was in L.A. for a three-month internship. I would move to
New York to become an (Extremely) Young Wall Street Wife: find a job
in publishing, go out on the town with investment bankers, and work
toward my dream of becoming a writer. I just needed to figure out
how. Judging by my idols (Joan Didion, Jack Kerouac), New York was
the place to do that, too. Since it was the height of the *Sex and the City*
era, though, my contemporary model was Carrie Bradshaw. That was

how young I was, young enough to venerate Carrie Bradshaw and to think myself ready for marriage at twenty-one.

Since my former fiancé was a tall, offbeat, enigmatic, problematic, charming businessman, and since our relationship could ultimately best be described as a wetland deposit of dead organic material, I'll call him Mr. Bog.

Mr. Bog came downstairs to the lobby and informed me that I was crazy and he was leaving on a business trip to Colombia in the morning.

"Inspecting a pipeline," he said, "in a jungle with gorillas. Could be dangerous."

"Gorillas?"

"*Guerrillas*."

We met later near his apartment on 86th and York. He was walking an orange cat on a leash. We ascended to his studio—all pizza boxes, analyst reports, and overflowing trash cans—and dropped off the cat. At the bar downstairs, he listened to my reasons why breaking things off was a mistake.

"If you move here," he said, "we can see."

East Village, August 28, 2001

From a friend's rooftop, the Twin Towers loomed above. I stared, almost praying, as if they were representations of deities at an altar: *Make my life in New York as sparkling and magical as you.*

Los Angeles, Fourteen Days Later

I only became more determined.

"Don't do it," my mother said. "There's anthrax there. The whole city's a mess."

Nothing would stop me. Not anthrax, orange-level terrorism alerts, or my mother.

Chelsea, April 2002

My roommate and best friend, Emir, moved with me. We stayed with my great-uncle in Chelsea for a few days, sleeping on couches in his theater space. He co-owned a theater company. Framed playbills and photographs from past performances lined the walls and the place was cluttered with antiques.

When my mother and I visited when I was little, we stayed there and went to the theater, the Empire State Building, and the Central Park Zoo. She was in the Foreign Service, so I didn't have a home in the traditional sense. Constant change was home, or wherever I put down my suitcase. Maybe that was why, Mr. Bog aside, I felt connected to New York. It was both a constant and a place where every misfit fit in.

Mr. Bog emailed. He'd been in a surfing accident in Mexico, shattered his ankle against rocks. A blood clot from the ankle broke loose and lodged in his lung. While he was in the hospital, certain he was about to die, he thought of me, making him realize he did want to try again.

Lower East Side, April 2002

In our new closet-sized fifth-floor walk-up, Emir and I assembled furniture from Ikea in New Jersey. Mr. Bog and I walked around Chinatown, and he came over to my little room where clothes hung on a wardrobe rack procured from my great-uncle's theater. We slept together for the first time since the broken engagement, but the following week, he said he "couldn't do this." Bog left me, but at least he left me with New York.

Midtown and Lower East Side, 2002–2003

My first job was in the notorious agent-trainee program at the William Morris Agency, pushing a mail cart around the Midtown skyscraper in a suit. Between mail runs, we sat in the basement reading

the trades and the *Times*. I earned four hundred dollars a week—enough to make my share of rent, then splurge on happy hour and the teriyaki-pineapple veggie dogs from Crif Dogs on St. Mark's.

In my tiny room with its distant view of the Manhattan Bridge, I wrote bad short stories featuring Mr. Bog. On weekends, I sought adventure in the city.

One of my mailroom colleagues used to work at *Saturday Night Live* and still got invited to the weekly after-parties thrown by cast members. "Tracy Morgan's party is tomorrow night," he mentioned nonchalantly one Friday afternoon.

The party was in an empty loft in a high-rise way downtown. I looked out the floor-to-ceiling glass at traffic rushing by on West Street twenty-something stories below. Naked women—high-class call girls, I presumed—wandered the party, men helping themselves as if they were appetizer trays, leading them over to only partially concealed couches in corners. Everyone was on something, and we stayed until the sun came up.

Welcome to New York.

I wrote in East Village cafés and wandered through Tompkins Square Park to meet Emir for gay-barhopping. I spent hours at the Met and in Williamsburg dive bars. I stood in line at three in the morning for the best pizza, Rosario's on the Lower East Side. In some small way, New York was mine, even though Mr. Bog was not. Sometimes he reappeared to help me do things like make decisions about my first 401(k) over cocktails at the Gramercy Hotel. I wondered whether we'd somehow become friends.

Chelsea, February–November 2004

At twenty-four, I was out of the mailroom and working for a literary agent. I had a small one-bedroom on 15th Street and Eighth Avenue and a boyfriend. An email from Mr. Bog arrived in my work inbox one snowy February morning, asking how I was doing. "Good," I replied, "but freezing." His response: an email confirmation for two

first-class tickets to Puerto Rico. For that weekend. I broke up with my boyfriend.

Four years after ending our first engagement, I married Mr. Bog at City Hall. I published some writing and left the agency to free-lance for magazines. I could say I was a writer in Manhattan married to an investment banker, so New York dreams came true if you stayed long enough.

East Village, September 2007

If you stayed long enough, they also unraveled.

When I interviewed author Anthony Swofford for an article and the topic of love in New York came up, he said, "New York City is a war zone for anyone looking for love. It's a city constructed for the ease of bad behavior and outright deceit. I loved it for that reason for many years."

So did Mr. Bog. One clue was naked pictures from another woman in his email, left open on our computer. She wanted to know when he would return to Argentina, where Bog had emerging-markets business. She was only a symptom of the larger problem: Mr. Bog and I were not actually compatible. He loved house music and bottle service on the expense account. I preferred plays and literary readings. I convinced him to see Joan Didion's *The Year of Magical Thinking* with Vanessa Redgrave (about, ironically, Didion losing her husband). Mr. Bog said, "Never again will I spend two hours listening to some old lady in an Adirondack chair." He gave me jewelry and tried to give away my books.

In the early morning hours after a night of clubbing for his thirty-second birthday, Mr. Bog, drunk, grabbed my laptop off a table and tried to throw it across the room. I knew he had problems with anger but I hadn't seen its propensity to turn violent until that night. It took that much to push me to end it. I couldn't be with someone who crossed that line, no matter how much history we had. We went through a Wall Street divorce, replete with Manhattan lawyers on five-figure retainers. It was difficult and sad as divorces are, and I longed to go back to a simpler time in my New York life. I moved back to the Lower East Side. Simultaneously defeated and triumphant, I still had the city.

I'd become one of those people who said things like, "When I moved here, Orchard Street was nothing but leather shops and Williamsburg was where you went for cheaper rent."

I never considered going elsewhere to start over. That's the thing about New York: no one ever wants to leave. Throngs of hopeful protagonists arrive with their dreams and diminutive bank accounts. It's only in disaster movies that you see anyone wanting to get out, and it's because a meteor is coming or aliens are attacking. Divorce didn't mean failure. Leaving New York certainly would.

Prospect Heights, Brooklyn, 2008–2012

Over fourteen-dollar cocktails at a faux-speakeasy, a friend complained that she was tired of high rent and a job that left her with no writing time. Many friends were writers without time to write; in New York, being there sometimes defeated the purpose of being there. She confessed she was thinking of moving to Pittsburgh or the South.

"That's a terrible idea," I began.

This scenario repeated itself with a small parade of disillusioned friends, starring me as stalwart for staying even when what they wanted most was to get out. In "Goodbye to All That," Didion says it never occurred to her that she was living a real life in New York. I thought living anywhere else meant you'd given up. Stay "too long at the Fair"? Preposterous. What was not true of my Bog marriage was true of the city: the successful people were simply the ones who stuck around. I was determined to become one of them.

This version barely resembled my twenty-two-year-old self: early thirties divorcée trampling around the city in six-inch-heeled boots giving directions in the West Village without pause. I had a faculty appointment teaching composition at Columbia, a Brooklyn

one-bedroom, a sketchily procured Park Slope Food Co-op membership, a literary agent, a Jungian psychoanalyst, and a by-referral-only tarot reader. That's New York: you wake up realizing this is what you dreamed of when you were younger, this is what it looks like, and yet there's still a long way to go, much more to do and accomplish. That is why I told the would-be deserters not to leave. Stay longer, see what happens. Ultimately, my friend who wanted to move to Pittsburgh or the South renewed her lease.

I had a couple of post-divorce boyfriends, but none lasted. One involved the guy taking revenge for my breaking up with him by shredding my clothes, trashing the apartment, and drowning my two laptops in the bathtub—the one Mr. Bog had tried to throw and one I'd acquired since. I don't know if such relationship failures had to do with trying to find love in New York City (see Swofford), being young, being me (impulsive), or some combination of any or all of the above. I settled into singlehood, for the first time thinking that would be all right. I thought I'd be lonely if I wasn't married in my thirties, but I wasn't lonely, even in a crowded city with so much room for isolation and so little for intimacy. I did hope I would meet someone. Specifically, at the Park Slope Food Co-op, while I, and possibly he, were sweeping floors or slicing cheese. But I didn't.

That I—who convinced people not to venture into the abyss of elsewhere—suddenly walked out on New York shocked me even more than the friends I talked out of doing this very thing. Emir, still my best friend (some things, even in the ever-changing landscape of New York, remain constant), quoted something he heard somewhere: "Good things happen gradually and over time. Great things happen all at once."

New York will invite you to pick up a quirky hobby. Mine was the Brazilian martial art capoeira. I trained almost nightly. The

capoeira group had locations in other cities, too. At the end of my tenth September in New York, visitors arrived for a performance. One of them, from Santa Cruz, California, was an elementary school teacher and the capoeira equivalent of a black belt. "He's a special guy," a mutual friend mentioned in passing, "charismatic and smart." She was right. I was instantly at ease around him. He was funny, interesting, easy to be with. I was glad to have made this nice new friend from California.

The nice new friend from California wanted to see the High Line, the former elevated train line on Manhattan's West Side that's been converted to a park. I told him I could take him and anyone else who wanted to go. We turned out to be the only ones.

He was at Starbucks when I arrived, eating a bagel. I would have told him to throw that Starbucks bagel away, that I could take him to get a real one, but bagels fell from my mind when he looked up at me and I never mentioned them. During that High Line walk, I had a better time in his company than I ever had on any date, and we weren't even on a date. He kept joking that I put up with him all day.

Two nights later, we kissed on the subway. When he went back to California, I didn't know if I would see him again but, also unlike my New York lovers, he didn't play games. I planned to visit for three weeks in November. Instead I got engaged, and stayed. It seems that when something is meant to happen, nothing can stop it, which sounds like something a by-referral-only tarot reader or someone who lives in Santa Cruz would say.

Santa Cruz, Today

I wear flip-flops in January and live in a house a mile from the beach. In August, my fiancé and I are getting married in a redwood grove. Friends and my mother have asked how I could move across the country and get engaged to someone I'd only known for a few months. The only answer I can give is that it felt right in a way that nothing did before, not even being in New York. That's true but not

the whole story: he did offer to move to Brooklyn, if that was what I wanted. But what I wanted was to join him. In this zephyrean beach-side paradise, sea lion barks under the pier replaced subway rumblings beneath sidewalk grates. Drivers stop if they see a pedestrian so much as eyeball a crosswalk.

Maybe I was wrong to convince those would-be Southerners and Pittsburghers not to leave. I wonder, if you come from somewhere else and stay long enough, whether New York is a place you inevitably outgrow, whether you take from it what you can, then go. If that was the case, I didn't realize it until I had a reason to leave—not because I failed, but because I found something worth leaving for, the kind of love I thought I was only imagining existed. Turns out I was only imagining it existed, for me, in New York.

REAL ESTATE

SARI BOTTON

"I'm hearing the words, '*Don't give up the apartment.*'"

It was my first of what would eventually add up to ten yearly appointments with Terry, a psychic who was popular among media types—a ritual I'd later refer to as my "annual checkup."

We were seated in the run-down, rent-controlled sixth-floor walk-up Terry herself had held on to for twenty-odd years at the corner of Mott and Prince Streets. In the fall of 1993 that neighborhood was still considered Little Italy. It would be another few years before realtors would rebrand it as "Nolita."

Petite and tomboyish in her forties, Terry sat across from me at a table strewn with tarot cards, alternately flipping them and pushing back her little-girl bangs with the heel of her hand.

"Yes, that's definitely the message," she said, after closing her eyes for a moment. "*Don't give up the apartment.*"

Well, no shit, I thought. I had a lease on a marginally decrepit but livable rent-stabilized one-bedroom in a tenement on East 13th Street, for which I paid about $600 a month. I didn't need a clairvoyant to caution me against relinquishing it.

Besides, real estate advice was hardly what I wanted for my $150. No, I wanted Terry to tell me what most people go to psychics to hear: that there was love on the horizon.

I was twenty-eight, two years out of an ill-considered marriage I'd entered at twenty-three. Add to the usual difficulties associated with finding love in New York that I was a bit of an odd bird, difficult to match. All my life I'd been a strange mix of loner, social butterfly, and musical theater geek, sometimes painfully awkward around people, at other times oddly charming and entertaining. I felt like some kind of alien, out of step with the kids I grew up with (even fellow theater geeks thought I was weird), my classmates in college, and my coworkers at the assorted publications where I worked over the years. I didn't like the same clothes, hairstyles, movies, music, and food that most of my peers did, and I had this insistent need to do most things my own peculiar way, even if it made no sense.

Not only would a man in my life have all that to contend with, but he'd also have stiff competition for my attention from the city itself. My idea of a good time—pretty much *the best time*—was walking leisurely around Manhattan and Brooklyn from neighborhood to neighborhood by myself, with no particular destination or goal. I preferred it to doing just about anything with anyone—other than singing, which I also did mostly by myself.

Walking the city aimlessly alone had been my favorite activity since I was fourteen. I got the idea after some older camp friends brought me along for an afternoon of simply kicking around, mostly in the Village. That day, New York City transformed for me. It stopped being some kind of Oz, the fancy place where you went to see Broadway shows, the Little Orchestra Society at Lincoln Center, my singer dad's operatic concerts, and all manner of culture with a capital *C*.

This New York, the one my friends showed me, was a different kind of exotic. It was gritty and real; a place to take your time and people-watch; a place where what was happening outside, in the streets, on the sidewalks, in the parks, was the main attraction.

Soon after that day, for the first of many times, I lied to my mother the way other girls lied about hanging out with boys, telling her I was taking the Long Island Rail Road only four stops to see a friend in Lynbrook, but instead riding all the way to Penn Station so I could wander the city for hours, as far as my babysitting money would take me. I would sip hot chocolate as I observed the skaters at Rockefeller Center. I'd eat soup in Chinatown and observe the other "bridge-and-tunnel" diners in from the suburbs as they greedily inhaled their spare ribs and chow mein. I'd browse vintage clothing stores in the West Village and hang around Washington Square Park so I could observe the buskers around the fountain and the colorful, loud tourists cheering them on. I liked to observe non-loner-alien people, and New York City was the best place to do that.

The bonus: I could do it all without having to ask my mother to drive me from place to place as I had to on Long Island. Here, on foot, I was free. Wherever my feet took me, I was happy to have the city as my sole companion. I loved the feeling of being alone but among people.

The preference for my own company naturally made it difficult to couple up too comfortably as an adult. I was horribly lonely and wanted to find that one other outsider who was put on this strange planet just for me—one who would, of course, give me plenty of space for my loner activities. So far, I only knew how to get that from guys who were difficult to pin down, emotionally withholding, and typically addicted to at least one substance, which is to say even less available than I was. Say what you will about unavailable guys, but you don't run the risk of making them feel neglected when you want to do your own thing. Dating them so I wouldn't feel hemmed in turned out to be a faulty strategy, though, because they drained me of my psychic energy—when they were around and when they weren't—so I never really got to be *alone* when I was alone, and when we were together, I was never fulfilled.

As for nice, available guys, I seemed to be utterly allergic to them as mates but great at being friends with them. And so I introduced one awesome male friend after another to my female friends. When the second of four couples married, they dubbed me "The East Village Yenta."

The matchmaker had no talent for setting herself up, though. This job I'd have to outsource. That's where Terry came in.

"I see the letter *B*," she said in her flat western New York accent. "Hmm. Who could that be? Pick nine cards."

When I was done choosing one and then another, she shifted them around into different formations. "Okay. So, this person whose name begins with *B*. He's got a goatee, maybe? I see him in a room with sharp angles, and a buffet with really mediocre food."

For years afterward, I would scrutinize intently the "angles" of one mediocre-buffet-filled room and then another to determine whether they might in fact be "sharp."

Just then Terry's cat jumped onto the table. "Oh, Edie," she said, stroking her. "You know what this means?" No, I didn't. "When she climbs on the table during a reading, it's usually a sign of true love. This guy with the letter *B*—this could be something! Yeah, look at that: the nine of cups," she said, pointing. "That card can mean marriage. You might have a marriage to a guy whose name starts with *B*."

Oh, great. I'd just divorced a guy whose name started with *B*. There went $150.

It's a wonder I went back a second time, a year later. At that first appointment with Terry, I didn't yet know about the strange, random accuracy of at least some of her predictions—like the suggestion I keep my eye out for a good job offer from "someone named

Horace—no, Horst" three years before I'd receive an assignment to ghostwrite a book for a guy with the unusual name of . . . Horst.

Incidentally, a three-year gap between a prediction and its coming to fruition was relatively short in Terry-time. As she explained, "What I see here could happen in ten minutes, or ten years from now. It's all very Agatha Christie. I'll hear a name, or I'll see an article of clothing, and ten years from now you'll go, 'Oh, my God—there's that guy with the red shoes Terry was telling me about!' And he might not actually *be* your guy. But you can bet he will have *something to do with* your guy."

Ten minutes or *ten years?* Couldn't she pinpoint the timing of her predictions just a little more accurately?

"But time isn't linear, dear." Whatever that meant.

I was also eager to hear from Terry whether there was a career break in my near future—some high-profile writing job or assignment that would both pay out and put an end to my six years languishing in the humdrum world of trade magazines. I'd wanted to be a writer living in New York City since I was a teen, after my grandparents took me to dinner at a restaurant in the East sixties and I spotted a woman eating by herself, with a notebook and pen as her only companions. I'd already been writing since I was in grade school. (I won the school-wide essay contest two years in a row!) But that woman writing and eating by herself put images in my head of a writing life located specifically in the city.

Not included in those images, to the best of my recollection, was one of me toiling endlessly at trade magazines with names like *Body Fashions/Intimate Apparel*, *Fashion Jewelry Plus!*, and *Home Furnishings News*, at the last of which I grudgingly covered the most bizarre assortment of beats: luxury linens, decorative pillows, air purifiers, and car alarms. I was always flying out from LaGuardia to housewares trade shows in Vegas and Chicago, where I'd moderate panel discussions on such exciting topics as whether HEPA air filtration was more or less effective than ionic particulation. I put in long hours at my desk, lunching and sometimes dinnering on salty soups and flavorless packaged salads from the nearest Smiler's deli in the bland, sprawling corporate park that is much of Midtown. That particular New York seemed galaxies away from the one I wanted to inhabit. I wanted Terry to tell me I'd soon get to put that all behind me and move on to more glorified and satisfying assignments. And, more importantly, success with my own creative writing.

"Well, I *am* seeing something," she said. "I'm seeing bookshelves . . ."

Oh, my god, *bookshelves*. I cut her off. "Do you think that means it's time for me to write my book?"

I was referring to "Adventures in Divorce," the memoir I'd been planning to write on the cheerful topic of my family's legacy of failed marriages, including my own at twenty-six. (Even my stepparents have stepparents.) If Terry didn't envision the book being published soon and to critical acclaim, I didn't want to put myself through the slow torture of sitting quietly at my desk after my day job, enduring loneliness and boredom, recalling painful and embarrassing experiences, and wrestling unwieldy sentences into submission. I wasn't going to take any chances if the time wasn't right and if I didn't already *know* it was going to be well received.

"Well, let's ask the cards," Terry said. "Pick seven . . ."

And the answer was . . .

"The cards are saying that any time from now on is a good time." That certainly narrowed things down.

Of course, it was the right answer. It's always the right time to get started writing. Duh. And it's always difficult, and there will never be any guarantees. And it's a process, a slow one. *Blah, blah, blah.* I'd resisted that wisdom when it was imparted by instructors at the two MFA programs I'd dabbled in before quitting, plus every self-help book on writing I'd ever read, and I was less than thrilled when the distilled essence of it was delivered again by a high-priced psychic.

I f I wasn't producing much writing, it wasn't for lack of space. My East 13th Street apartment had an extra little room for me to write in, and I did, some—mostly freelance articles and essays and a lame proposal for *Adventures in Divorce.* But I never pushed far enough through the difficulty of writing any one piece of the book for it to really go anywhere.

I had any number of ways to distract myself from that difficulty. There were countless hours of mental gymnastics trying to figure out one intermittently interested guy after another. There were longer and longer runs around the East River Park. There was singing, at the top of my lungs, in my apartment (my upstairs neighbor once popped down to ask, "Can we move the Joni Mitchell hour to a time when I'm not home?") and at the weekly jazz open mic at Cleopatra's Needle on the Upper West Side and Rue B in my neighborhood. I took to the task of organizing casual dinners among the group of friends I considered my East Village family as if I were a professional event planner.

I had a place I could afford to write and live in alone in New York City, and I was squandering my time there. I tried not to think about that, and so I stopped noticing. But the years ticked by, quite linearly I might add, and somehow one day I was twenty-eight, and the next I was thirty-eight. I assumed I'd have that rent-stabilized apartment forever, which at twenty-eight seemed like a great thing for a struggling writer. But at thirty-eight, still lonely and with few details of my life changed, I started to imagine that I'd grow old and die alone in that run-down shoebox, and it scared me.

et me cut to the chase here. Ten years almost to the day after my first reading from Terry, in the fall of 2003, I met a (goateed) guy named Brian.

Brian. *Whose named starts with* B.

An hour after our first date, brunch at Life Café, I attended a wedding reception—*in a room with sharp angles and a buffet with really mediocre food.* Well, the closest any room's angles had come to being "sharp" in the decade since Terry had predicted that detail. (The wedding was at the industrial-chic, poured-concrete-walled Tenth Street Lounge, where there were no soft edges. Whatever. Work with me.)

Brian was a really nice guy, and fortunately, thanks to roughly $20,000 worth of psychotherapy, I no longer had a strong aversion to that. He was cute, smart, funny, creative, and, I would later learn, totally cool with me being a weird loner when I needed to be. He'd also soon come to encourage me to stop making my singing a private affair, and accompany me on pretty much every instrument on recordings we'd make together.

But let's get to the important stuff: he had *real estate,* specifically a rambling below-market-value loft in a Gothic Victorian former yeshiva on Avenue B, across from Tompkins Square Park. After our third date, he invited me up. As I stepped in behind him, I couldn't believe my eyes—1,800 square feet on two levels, three bedrooms, high ceilings, exposed brick, big windows, an arched entryway, and other interesting architectural details. It was run-down with chipping paint, which gave it a bohemian feel similar to that in my apartment. Brian and I shared the same threadbare flea market style, with mismatched furniture, some of it picked up right off the curb—the same place I'd found the desk where I still write.

Only a few months after we started dating, I moved, unofficially, into that incredible, gaping loft, and began illegally renting out my place on 13th Street—by the weekend, by the week, by the month. Eventually, though, toward the end of 2004, my super warned me

that I was in danger of getting busted. "The landlord's been asking me if you really live here," he said. Brian and I were engaged. There was no question we'd ultimately choose his 1,800 square feet over my 350. Maybe it was time to hand over my keys.

My last day in the apartment, after all my stuff had been moved out, I sat for a while on the scraped-up hardwood floor. I couldn't decide whether, now that it was empty, the place looked like a spare art gallery or a seedy slum. New York City real estate is like that. How you perceive it is relative, mostly to time and to what other conditions you've lived in. The $600 dump I'd moved into with lumpy plaster walls, lopsided floors, and peeling paint hadn't changed much over the years. Even with new windows, it was probably still a dump by many people's standards. Although the next tenant would pay $2,150. *Tenants*, plural, that is. When I stopped by a few months later, the super told me there were four young women, NYU students, sharing the space.

Without my furniture, clothes, books, the memory-steeped markers of my time there, the place had a peacefulness to it that I wanted to inhabit for one moment longer. It struck me that the sunlight streaming in was the same golden hue it had been when I moved in. I swear it could have been the same day. Had any of the things I remembered actually even happened here? The many lonely, gloomy days interspersed with relatively brighter ones? The all-nighters to meet freelance deadlines? *Twelve* birthdays? The parade of bad boyfriends, first nights together, tearful last nights, promises made and broken? Was this the moment before or the moment after? Maybe time *isn't* linear.

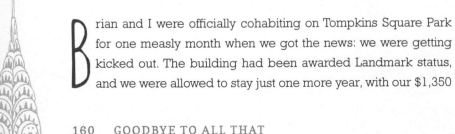

rian and I were officially cohabiting on Tompkins Square Park for one measly month when we got the news: we were getting kicked out. The building had been awarded Landmark status, and we were allowed to stay just one more year, with our $1,350 rent nearly tripled. The week after we eloped, at thirty-nine and forty-two, we welcomed two roommates to help us afford the place. Yes—we got married *and then we got roommates.*

The building would undergo major renovations, and the rents would skyrocket to $6,500 and higher. Michel Gondry, followed by Matt Dillon, would each spend a couple of years living in our space.

First, though, we'd spend a bitter year in housing court trying to fight it. Toward the end of the expensive, infuriating legal process, when it became clear that we were probably going to lose the place, one of our lawyers asked each member of the tenants' association, "Have you got some other place to go?"

And that's when I heard it—Terry's voice. *"Don't give up the apartment."*

Shit! I gave up the apartment! *How could I have given up the apartment?!* I was suddenly sure those words Terry had uttered so many years before pertained specifically to our current situation. I couldn't believe it. I began to kick myself.

But also at some point during that struggle, Brian and I both found ourselves feeling soured on the East Village and the city as a whole. Never mind that we were getting priced out. The city wasn't the same anymore. Of course, New York is never the same, from one day to the next. But now it seemed there was a more extreme, rapid level of gentrification. Every neighborhood was starting to appear and feel the same. Each one lost its individual character as one deli, pizza place, shoemaker, or thrift shop was replaced by a Chase or a Duane Reade or a Chipotle, or a pricey, twee mini-cupcake shop. One by one, our favorite restaurants and shops went out of business. A three-dollar umbrella was now five. The Second Avenue Deli was now on Third Avenue. All this made it mercifully easy to leave the island we were getting kicked off anyway.

We moved upstate to Rosendale, a depressed, funky little river town that's become an outpost of what I've labeled the Downtown Diaspora. Nearly all our friends there moved up from either Lower Manhattan or Brooklyn. Rosendale reminds me of Cicely, the town where the early 1990s television series *Northern Exposure* is set, with lots of hippies, theater geeks, and other offbeat characters flying their freak flags. I fit right in.

The first few years upstate, we didn't really miss the city. We'd take the Trailways down as needed. One summer weekend, when we stayed at a friend's West Village apartment, we went to breakfast at La Bonbonniere, a long-standing greasy spoon on Eighth Avenue near Horatio Street. (I'm obsessed with patronizing old, authentic, non-corporately-owned establishments before they perish.)

Seated next to us was a heavily made-up woman in her eighties who wasted no time striking up a conversation with us. She seemed to be one of those New York lonely people who spend so much time by themselves that as soon as they come into contact with other humans, they start babbling, almost involuntarily. I'd once been terrified of becoming one of them.

The woman, a onetime musical theater actress, asked us where we were from, and we somehow wound up on the topic of the apartment I'd let go. "I still sometimes kick myself," I said.

"Listen to me," she insisted. "A rent-controlled apartment can be a life sentence! I've been in my place for over sixty years, and it has kept me from the other things in life." She said she'd forgone year-long U.S. and European tours with shows for fear of losing her studio—now $150—if she'd sublet it. The place wasn't big enough for two, and anytime living with someone or getting married was on the table, she felt too shackled to her low rent to take a chance and move out. There had been two broken engagements. She was filled with regret. "You made the right choice," she said. It turned out New York City fell short as a life partner.

For a while afterward, that encounter helped me make peace with having forgotten Terry's first words to me when I finally needed

them. But now, eight years after having left, I am back to kicking myself—sometimes. Rosendale has a one-block "downtown," where my house is, with a whole 2,000 people in my area. On Main Street, there are exactly four restaurants, a cheese shop, two thrift stores, a tattoo shop, a pet groomer, and a used guitar shop. There were probably all those things within a one-block radius of my old place in the East Village.

I love my life in Rosendale. But I also miss New York. I yearn for it something awful, the way you'd yearn for a lost lover. So what if the Lower East Side is now littered with gleaming glass buildings? So what if the familiar is steadily replaced by the unfamiliar? So what else is new? I miss the crowds. I miss the variety—of *everything*. I miss Vietnamese food (and takeout in general). I miss having perfect knowledge of where to eat and the latest rerouting of the B, D, Q line. I keep a MetroCard in my wallet at all times to ward off the feeling of being "bridge-and-tunnel" again.

I miss my cute little apartment. I miss having a home base, a place to drop my bags or even just to pee. Most of all, I miss the serendipity of simply walking out of my building and seeing where I land.

Every now and then, even without an appointment of any kind, I'll hop on the Trailways to Port Authority the way I'd once hopped on the Long Island Rail Road, and I'll walk for hours. I don't make any plans. I don't call any friends. I want it to once again be just the city and me.

MAYBE I LOVED YOU

MARCY DERMANSKY

I left New York City about a year and a half ago for Germany. I still can't entirely believe it. I mean, what the fuck did I do? I lived in New York for ten years. Maybe ten years is not a long time. Sometimes, a day can take forever.

I grew up in Englewood, New Jersey, and went to the city all my life. In the eighth grade, I invited three of the popular girls in my class to go shopping at Canal Jeans. My mother drove us in. We bought clothes and then went to Washington Square Park. This venture, however, did not make me popular. As a child, I used to go with my family into the city for museums, dinners in Little Italy, shows on Broadway. I went to my first concert in Central Park: James Taylor in the Sheep Meadow.

But I was always a little bit scared of New York, too. When I got older, I would go in on my own. I didn't like the trip: the porn shops that used to line 42nd Street, the grime, the homeless people. That part of New York seems strangely gone, wiped clean, though I don't particularly like the shiny lights either. All the shopping, stores you could just as easily go to in just about any mall. The tourists. The crowds. And where are the homeless people? Where have they gone?

I didn't move to New York after graduating from college; I went to San Francisco because a friend told me I would like it there. And I did. I loved San Francisco, but I left after five years, quitting a high-paying administrative job to go to graduate school in Hattiesburg, Mississippi. People thought I was crazy. Even the UPS man delivering boxes to my new apartment thought I was crazy. I still miss San Francisco but have never made it back for more than a brief visit.

I didn't make it to New York City until I was thirty years old. When I rented my first apartment, it wasn't in Manhattan and it wasn't in Brooklyn, either. I moved to Astoria, Queens. The neighborhood had been on the cover of *Time Out* the week we started looking for an apartment. I had been married for all of two weeks, marrying my German boyfriend from graduate school at City Hall. We found an apartment we could afford, seven blocks from the N train, much too close to the Grand Central Parkway. We didn't know any better.

Astoria, famous for its Greek restaurants. I never fell in love with the Greek restaurants. Honestly, I never fell in love with Astoria. Some people do. I understand why. There were a great many things about the place that I liked. I have not been completely happy anywhere. At least not yet.

In the ten years I lived in Astoria, I wrote and I published two novels. I had the same job for nine years, a content editor for a start-up, Screaming Media, a hip company with free M&Ms and granola in the kitchen, a company that got bought and sold, and then bought and sold again and again. Every time, I was rehired. At some point, I swung benefits, vacation days. Wow, that job—it was like an NEA grant. Mornings, I worked. Afternoons and evenings, I wrote. Which was all that I ever really wanted to do.

Every day, I took the subway into Manhattan. In our one-bedroom apartment, I did not have a proper desk. At the Writers Room, where I was a member for almost a decade, there were more than forty desks, but I could write at maybe six of them. The desk had to be near a window. I couldn't sit next to a loud typer, a heavy breather. If a good desk wasn't open, I would wander the streets. Which

was okay because the space was in the East Village, and I liked that. I'd go to Union Square, buy produce at the farmer's market, and later, when Trader Joe's opened, I would go there, too, buy bags of groceries and wine, and carry the heavy bags home on the subway.

I'd wander into the St. Mark's Bookshop and gaze at the shelves of new paperbacks on the front wall. I always wanted to write a book; I always wanted my book to be there, on *that* wall. Later, when my books were published, they never quite made it there. St. Mark's carried my novels but shelved them in the stacks.

Sometimes, I worked at the Writers Room late into the night, when all the good desks were open. I would take breaks, walk the empty aisles, stand in front of the big picture window, and gaze at the lights of the Empire State Building.

The magic of New York was not lost on me. Do not think that I didn't eat my share of Thai food. Or Indian. Or Japanese. Often, I long for the crispy squid served at a Vietnamese restaurant downtown, not far from City Hall, where I got married, across the street from a prison called the Tombs. Don't think that I didn't go out for bagels or eat pizza or, on indulgent days, have sushi delivered for lunch. Do not think that I didn't go to movies, readings, gallery openings, and free concerts in the park.

My older brother lives on the Upper West Side. His apartment is only blocks from Columbia University, close to Riverside Park. Going to his apartment felt like entering another world.

Michael would visit me in Queens. He called it "the land of junk." He had a point, of course. My brother reveled in the dollar

stores. He bought Elmo T-shirts for his daughters, random plastic toys. I took him out for huevos rancheros. He was polite, picked at the refried beans, but did not like them. His wife once told me she loved Queens because of the U.S. Open, but the tennis tournament was not part of my life in Queens, even though I used to go to the Open with my brother when I was a teenager.

We would have fun, my brother and I, watching matches in the outer courts. There's a picture of me taken with him and a woman who was in the tournament that year. She was a tall, beautiful, black tennis player named Camille Benjamin. My mother framed this picture. It was the year I was fifteen, the year I had short hair.

I was also a film critic at About.com during my years in New York. I loved to see movies in screening rooms, to sit on the plush leather couches in the Sony building, so comfortable that sometimes I would fall asleep, regardless of the movie. I used to attend film parties and drink free drinks. I went to press junkets, and I loved that, too. To wander into fancy New York hotels, sit at a crowded table full of overeager online film critics—nobodies, all of us—across from genuine famous people: Woody Allen, Scarlett Johansson, Sean Penn, Maggie Gyllenhaal, Sofia Coppola, Gael Garcia Bernal, Cate Blanchett, Parker Posey. I interviewed French actress Isild Le Besco in a café. I once stood next to Daniel Day Lewis at a premiere. He was surprisingly tall. I would go to the morning press screenings at the New York Film Festival and Rendez-Vous with French Cinema at Lincoln Center, and then out for the lunch special at Ollie's, the Chinese restaurant down the block.

I think about that, those days of movies, riding the subway into Manhattan. I miss it. Wonder how I gave it up. So what that About .com, like Screaming Media, also got bought and sold, bought and sold again? That my pay there was cut in half. That I felt a little bit

dirty, sitting at those press junkets, watching stars cringe as they were asked questions they clearly did not want to answer. I still want to go back. Back to the movies. Back in time.

But honestly, for the last two years that I lived in New York, I went to very few movies. I had a baby. I was laid off. I could not afford child care to go to the movies. Irrationally, I did not want child care. I wanted to take care of my daughter.

I was in love with her, Nina, a burning crazy passionate love. My life in New York City pretty much fell apart after she was born.

I did not know when I moved to Astoria that I would be there for ten years. Once, when the lease ended on our first apartment, my husband and I looked at apartments in Brooklyn. We were discouraged by the higher rents, the smaller spaces. We gave up, perhaps too easily, found another apartment, a better apartment, not aware that the auto repair shop next door, so quiet in the winter, would make us feel crazy on beautiful spring days, when we would open our windows to the sound of its industrial noise.

The truth is, of course, that I have always envied what money buys in New York City. I envy the Brooklyn writers. I wished then, as I wish now, that I could be better at making money.

I wrote and I published those two novels. *Twins. Bad Marie.* I hired a publicist, bought dresses, had book parties, was reviewed and later profiled in *The New York Times*, and was written about in glossy magazines. I got to feel a little bit fancy, a little bit proud of myself. A lot of people go to New York City to be artists, to write books, and end up doing something else. I published two books, and somehow, it wasn't enough. I sound like a petulant child. Often, I feel like a petulant child.

I made money from my books, but really, I made rent and health insurance through my job. It was the job—not reviewing films, not writing fiction, but editing headlines for corporate websites—that

paid. I knew not to take it for granted. New York is an expensive place to live. Nina was two months old when I was laid off.

Nina is three and a half now. I no longer live in New York City. I have been gone for a year and a half, but it feels like forever.

I moved to Wiesbaden, Germany.

I actually did that.

We left New York for Germany to get affordable health insurance, something I lost with my job after COBRA ran out. My husband promised to find a job in Germany, where social media was only just beginning to take off. I could almost picture it. Monthly *kindergeld*. European vacation time, six weeks a year. Free babysitting. My husband's parents are much younger than mine. They promised to help with Nina. I would have time to write. *I would have time to write.*

I think that, alone, was what sold me.

I had left San Francisco, after all, for graduate school in Hattiesburg, Mississippi, and the chance to write.

Many people think it's cool to live in Europe, raise a bilingual child. Leave America, which was steadily going downhill. That is what they told me, before I left. What do they know?

I am homesick.

I am waiting to hear from my agent about the new book I am writing. I am waiting for emails from my friends back in New York. There is a six-hour time difference, and I am often waiting for my friends to wake up. I am in a constant state of waiting.

I lost my job the year *Bad Marie* came out. It didn't seem like such a terrible thing. I would be able to get another job. I received severance pay. I was able to go on unemployment, stay home with my child.

The day my novel was written about in *Time* magazine, I went for my first appointment at the unemployment office out in Flushing.

It felt surreal to me, sitting in a crowded room full of newly jobless people, a room full of immigrants and white, middle-class me. I felt like I had a secret: I didn't belong there. Of course, I did belong there. I had lost my job and my benefits. The advance I received from *Bad Marie* would not pay my rent. I had a five-minute session with an employment counselor who, befuddled by my résumé, told me about a new racetrack opening up on the edge of Queens that was looking for cashiers.

Then I went out for lunch. I loved that lunch, how decadent it felt, to sit alone in a restaurant by myself, eating Chinese broccoli, drinking tea, out without the baby. I had been to Flushing only once before, for dim sum.

Months later, I would have to go back to that unemployment office to prove that I was still looking for work. I was, but I also wasn't. I was promoting my novel. I was taking care of Nina. I was getting by. The appointment was early in the morning. My Romanian babysitter couldn't make it. My husband, sick in bed, couldn't watch Nina. And so I put her in the stroller, packed the diaper bag, and went on my own, all of it so much harder with a baby: taking the subway, transferring trains, finding the elevators in Roosevelt Station. I remember missing my second train, the door closing in my face. Almost panicking when I couldn't find the elevator at the Flushing station, taking the escalator up instead, and then racing through the crowded streets of Flushing, only to get there late, fifteen minutes late, more than twenty minutes by the time I made it to the front of the line.

That was me: writer, new mother, beyond exhausted, in a shirt covered with spit-up and milk, sweaty and flushed because it was summer and I had been racing to get there, pushing a stroller. Nervous. Wildly nervous. I had missed my appointment.

"Too late," the Asian woman behind the counter told me, not coldly, just indifferent.

There was, of course, a line of people behind me. I started to cry. I think now: *Why didn't I tell my mother?* She didn't know then that I

was on unemployment. Why didn't I tell her? At the very least, she would have told me to take a taxi. She would have paid for the taxi. All those years in New York, I never took enough taxis.

My parents had helped us with the hospital bill after Nina's birth. Nina spent the first four days of her life in the neonatal intensive care unit at NYU Hospital. We had good health insurance then and still could not afford that hospital bill. This is the same NICU where sick babies were carried down nine flights of stairs by nurses when the backup generator failed after Hurricane Sandy. I remember those stairs. Those four long days, I was a floor below, being treated for complications from the birth. The doctors had told me to take the elevator when going from my room on the eighth floor to the NICU on the ninth, but often, I couldn't wait, and I walked.

I stood there and cried at the unemployment office in Flushing, and the woman behind the desk looked up at me, reconsidered. She decided to accept my updated résumé and the piece of paper on which I had diligently written the jobs I had applied for, the jobs I would apply for. The woman processed a form for me; she told me that I was fine, until the next time.

And this is what I think of when I remember my life in New York. Not the plush couches at the Sony screening room or the hip bars in Nolita or the book parties. I think of the unemployment office in Flushing. And my Romanian babysitter Mary and her overweight teenage daughter whose name I can't remember, who had recently been released from the psych ward. They would pick up Nina at my apartment and take her around the neighborhood, while I tried to work. I am surprised by how often I think about Mary, wondering how she is now, what happened to her daughter.

I think about how scared I felt, how out of control.

Those ten years I lived in New York, why did I never fall in love with the city? I had the screening rooms. The takeout sushi. A place to write. I had my friends. I had my family.

But I always had something to complain about. The subway. The cost of brunch. The lines for brunch. How crowded it would get at the bagel shop. Sometimes, I couldn't even get a table. The noise. The crowded streets. The tiny aisles in the supermarket. My neighborhood and how ugly it was.

I don't fall in love easily. My husband had to work to woo me, and I mean hard. It was months and months before I would kiss him. I had to get over my life in San Francisco first and a former boyfriend. Sometimes, it takes me a while.

Like now. Writing this essay, sitting on a couch in a café in Wiesbaden, irrationally angry at the Germans not far from me, angry at them for speaking German, for being German, I think that I might have actually loved New York. That I could have figured it out, found Nina regular child care back home. Not crossed an ocean to get steady writing time. Here, I take the bus almost every day, and I miss the subway.

Only now, living in Germany, where I don't speak the language and the people seem impossibly cold and distant, do I think: *Maybe I loved New York.*

And maybe I didn't.

Maybe I don't.

Maybe I just don't like where I am now.

I am not sure how, but I want to go back.

LONG TRAINS LEAVING

EMILY ST. JOHN MANDEL

1.

I came to New York City by train on a cold evening in February. I'd been living in Toronto for some years, ever since I crossed 2,800 miles of Canada to attend the School of Toronto Dance Theatre at eighteen. Now I was twenty-two, and it turned out my ties to Toronto were so light and so few that it was possible to decide to move to New York City and then leave ten days later.

My friends' reactions to this decision varied. "She's moving to a foreign country to live with a man old enough to be her father," someone close to me said. This was factually correct, although the man in question—let's call him Owen—would've been a young father. But the point wasn't really Owen, although I did love him at the time, or his age, which was inconsequential to me. The point was the word "foreign." The point was that I longed for change.

I'd come to Toronto to dance, but now that I'd graduated, I wasn't dancing. I was working twelve hours a day as an assistant to a designer, and I was aware that I was drawn not to the work, exactly, but to losing myself in it. All I'd ever wanted was to be a dancer, but now I wasn't sure I wanted that anymore and there was nothing in that moment to replace it.

I had slept very little the night before I boarded the train, and sleep deprivation lent the passing landscape a hallucinatory glaze. I read *Pale Fire* and gazed out at southern Ontario. I'd never been to New York and didn't even have an especially clear mental image of the place. When I thought of New York I thought of *Law and Order* and *Seinfeld,* of towers collapsing six months earlier on the morning news, of the piles of flowers outside the U.S. consulate.

Somewhere near the U.S. border the train tracks curved close to Lake Ontario and I saw Toronto for a moment across the brilliant water, a collection of towers and spires rendered ghostly by enormous distance, pale against a milky sky. The city flashed out of view and receded into memory. Can you isolate the instant when a place ceases to be home?

"I'm visiting my boyfriend in Manhattan for a few weeks," I told an agent at the border.

"Are you planning on working while you're down there?" the agent asked.

"No," I lied. He stamped my passport and handed it back to me. As the hours passed, rural New York State faded into twilight, my reflection appearing on the darkening train window like a Polaroid coming into focus. Even before I arrived, the story was beginning to seem improbable: I slipped like magic across a guarded border and arrived in Manhattan with sixty-five dollars, two suitcases, and no Social Security number. I don't mean to imply that it was an especially hard landing. Owen met me at Penn Station with a rose.

But the only one of those details that remains truly relevant, all these years later, is that when I disembarked at Penn Station I found home.

2.

I found a job selling expensive objects in a store in Soho. Every two weeks they gave me an envelope of cash, because a year would pass before I realized that the fact of my father having been born

in California made me a U.S. citizen by default. Once freed from the sales floor, I went for long walks through the streets of Lower Manhattan. I watched old men feed pigeons in Father Demo Square and listened to musicians on the street. I stumbled upon Ground Zero—machines grinding down through the basement levels of the towers, a sense of disaster still hanging in the air—and had dreams about towers falling. I wrote in cafés. I'd been writing all my life, but in New York this habit acquired a new force. Perhaps, I thought, writing was what would come next. Spring arrived, flowers on trees. In Toronto I had walked the streets for hours, looking for something I couldn't name. In my first days in New York City, I realized that I'd found it. This was the city I'd been looking for.

But neither of us was really making enough money for New York City. We were behind on the rent. The thought of leaving the city was wrenching to me, but in May we decided to move to Montreal because it was a new adventure and because the rent's cheap there. In July we packed our belongings into a bright yellow truck and drove north. I was aware of New York City receding behind us.

"Welcome home," the Canadian customs agent said at the border, but I couldn't shake the uneasy thought that home was behind me.

3.

We had a blue apartment on Rue de la Visitation, which I had a difficult time pronouncing, because I'd never studied French. French is, of course, one of the two official languages of Canada and a core subject in English Canadian schools, but I was homeschooled as a child and French had never quite made an appearance in my parents' improvised curriculum. In fairness to them, it can't have seemed very relevant. I was born and raised in British Columbia, three thousand miles to the west of Montreal. Before I came to Quebec I'd heard French spoken in passing perhaps a dozen times, and it had the inscrutability of any other perfectly unfamiliar tongue. It

slipped past me in a blur of sound. I couldn't differentiate individual words. I'd been under the impression, based on one or two brief visits, that I'd be able to get by in Montreal speaking one out of two official languages, but it was immediately obvious that I'd been horribly naïve. Not long after we arrived, a man approached me when I was walking alone, and I understood that he was asking for directions. "Je ne parle pas français," I said, the one phrase I pronounced with confidence in those days. "Je suis désolé."

Is it fair to say he spat at me then? I'm never entirely sure how to describe the moment that followed. He made a spitting gesture at my feet—I jumped back, realizing what was coming—but it was all sound and motion and contempt, no actual spit.

"He was just expressing an opinion," Owen said. Owen loved Montreal. He spoke French.

The week we arrived, I set out walking with a stack of résumés. I was beginning very tentatively to describe myself as a writer, and writing, I'd realized, would require the same split life I'd become accustomed to as a dancer. Almost every dancer I knew had a job or two on the side, and in the years since I'd started supporting myself at eighteen I'd built up the sort of aimless work history that only happens when one's interests lie emphatically elsewhere: I'd made sandwiches, martinis, and lattes; I'd sold everything from sofas to ballet shoes; I'd been a janitor and a designer's assistant. Now that I'd arrived in Quebec I knew my inability to speak French would make finding work difficult, but I thought perhaps someone might hire me to move boxes in a retail stockroom, far from customers. I'd held such jobs in the past.

"Est-ce que vous parlez français?" a long sequence of retail managers asked.

"No," I said. "I'm trying to learn. I was hoping it wouldn't matter so much in a stockroom position."

"Well," one told me helpfully, "not being able to speak French is really not an asset."

"I've noticed that," I said. I felt a slight vertigo sometimes—how

had I landed in Montreal when I'd set out so recently for a new life in New York?—but I was determined to adapt. I learned that Quebec offers free French lessons to new arrivals in the province, which was exciting, but it turned out these lessons were available to everyone except English Canadians. ("It's policy, madame. You'll have to go to a private school.") I didn't think there could possibly be any lessons that I could afford, so I studied in cafés with a French-English dictionary, translating the newspaper, trying to memorize words. There were wonderful surprises. I was delighted to learn that *trombone* could refer to either a trombone or a paper clip. I spent hours walking, stopping with my dictionary to translate the signs. I was trying very hard to fall in love with the city, but the trouble was that New York was at the edge of every thought.

"How are you liking Montreal?" my boyfriend's friends would occasionally ask. Owen had lived here before and had friends in the city. I didn't know anyone in the city but him.

"It's actually been a bit difficult," I would say, understating wildly. "I don't speak the right language. A guy sort of spat on me on the street." There were things I liked about the city, but I was having a hard time getting that episode out of my mind. It was only the most blatant expression of a low-level hostility that I sensed all around me.

"Montreal's just a *great city*," they would say, as though I'd said something entirely different. Their willful deafness was eerie, but it occurred to me later that they weren't necessarily wrong. Edmund Wilson once wrote that no two people ever read the same book, and I've come to believe that no two people ever live in the same city. I've met people who find New York to be desperate and gray.

4.

I found a job where it didn't matter that I couldn't speak the right language. Every morning at 7 AM, I met a delivery truck in front of the Caban store on Rue Ste.-Catherine and helped shift boxes into an underground stockroom. I spent the next seven hours putting price

stickers on martini glasses, bubble-wrapping mirrors, unpacking scented soaps, and stacking objects and boxes on metal shelves. The pay was $8.50 an hour. My coworkers were a mildly burnt-out anglophone musician and an Iranian film student. We listened to English-language radio all day.

I didn't mind the work. It covered my rent, and there was time to write in the afternoons. The problem was that occasionally I'd have to walk across the sales floor, and customers would invariably approach me in French. I wasn't progressing very rapidly with the newspaper-and-dictionary method, but I did know how to say, "Pardon me, I don't speak French," and then I'd offer to find a French-speaking sales associate. Sometimes the customer would smile and switch to English without skipping a beat, and I was secretly so grateful that I could've kissed them, every time. Sometimes they would gaze coldly at me and say, "I see." On two occasions a customer glared at me, turned, and stormed out of the building rather than be contaminated for one more second by my Englishness.

"It's no big deal," my manager told me. "People are crazy."

But I was shot through with dread, because while people throw phrases like "language police" around all the time, Quebec actually has them. There are laws in Quebec to protect the French language. Businesses over a certain size must conduct their operations in French. There are complicated regulations involving signage: if English appears on a sign, it must appear after the French and in smaller letters.

These laws are enforced by means of a tip line for citizen informants. If you spot a business sign in which English appears before the French, for instance, or if you walk into a store and the sales associate greets you in English, or if, as in one particular instance I remember reading about, a bartender gives you a coaster for your drink and you realize—*quelle horreur!*—that all the words on said coaster are in English, you can call a 1-800 number and report the infraction to the French language commission. Penalties can include fines and revoked business licenses.

Every time a customer looked at me, I feared offending them by speaking the wrong language, and then what if they called the tip line and reported the store? If the store were fined by the language authorities, would I lose my job? I worried that if I lost this job, I might not be able to find another one. None of the recipients of the other twenty-five or thirty résumés I'd distributed had called back. My résumé was in English.

The weight of speaking the wrong language followed me everywhere. There was a graffiti message that I walked by on my way to work every day: MONTREAL EN FRANÇAIS: 101 OU 401. Bill 101 is a Quebec law that restricts the use of the English language. The 401 is the highway out of the city. This, then, is the translation: MONTREAL IN FRENCH: SPEAK FRENCH OR GET OUT.

5.

At the end of the summer, Owen announced that he'd prefer to be single. He broke up with me, then changed his mind and took me back, then broke up with me again, and after that I was dazzlingly alone.

There are times when life goes dark and still. I moved into a cheap apartment share in the Latin Quarter. I drifted through the hours of my workday. I'd worked for the Caban store in Toronto until six months before I'd left for New York, and in the winter boxes arrived with my handwriting already on them, surplus inventory I'd boxed up in another city the year before. Now they were surfacing out of far-off warehouses, like bottles rising out of the sea. I went alone to the English-language movie theater on St. Catherine Street and watched whatever was playing—anything, it didn't matter. I just wanted the hours to pass. I saw *Chicago* twice.

"A quiet room in Brooklyn," I wrote in my notebook. The idea was a fixation. *If I could only find a way to return to New York,* I thought, *then perhaps I would be less sad.*

By the end of November it was so cold that when my eyes watered, my eyelashes would freeze. I wrapped a scarf around my face,

but then the condensation from my breath froze too, a thin layer of ice between the scarf and my skin. I didn't own a watch, so I carried a tiny travel alarm clock around in my coat pocket. It got me to work on time, but usually it was six hours behind by nightfall, because batteries fail as the temperature approaches −18 degrees Celsius, 0 degrees Fahrenheit. I felt a curious compassion for my alarm clock; I wasn't holding up very well either. Every sound was too loud. Every light was too bright. I stepped outside and felt translucent, the cold passing through me. I'd stopped trying to learn French.

"Marooned in a hostile city," I wrote in my notebook, but there were moments even in the dead of winter when the city of Montreal was beautiful to me. These streets of gray stone and ice, spiral staircases with their burdens of snow. Moments of friendship and grace. I adored my roommates, a brother and sister from Ontario who spoke English at home.

We couldn't afford to turn the heat up very high in the apartment. I would sometimes go to bed at 6 or 7 PM because it was warmer under the covers. I would wake at midnight or one in the morning, rise in the freezing darkness, and go out to write. A ritual: I dressed in my best clothes, sometimes put on a tie. I gathered my papers and my laptop computer, bundled up as best I could, and stepped out into the breathtaking cold. It felt like embarking on a profound adventure.

At the open-all-night Café Depot on St. Lawrence Boulevard, two blocks away, I took a table near the window and wrote through the night. A memory of a ballet class when I was a teenager, a teacher glancing at me as I struggled through a difficult adagio, nodding approvingly at how hard I was working in that moment: "That's the work," she'd said, and the line stayed with me. *This is the work,* I thought, writing by the hour in the café. This is the discipline. This is what writing will take. I worked for hours at a time, trying to distill my wild fragments and false starts into a novel, drinking cup after cup of tea. I watched the night progress in stages. The freezing club kids ferried away by a fleet of taxis at 1:30 or 2 AM, the last few strag-

glers stumbling homeward with greasy pizza slices at 3 and 3:30. By 4 AM the street was quiet, scoured by salt and ice. A line from my first novel: "Outside the café the cold deepened until the streets froze white."

By 4:30, the first movements toward daylight. More cars on the street, a few tired workers coming in for coffee. By 5 AM, I saw the bread trucks, and by the time the bread trucks came, I was too tired to write anymore. I had been reading Jeanette Winterson's *Art and Life*, with its fractured plot and half-grammatical incantations: "My city, and long trains leaving."

In the early mornings I walked back to my apartment and lay shivering under the blankets until I could fall asleep. Writing held me together, but it wasn't enough. I was desperate for the moment when I might look back on this place from the window of a long train leaving, anguished and exultant and perfectly free.

6.

I don't come from a family with money. We were never even middle-class. My education was made possible by student loans. But the year I was in Montreal my grandmother died and left my father some money, and he sent me a money order for a thousand dollars. I remember opening the envelope in the living room in Montreal, staring at the unfathomable sum on the scrap of paper, and thinking of train tickets.

A few weeks later, in late January, I received an unexpected' phone call from Owen: someone he knew in Manhattan was leaving town for two weeks, and would I like to sublet her apartment while she was away? He knew I wanted to return to New York, and it would be a cheap place to stay while I looked for an apartment and a job.

Six days later I took a taxi to Station Bonaventure in the freezing morning and stepped aboard a southbound train. It was the second day of February, a year minus three weeks from the day I'd first set out for New York. I took photograph after photograph of Montreal as

the train departed, trying to freeze the moment of escape. I crossed the U.S. border without incident and continued south through the afternoon.

This is the future: In a few hours the train will arrive in Penn Station, and I'll set out walking into the winter night. In twenty-four hours I will meet my future husband and in eighteen months he'll propose in Central Park, fireflies rising from the grass around us. We will marry a year later and walk home up Fifth Avenue after the reception, me in my wedding dress in the cold spring night; we'll stop for eggs in a diner at two in the morning where the waiter will take our order without comment, deadpan, as though women in wedding dresses order eggs in his diner every day, and perhaps they do. It's New York.

There will be years of quiet rooms in Brooklyn, years of books and cats. In 2012 my French publisher will bring me to Paris and we'll wander the streets, my beloved husband and I, in love with the city, the country, the language, trying out our terrible French on waitresses. I'll have been studying French for six months by then. "Mais c'est fasciste!" a Parisian journalist will exclaim, when I tell her about the Quebec language laws, which feature in the book, and we'll agree that Montreal and Paris are very different.

But first there was a year of long trains leaving, of traveling between countries and cities and lives. On the train from Montreal to New York I stared out the window and wondered what would become of me. I was twenty-three and felt very old. Night fell and there were only occasional lights and deep shadows, the small stations of upstate New York. The manuscript pages that would eventually become my first novel were bundled together with old shoelaces in a bag by my feet. I tried to write, or to read, but my impatience and my longing to see New York City again grew with each passing hour. I eventually gave up and just watched the landscape, the movement, the passing stations and lights.

SO LONG, SUCKERS

REBECCA WOLFF

I first said goodbye to all that—though I don't hold New York to be *all that*, a monolith precluding the *all that*ness of other places— a long time ago, in 1985, at seventeen. I had been the sort of manor-born Manhattanite to whom that famous *New Yorker* cartoon, the one that shows everything west of the Hudson River as a perspective plain of diminishing signification, didn't seem funny at all. *What's funny about that?* It's totally true, and everybody knows it.

Yeah, arrogance. New York is full of it; I was full of it: the kind of arrogance that's extra numbing, mind-stuffing, because it's backed up by what I've come to know as "seeming inevitability," that anyone who's anyone will at some point move to New York. Or die in obscurity with failed dreams. Yeah, all the brilliant people are here. Yeah, here's where it's really at, and you know it's true, and anyone who says anything else is just not up to the challenge.

In the diffused sparkle of refraction of Joan Didion's adorable and probably accurate portrayal of what it's like to be from somewhere else and move to New York and get what you can from it and stay a little bit too long and then leave, I proudly and grouchily represent the bright lights of the native. For visitors—you can stay a lifetime and be a visitor—what is at stake, according to Didion, is the dream of New York, the abstracted coordinates of its glamour and legendariness. You want to be there because it is like living on a Monopoly board. It is like living in Oz. Natives get that, are fed it along with their mother's milk, plus they get the extra added glamour of secret knowledge and self-exile and hardwired urbanity. Didions bring a knowingness to their efforts at urbanity: *rubanity*, I'll call it. Natives just bring it.

In high school I went out a lot, to nightclubs and bars. Danceteria, the Mud Club, Limelight, Save the Robots, Pyramid, Area, Beirut, bars in the East Village, which at that time ended at Avenue A. Beyond, purportedly lay a river. I snorted lots of cocaine and made out with bouncers in exchange for free entry to clubs. Bouncers—Nigerian bouncers, bouncers from Berlin, underage bouncers I had known in grade school—waved my friends and me out of the crowd, to the front of the line, ushered us inside where we would shed our coats and get free drinks and dance dance dance until five in the morning. That's what I did in high school. By the time I left for college, I had renounced a bunch of things, including the high life, and was leading with latent bookishness and vegetarianism and a closet full of attitudinal old clothes I had amassed at the Salvation Army on my corner next to the gay bar, long before old clothes were called "vintage."

Goodbye to all that, hello end-of-the-world rural pinhead Vermont, for college, dropping out to live in Boston "You-Call-This-a-City" Massachusetts for a couple of years, then back for more college in the Happy Valley of Western Mass., where I had my first sweet taste of real small-town, albeit college-town, life.

I moved to a very small city, really a town, in Iowa for graduate school. There at the outskirts where true rurality abruptly swelled I witnessed organic vegetable farming, cooperative living, and the fulsomeness of rubes and radicals and serious artists doing their business in generative ease, relative privacy, and cheap comfort. Lots of bands and visuals and ideas. I did not miss the compression of the city; I did not miss my parents, who I felt in their high-mannerist urbanity had taught me nothing of worth. I spent summers on screened-in porches and went back home about once a year, and when I walked the streets in the late 1980s to early 1990s, it made me cry. This is before the home*less* people were stored wherever they are currently being stored: then they were living, eating, shitting, sleeping all over the streets, and one had to step over them at every corner, doorway, subway grate, and step over them everyone did, as though it was an acceptable situation. Seemingly inevitable: oh, it's just so fabulous in New York, you can really just learn to step over people's suffering bodies. Cities are so cool, and this is the coolest, so hard-core, and you can learn to live with this. No one spoke of it. I would come home from my night out and ask my parents how they could live like this. They honestly had no idea what I was talking about: this was their fabulous city. I was inured to the fabulousness by the dirty, hungry people lying around on the street; they were inured to the dirty, hungry people lying around on the street by the imprint of fabulousness, the fabulousness impressed upon them when they arrived in the West Village in the 1950s from their respective outposts.

At the age of thirty I came back to New York to be literary, and it worked. Return of the native in the clothing of the naïf. Wolf in sheep's clothing. I had abruptly tired of outposts, of decentralized living—the city still an epicenter—and I had something very specific I wanted to do within the specific culture of the literary. And I had noticed that every time I came back to visit I had a marvelous time, suddenly, in that specific culture, at parties and drinky lunches and magical, hidden offices. So I came back, and said hello again to all that, and it genuflected back at me. I sucked up the transitional, transactional energy like a newborn mosquito. That's where language is. I get my total buzz on when the buzz is there to beget. It turns out I am supremely familiar, you could say "comfortable," with cityscape—noise, bustle, crowds, action; stimuli such as the very poor, the very rich, the very beautiful, and the degraded; lights and smells of food on the street; shouts of people selling things for lots of money or begging for money or scamming with infants in their laps. Bumping into people I know in parks and bookstores and art houses. For six or seven inexhaustible years I was one of those culture workers who expend themselves beautifully, for whom the city is working, and what I did there I probably could not have done anywhere else. Once I had accomplished that, I was just as abruptly done with New York.

New York is a place for being public, for *wanting* to be famous. I achieved a degree of recognition in my field and became a public figure and found I didn't like it. I didn't like being public, the attendant flush and two-facedness and gaze. It served me well in launching my Literary Project—*Fence*, a journal of poetry and fiction, and Other, and later Fence Books, a press—but did not serve my soul well, my soul, which had been forged in that very vault.

When I left the city I was surprised at how complete I made the break. I did not invite friends to visit me; I did not come back often. I made new friends and found new ways to keep my Project visible and sustainable. *Fence* eventually required less and less of my long-distance personal spiritual life force—my precious ectoplasm—and just as though it were an infant, I have been able to cut its cord. The labor of love does result in independent life.

I didn't move far away—up the river to the tiny, quixotic city of Hudson—but I will never move back and I still don't visit as often as you might think, and when I do I am happy to leave again, often on the same day. SOHO GIVES ME HIVES: that's a T-shirt meme I brainstormed in the late 1990s, as the transformation of that deathly quiet neighborhood from artists' cheap housing and site of freewheeling conceptualism to Mall of Outrageous Crap was completed. There are lots of neighborhoods and enclaves and scenes and nodes of NYC behavior that give me hives—too many to give shout-outs to.

There are wonderful brainy sexy people I see only in the city, who stubbornly refuse to get on the train of diminishing signification and whom I sadly bid farewell after each brief encounter.

I go down about once a month, two hours on the train with the other suckers, usually to attend or present or facilitate a potentially dazzling literary event. In New York City, in the dusk-filled streets or in the cold wintry streets, in streets when the light is pretty or streets when everything looks crappy and grimy, I see a tremendous amount of samey-ness, the kind that didn't used to be there. Poseurs and wannabes and money-hounds EVERYWHERE, when in my youth they were restricted to the bridge-and-tunnel funnels of Eighth Street and Midtown, Lexington Avenue and Central Park and, eventually, Soho. You could spot these chumps a mile away, and they were different from tourists, who came to gawk and then went back home; they were tourists who overstayed, put down roots for no good reason, who could lay no legitimate claim to the greatness of the city's historic convergent energies, who could simply make money anywhere and could therefore make it here. New York City manifests itself now shamefacedly as a chump-factory, a chump-house. It's Chumptown. Artists who live there are living dangerously, close to extinction, dangerously close to the source of their art's diminishment, an ouroboros of economic exigency. It's well documented: chumps need artists and artists need chumps, but they're supposed to stay out of one another's sight in order to maintain the necessary illusions! There have always been chumps in New York, but they used to be bashful chumps who bought the brilliant ones their drinks.

There's this thing that happens, where I speak to a twenty-something or thirty-something sweetheart, a Joan Didion who's moved to New York recently, and I realize at a certain point that their expectations of it are actually very low, compared to my own, because they cannot possibly imagine what it used to be like, the New York of the recent past, of the late 1970s, 1980s, 1990s. They have no idea how far any of it has fallen, how sterile Chelsea, how horror-show

Soho, how lame-ass the Lower East Side. All by comparison. I'm not even going to mention Brooklyn because Brooklyn is nothing but a brand name. Forget Queens. Visual culture does not often represent what's past; I'm sure a slew of movies soon will, but right now with the exception of *Chico and the Man* and early, secret, legendary Madonna as incarnated in Lady Gaga, I don't know what is widely culturally understood of what was cool in those times. Whit Stillman? The 1980s art world via Basquiat? Graffiti? Michael Douglas in *Wall Street*? I'm afraid this latter giant face has eclipsed the faces I knew, the faces of the brazen, the bold, the class- and culture- and gender-vultures, nonrich aspirants to splendor, gamy artist-class fast-talkers, children of choreographers, children of sculptors, excitable children of alcoholic Midwesterners, those for whom there was no money involved in the transaction.

There is the fallacy of nostalgia, and there is the fallacy of the fallacy of nostalgia. You're not supposed to ever say that something used to be better, because then you are vainly trying to hold that something in stasis, cold in the frame of reference in which you knew it, and this is narcissistic and regressive and cranky and blindered. It is ungenerous to those whose references are framed more recently, to those whom we must make way for and learn from: to the young. Those who are making their way in the world, and making the world. Those who could, at this point, be our children, if we had given birth to the children we aborted in high school and college and graduate school.

But we have already said goodbye to all that dualistic relativism, in this new world. It's a "both/and" world we live in: every cranky, aging generation feels that things used to be cooler or more imaginative or riskier; many things actually *did* use to be cooler, riskier, et cetera, and this argument against the insistence that something could actually have been qualitatively so—probably quantifiably if you had the time—serves most those for whom the status quo is best maintained: chumps. For if it's never true that things have degraded, deteriorated, absolutely—and, of course, the same is true of improvement—then there's never any impetus to halt the degrada-tion. Or to look for something better elsewhere. You'll keep paying rent until you can't.

So yes, it's true. New York City used to be cool, and now it's not. It's not at all. It is boring and dismaying and stymied; everything potentially cool in it is overwhelmed and inflated and parodied and sold. You can't even love the absurdity of it because it's too pain-ful, and we cannot be allowed any more to callously love, for their absurdity, systems that oppress and impoverish. New York City is mediated by money so visibly. Everywhere everything is mediated by money, so perhaps you could make a brutalist argument for how fabulous it is to live with that so in your face, but my face hurts. New York is a giant sinking pile of crap compared to what it used to be. Literally sinking, now that the waters rise so much more quickly, the winds blow so much harder than even scientists predicted. Lately I like to imagine that I will have the privilege of seeing in my lifetime real estate values in the city plunge wildly, in free fall, as Climate Events force Permanent Visitors to admit that they pay Top Dollar to perch on Coastal Landfill. But I hope that my parents sell off their holdings before this happens. I still love to visit them in the apart-ment I grew up in, on the tree-lined residential block I grew up on; love the first ten exhilarating hours of each overnight stay at the beginning of which I swing down Seventh Avenue like Georgy Girl, join an audience of haters or buyers or tourists to see some pasteurized, predigested art or film or poetry; hate the twin mat-tress perched on top of a desk in my father's office; hate the last six hours in which nothing has been as brilliant as I thought it would be and I am left hungover, teeth-grindingly claustrophobic, chock-full of morbidity.

In New York City these days I see loads and loads of formerly brilliant people—gender champions, visual whizzes, start-up ho's, crackerjack dancers, actors, journalists, and chefs—who have "stayed too long at the Fair," to use Joan's wistful archaic turn of phrase, who are baffled and internally conflicted as to why they can't admit that New York sucks so hard. Why they can't draw the proper conclusion. That if they are to work all the time in order to pay super-high rents that make it impossible for them to do their art, if they never have a chance to see the people they came here to see, who are also less brilliant now that they are muffled by the smog of wrongness that hangs over New York (thicker than the smog of smog that hangs over Los Angeles, another city that's not even half as cool as everyone who's moving there says it is), if they are living somewhere that is giving them less than they are giving to it, then they should leave. (What goes on in Queens is hysterical. Why do you need to displace natives of Queens from their apartments in order to be a member of a community of artists who do not want to go to Manhattan, ever? Or who never get to be at home in Queens because they can't afford to waste the time going back there? Why not populate Detroit? Or Albany? Or Pittsburgh? Or some other charming small city with a low profile and vacant properties you can buy from the city for a dollar? From there you can FTP your PDFs for a fraction of the cost of living and when it's time to have babies you can stay where you are because your apartment is big enough! Or you live in a house. You live in a house with a door that opens onto a yard. Maybe you share the house with friends.) They should find somewhere to live, perhaps collectively, perhaps not individually; perhaps they should try to make sense of this whole living-somewhere thing in a way that doesn't pretend, as New York City does, that we are all ruthless rock stars with amnesia and aphasia and lifetime amniotic sacs.

The brilliance of Didion's essay: She makes no claims for New York City but that it is what it is to those who regard it. She claims only that for various ineffable reasons having mostly to do with aspirations and the qualities of light at different times of day, people come to New York bringing with them their youth and they apply their youth, and they ought to leave before their youth is exhausted and it no longer applies to New York. This seems to happen just as their prime breeding years clock in. As a native of New York I grapple herein with a different set of coordinates for departure: I must leave behind my love, my home, my turf, my territory, my breeding ground. I must punish New York for its lameness by my desertion. Reprove and improve. How can *you* help New York City to rise to some of its former coolness? Leave it before you yourself are a chump, and perhaps by attrition it will float up.

CRASH AND BURN

EVA TENUTO

I t was the summer of 1991, and at eighteen, I was finally getting the chance I'd daydreamed about for years: I was packing my bags and moving from the sleepy Hudson Valley to New York City to become A Professional Actress.

I grew up only ninety miles from New York City, but worlds away from it in rural New Paltz, on five wooded acres along a silent, dead-end road. Having spent very little time in the city as a kid, I could only imagine it was like my favorite television show, *Fame*. I wanted to "learn how to fly"! I wanted people to "remember my name"!

Then, in my senior year of high school, I cut school a few times to hop on the Metro North train from Poughkeepsie to Grand Central Station. From my first hit of New York City, I was hooked. I got high off the energy and craved it when I returned to my quiet, boring country home. I found comfort in knowing there were freaks in abundance in the Village, discovered how easy it was to buy pot in Washington Square Park, and quickly learned no one cared about the legal drinking age in this city.

My next moves became perfectly clear: move to New York City and go to acting school. I auditioned and got into the American

Academy of Dramatic Arts. It seemed my acting dreams were about to come true.

I was fiercely dedicated to "the craft" not only because I wanted to be famous, but because when I was eleven, acting saved my life. I was the eldest of three girls. We lived in a small two-bedroom apartment temporarily while my father, with his own two hands, was building our family's dream home. But in the short six months when he was building from the ground up, my world came crashing down.

In the space of just a few weeks, first I overheard my mother talking on the phone to a friend about a son she'd given away when she was much younger and whom she was looking to find. Then I stumbled upon her journal, in which she wrote about an affair she was having and how she was contemplating divorce.

I have a brother? My mother is having an affair while my dad is building a new house for our family? My parents might get a divorce? *No one must ever know*, I told myself. *My sisters and father must never find out. It's my responsibility to keep this to myself, or my family will fall apart.* And so, in an effort to make sure nothing ever slipped, at eleven, I stopped talking and started eating.

Since my parents didn't know what I knew, they also didn't know what came over me. I became a mystery. My sudden outbursts and crying fits. My mysterious weight gain from sneaking downstairs in the middle of the night and stuffing the secrets down with food. By the time the house was finished and we moved in, I had shut down and blown up. I gained weight and lost friends. I was teased ferociously. Practically overnight, I'd gone from being a happy child to a damaged reject.

That's when my mother decided to enroll me in an acting class. There, miraculously, I was reborn. I found my voice again. Well, not *my* voice—I found I was able to channel the voices of others through me, which felt so much safer. I could be emotional and open and free, and not have to worry about leaking any of my own material. It was true love.

In my freshman year at the academy, I discovered my second love: booze. With alcohol, I no longer needed food at all. After my

first sip of beer, I felt all the discomfort I had been carrying around, all the self-consciousness and fear, slip away. I started limiting my food as obsessively as I'd previously consumed it and lost a lot of weight in a very short period of time.

The first place I lived was a residency hall on Gramercy Park run by the Salvation Army. It housed elderly women, mentally re-tarded women, and actresses. For $650 per month, two meals a day were included—meals like beef cubes and gravy, canned peas and potatoes with meatloaf—not the diet of an aspiring actress in New York with a mild eating disorder, that's for sure.

But I didn't really mind starving myself. There was so much to do and see. We got free tickets to everything. I got to see Al Pacino in *Salome* and Glenn Close, Richard Dreyfus, and Gene Hackman in the preview of *Death and the Maiden*. I saw Laurence Fishburne in *Two Trains Running* and bumped into Tony Randall in the audience. I fell in love with the off-Broadway production of *From the Mississippi Delta* because it was a powerful story told simply, with three actresses playing multiple characters and no set—just a few boxes onstage. I couldn't wait to be done with school and join the actors onstage.

I loved New York City. I welcomed its grit. I felt relieved to be in an environment where the secrets lived so much closer to the surface. There was no wondering what lay beneath when homeless men masturbated in Midtown delis and junkies shot up drugs on the street. Although when a dead prostitute lay on display on the steps leading up to the building of my second apartment in Hell's Kitchen, my roommates and I decided we should probably move. We relo-cated to the East Village. There, I felt I had found home.

In the beginning, New York City seemed to love me too. When I started acting school, I was a teachers' favorite. I was asked repeat-edly how I was able to exhibit such a mature range of emotions at such a young age. But as the year progressed, I became less and less confident. The critiques and competition with my colleagues made me feel pressured and extremely self-conscious. I found my-self reaching for what had previously come so naturally. By the end

of the year, I was fully aware that I was not nearly as good as when I'd begun.

Still, I was invited back to the second-year program—a highly coveted invitation, as only a quarter of the students were invited back. I looked around at the others who were invited. They were not the most talented of the lot. They were *marketable*. They were thin and blond and would look great in the school's brochure. Others, much stronger in skill but a little less easy on the eyes, were rejected. The stench of the business was seeping through the selection process. I could feel some of my love for acting being compromised by a growing disgust. I declined the invitation. I claimed feminist objection, but mainly I was terrified of getting worse and being rejected the next time around.

I changed course and went to Hunter College, where I became a women's studies major. I moved to, and immediately hated, Murray Hill. There were no artists living in this Midtown span of mediocrity. I shared an overpriced, roach-invested apartment at the top of a steep six-floor walk-up with a Bulgarian woman who inhaled canisters of Whip-Its for breakfast. This was not the New York City experience I'd dreamed of.

While at school, I started a women's theater group. I decided I would rather spend my time creating the work that I believed in than auditioning for someone else's work. *Who wants to stand in line to land a commercial and end up playing an anal polyp, or some poor woman who needs relief from vaginal itching?* I asked myself. Not me. I was going to be in control of my destiny.

Unfortunately, my coping mechanism for living in the city derailed me from that destiny. I became exactly what I did not want to be: a drunk waitress dreaming of becoming an actress. The club scene, a major escape for me, started to matter way more than the theater scene. The once-ostracized child in me got high on being part of a group that didn't have to wait in line at all the clubs in the East Village and the Lower East Side. I was a regular at Bob and Sapphire Lounge, and went to Lucky Cheng's when it was still called

Stella's. I started to explore my sexuality. I bedded the hottest men and women I could find. I chose men who could have had careers in modeling, but in reality were bouncers, drug dealers, or guys who eventually admitted to being unemployed and still living with their mothers. The women I chose were beautiful too, tall and thin—they had the bodies I dreamed of having. I found the ultimate validation in sleeping with them all because it meant I was wanted, and hopefully hot by association. Despite my better judgment, I was now using people to silence the echoes of the teasing from grade school, the shame I carried for my mother, the endless critiques of the acting business—all of which boiled down to a constant inner critic that said, "You are not good enough." What I wasn't expecting was to fall in love with the women I got involved with. But I did. And then I had something else to hide.

For years, my work life mostly consisted of waiting tables at a chain of greasy spoons, but eventually, after eight years of wait-ressing, in 1999 I moved up the ladder to a fine Italian restaurant in Tribeca, Rose Marie's. It's there that I found myself waiting on Robert De Niro. I was so nervous but tried to appear casual. He ordered a Cosmopolitan—my favorite drink at the time. We had something in common! But, when I returned to take his dinner order, he sent the drink back because it had a bug in it. How could I have missed it floating in the martini glass? I joked with him, "Would you like me to scrape it off the top or make you a new one?" He laughed! It would have been a great scene if I had been playing the part of a waitress in a movie opposite Robert De Niro playing a customer. But there were no cameras, no crew, no one coming over to touch up my makeup between takes. I was just a waitress, waiting on Robert De Niro, playing himself. I couldn't stand the thought of being a waitress for another day and decided to go back to school.

I went back to Hunter, this time for a master's degree in elementary education, because one thing I'd learned in the city, living the cliché of the out-of-work actress, was this: you must have a backup plan. But backup plans aren't as exciting or fulfilling as

dreams. As I moved away from my dream and became more invested in my backup plan, I became depressed and started drinking more. I could no longer afford the skyrocketing rents in Manhattan and jumped from one bad neighborhood in Brooklyn to another. I spent countless nights barhopping and driving drunk, cruising up and down the Brooklyn-Queens Expressway as if I were riding the Cyclone at Coney Island. I bordered on nonfunctional. I cried everywhere. I was teaching preschool on the east side of Prospect Park at the time. I would show up to work late and hungover. I'd cry on the playground, in the director's office, on the subway to and from school, jogging around Prospect Park in the morning. I cried more than the four-year-olds in my class.

In the fall of 2001, though, I regained some hope. My theater company was doing cabaret now and booking gigs more frequently and at bigger venues. Instead of getting stiffed at Ludlow Bar, we were being offered hundreds of dollars for a three-minute set at Shine, a hot club on West Broadway. There was promise on the romantic front, too. I was playing phone tag with an old friend, Dylan. We had known each other for years, and then one night at a party, after we talked into the wee hours of the morning, he looked me in the eyes and said, "I've never seen you this way before." I knew exactly what he meant. I had never seen *him* this new way either.

Perhaps we were just drunk, or perhaps a shift had actually occurred. But the possibility of it excited me. He was different from any of the other men I'd been interested in before—usually noncommittal, dysfunctional bad boys. Dylan loved his mother but didn't live with her. He was a firefighter and good with kids. With his loyalty to his family, he reminded me of my father. I respected him. He had a thick Queens accent that somehow made it irresistibly charming when he called me "sweetheart" and "baby." And he was a male! I wouldn't have to hide him! I could introduce him to my family! We played phone tag, missing each other while on vacations and not getting messages left with roommates. When we finally touched base, it was early September and we made a plan to go out for dinner. I was sure that New York was finally about to be mine. I would have the career I dreamed of and a decent man by my side. We could live the dream together. We set our first date for that Tuesday. Tuesday, September 11, 2001.

The house I lived in at the time was in Vinegar Hill, a neighborhood near the Brooklyn Navy Yard between DUMBO and Williamsburg. (My roommates and I called it "Dumbsburg.") It was on the edge of Brooklyn, right across the water from the towers. That morning, our yard gathered a flurry of burnt paper documents. When we discovered the reason for the hours of incessant sirens, we ran around and closed all the windows to relieve ourselves of the stench of burning bodies in the air. I began to panic. Instead of our dinner date, I watched the firefighter death tally on the news go up for three straight days and was convinced that Dylan was dead.

He finally called on the third day, explaining that he'd lost his phone in the rubble. After that, we talked on the phone often. After thinking he was dead for seventy-two hours, I wanted to see him more than I had ever wanted to see anyone. I wanted to hold on and be grounded, but a traumatized man in combat is not a good choice when searching for stability. He worked around the clock at Ground Zero, finding arms and legs and putting them together with other body parts, hoping they weren't parts that belonged to friends he worked with. He went delirious from a combination of sleep deprivation and trauma. He stopped returning calls and started to just spend time with other firefighters. He pulled away from his family and his friends outside the department. He could only be with people who understood what he was going through; we could not understand.

He lived, but he was gone. And so was my theater company. The big show we were looking forward to at Shine got canceled with no rain date. It was just blocks away from Ground Zero. They were shutting their doors with no immediate plans to reopen. Trying to find other cabaret work didn't seem to make sense in this new city.

The plug was pulled on my artistic pursuits, my hope for love, and the electricity of the city that once got me high. New York and

I crashed and burned at the same time. I went into severe with-drawal, as if I had gone cold turkey too fast. On the outside I was a well-respected preschool teacher with a master's degree. Parents were fighting to get their kids into my class. But if you scratched the surface of this mirage and looked underneath, I was clearly a depressed alcoholic hitting a low I never knew possible. Everyone kept saying, "We will never forget," but forgetting was all I wanted to do. I started drinking during the day and fantasizing about suicide.

Despite my emotional state, somehow I managed to hold on to life in New York tightly with both hands for another four years. In 2005, though, I finally unraveled and could not hold on for a moment longer. I was done. I quit my job, sublet my apartment, sold all of my shit on the street, and moved back home.

I never expected to stay in New Paltz. I thought I would return to the city one day. Despite how treacherous the end had been, I was still committed to the city the way I'd been to so many bad lovers. But when I returned home, I could feel myself relax. I could breathe again. I started to get in touch with a side of myself I'd forgotten even existed; I started to sit still. In the country, I was able to get sober. As I detoxified myself from the booze, the dysfunctional relationships, and New York City, I started to hear the voices in my head—the ones that told me how awful I was. The voices of the kids who tormented me at school. The voices fueled by the shame of my childhood se-crets. The voices I tried to run away from, first with food, then with booze and sex, and then with New York City. I let them wash over me. I sat and listened without the distractions of crowds and sirens. I found the space to go to the core and reprogram the thoughts I was left with when finally alone.

Once I got myself together, I knew I was in the right place; this wasn't the short break from the city I'd imagined. I bought a house on the river—a worn-down, disgusting little shack I rebuilt from the ground up, in the same way that I was rebuilding myself. We got re-habilitated together. I created a space that could comfort me. In that comfort and safety, I started to find the courage to finally tell the truth.

I stopped using people for validation and stayed single for four years, focusing on getting better and reconnecting with my creativity. It now makes perfect sense, that right there, in my living room, I started TMI Project, a nonprofit organization that offers storytelling workshops, helping people unburden themselves of their secrets, using the stage as the platform for telling the truth. My mom came and saw me in one of the performances. Even though I was telling the secrets I had been keeping for a lifetime, when the show was over, she hugged me with tears in her eyes and told me she was proud.

Through this work, I also found real love—with a sober woman who is also an actor. I got a chance to come out to my parents, to my ninety-four-year-old grandmother, and then, onstage, to my entire community. For the first time, I was all of myself with the whole world. I never realized how bad it felt to hide until I got to experience how great it felt to be fully seen. Julie and I are now engaged. And my affair with New York City is over.

HEEDLESS, RESILIENT, GULLIBLE, AND STUPID

JANET STEEN

I think some part of me knew I was going to leave New York before I even moved there, and even knew the place, unconsciously,
that I would leave it for. It was as though the next chapter were
already being written before the current one had had a chance
to unfold. But you could not have guessed that from the way I threw
myself into New York. And throwing yourself into it is really the only
way to do it. So I did that, or tried to, for fifteen years.

You're heedless, resilient, gullible, and stupid at twenty-one. I
was all of those things and also deeply enamored of the city's mythol-
ogy when I moved there, especially its artistic and literary lore—all
those suffering artists, the legendary bookstores, the places where
writers gathered and drank, the places where they lived and died.
This feeling came in no small part from the reverence that my father
had shown for books and writers. But that didn't mean that, even in
my young enthusiasm, I had illusions of becoming the stuff of legend myself. I was from Pittsburgh, after all, from a very self-effacing
family. You didn't dream too big. But I could still stay up late in my
railroad apartment writing short stories at a flimsy card table that
served as my desk, getting a little loaded on peach schnapps, and

feeling as though I were carrying on an illustrious tradition. I could try this thing out for a while.

I had to have three roommates and live in Jersey City at first, but it still counted as living in New York. The Manhattan skyline was right outside my backyard, across the Hudson. "Dazzling" was the word that came to mind. I also had to find a job. Through a friend I found out about a proofreading job at *Esquire* magazine, and I got it before they had time to advertise the job. Tedious work, but there were writers and illustrators and photographers coming in and out of the office, and there were parties and drinks after work. It was all a very smart and normal way to go about things. You got a job and tried to work your way up.

There were three of us young women in the railroad apartment, and one young man. Apparently he had been accused of raping someone while at his Ivy League college just a couple of years before. I didn't know this until after he had moved out. In the apartment below us were two Frenchmen, and in the apartment above, two young Italian men. Frequently one pair or the other would make dinner for us girls. One of my roommates was narcoleptic and would regularly fall asleep at the dinner table; one time she fell asleep on the escalator in Port Authority bus station. She had a poodle she liked to French-kiss. We were an odd little family. But there was always the skyline to look out at, to dream on. I was smart enough to know that your early time in a big city is something to be greatly sentimental about, and I was, even as it was happening. I had instant nostalgia for a place that I felt was more glamorous than I could really take in.

There were other apartments, other jobs, other roommates and friends. This was the New York of pay telephones that never worked, indecipherable announcements about subway delays, mentally ill street people not shunted away but highly visible, freezing at night under cardboard boxes. At the time you could still go to see double features at the old movie houses. A man once came in and sat down next to me at Thalia Uptown and started masturbating during the 1970s post-Vietnam movie *Cutter's Way*. Not exactly erotic material, but in New York you never knew what was going to happen. Many nights were spent going out to see bands—the Feelies, the Mekons, Camper Van Beethoven, Yo La Tengo—bands that attracted a very white post-college crowd that could be easily typified. I was perhaps a type: I looked like part of the crowd, but I felt unmoored a lot of the time. Still, in that period New York felt like the only place I could possibly be.

B ut before this I had taken a road trip the summer I was nineteen, with my sister and my best friend. They were driving me up to a college in Vermont, where I was going to spend two months studying French. I have no idea how we came up with the route we took—I don't think any of us was very good at reading a map. We ended up spending a long time driving on twisty back roads through mountains and valleys somewhere in upstate New York. In my memory there are glistening lakes around almost every turn. And there is a VW bus parked somewhere, and a bunch of hippie-looking people just a little older than I am making their way down to a swimming hole. A lot of the houses look built by hand—they're ramshackle and added on to in makeshift ways. At the time I thought back to a high school project I had done for a history fair. It was titled "The Counterculture" and consisted mainly of a lame, thrown-together cardboard display with pictures of hippie types and antiwar demonstrations, and it was accompanied by a taped narration I did interspersed with bits of Jimi Hendrix, Bob Dylan, and other obvious choices. I looked out the car window and thought, *This must be the Counterculture.* I had never really seen it like that before, at least not in that untamed country setting, which made it look all the more appealing. I was too young to have ever been a real hippie, a bit too modest to have ever gotten into free love, but I still liked what I saw.

T here were the garden-variety late-twenties depression and the first visits to a dim therapist's office on the Upper West Side. Life was supposed to feel edgy, a little bit off to the side and out of the mainstream, but it seemed less and less so. Nine-to-five jobs were draining and claustrophobic. Then when you didn't have one, you just worried about money. But most people I knew were in the same predicament.

Certain parts of the city still thrilled me, the parts where the buildings were lower and people looked like they were doing something secretive or subterranean. The East Village was where my (requisite musician) boyfriend rented studio space with his friends for band rehearsals. It's where we ate because it was cheap. One friend started writing "manifestos"—Xeroxed statements about the crassness of the music business and mass entertainment, bands that had disappointed him, and various other things he felt like announcing to the world—and pasted them up on telephone poles around the neighborhood. They were often cryptic little anti-establishment messages that eventually got torn off and rained on and pasted over. KILL THE MOVIES AND SET YOURSELVES FREE, one said; another proclaimed, THIS POSTER WILL WRECK YOUR LIFE. For some reason they're some of the things I remember most fondly about early 1990s New York.

But strange things started happening. I broke down crying on the subway coming back from Coney Island one Fourth of July. There was too much humanity out there in one place. I started loathing certain parts of town. I dog-sat for a friend on the Upper East Side for a month and lived in her studio apartment in a doorman building, a place that should've felt swanky and nice but instead demoralized me. All those people down there on the sidewalk, all those things to buy. I couldn't get over the thought that my friend, an older woman, was living out her days in that little box on the seventeenth floor. She was perfectly happy there as far as I knew, but I didn't like to think anyone could end up so alone.

Then another equally odd thing happened. Things started to improve. Through chance I climbed up a few rungs on the ladder and became an actual editor at a magazine. I moved to Brooklyn, the obvious place to live at the time, and later the boyfriend and I found an apartment together with a garden. Things were *falling into place*. Apparently this could happen if you slogged away in one place long enough.

But back then a subtle but persistent guilt settled over me whenever things were going too well. It was a bland, uninteresting sort of Protestant guilt. Not as dark as Catholic guilt, not as entertaining as the Jewish variety. It was more like a sense that I shouldn't be having too much fun or feel too self-satisfied, because there were others out there who weren't feeling as good.

The guilt was altogether tied to my father. He was a man capable of great joy who had tremendous sorrow in him. He and my mother had a troubled marriage but soldiered on, together but emotionally separate. By leaving my hometown, I had, I thought, forsaken them to deal with it on their own. Not that I had ever been able to help, but there was always the illusion that if you were nearby or willing to suffer as well, you were at least providing some sort of company. But instead I had gone off to New York, slightly embarrassed that my ambition had become larger than my parents' ambition had ever been.

On the weekends sometimes we borrowed a friend's car and drove north, out of the city and into the country. And for the first time since that college road trip, I got that warm counter-cultural feeling again when I saw the ragged fields and old cars parked next to farmhouses and bungalows, the messy way the women dressed (as opposed to the fashion obsession of New York),

the general scruffiness. I liked the way people were just throwing their lives together. I was romanticizing, of course, but that's how I'd always gotten drawn into things.

We bought an old gray Volvo, the most respectable-looking car I'd ever driven, and rented a cabin upstate for the whole summer, using it on weekends. The boyfriend became my husband. We were now in between things—in between the claustrophobia of the city and the expansiveness of the country, in between the subways and the open fields. We were literally stuck in heavy traffic trying to get up there much of the time, the feeling of wanting to escape becoming more and more intense.

We kept renting our apartment in Brooklyn, but we took what money we'd saved and bought a house. Upstate. After we signed all the papers at the bank and made the place officially ours on a beautiful day in June, we went to the empty house and I lay down on the wooden floor of the living room in the middle of the afternoon and fell asleep. I was feeling overwhelmed, nearly depressed, but I always did, at least momentarily, when something monumental happened. And this counted as that, mostly because I knew that New York was fading away.

We gave up the apartment in the city. We had a baby. And true to form, I was overwhelmed, could barely eat for a while. She was a gorgeous little creature who spent most of her time crying. I sat in the living room of our farmhouse and looked out at the road, at people driving by, going places (there they were, free to come and go as they pleased), and I thought, *I'm really stuck now.* I missed New York painfully. Maybe a loud, frenetic city could get a baby to stop crying more easily than I could. I remembered those years of living in Park Slope—the baby-making capital of New York—and thought of the camaraderie I'd have with all those lactating new mothers who looked just like me, exhausted and pushing forty. I could just stroll down the street and sit in a café, where I'd breast-feed and chat and not be alone. In the country I had to strap the little creature in her carseat and snap it in place in the car before I could do just about anything.

And then, once again, things improved. The creature started to blossom into a funny, beautiful little girl. And we lonely former New Yorkers tended to find each other in the hills and valleys. One friendship seemed to lead easily to another, and many of my new friends had the mordant sense of humor you find in New York, which I had always loved. But there was something different too because they were people who had chosen to leave. And that meant something, more than people realized. It meant they were trading in a certain protection that the status of the city afforded them, and that was something to get used to. They risked a certain ordinary life.

But in subtle ways, life became much richer than ordinary to me, even while things went wrong, even when work got slow and cars broke down and storms knocked our power out. If this was throwing life together the way I'd imagined it, well, it was harder than I'd thought it would be, but it still made some kind of sense. The sweetest moments came during outdoor summer parties, when my little girl and my friends' children ran around in fields as the adults sat and drank and talked. The kids ran themselves ragged until dark, staying out long after the sun had set, sometimes holding glow sticks that made trails of colored light in the distance.

And I did sometimes make it into the city, to see friends, to keep a semblance of a high-powered professional life. But by then I had been gone a while. I took the train down one fall evening to go to a publishing party given at my favorite bookstore, Housing Works, in Soho. The place was packed; it was hard to maneuver around the smart-looking, well-dressed crowd. I felt clumsy and out of practice. Everywhere around me were faces of people I'd dealt with in the business at one time or another: writers, editors, agents, publicists. I'd gone to lunch with these people, assigned reviews of their books or their authors' books, written articles myself about some of them. I saw one woman coming toward me, a woman who had chipped away at me over the years to cover her authors, who had taken me out for drinks, invited me to numerous events. Her eyes met mine, hovered for just a second, and then drifted off over my shoulder as she made her way past me. It was that classic moment of reckoning: I had outlived my usefulness to her. I suppose I wasn't all that surprised, although at the moment it stung, both her disregard for me and the realization that I wasn't who I used to be. And then, a wave of relief. I went back to talking to a friend who was a friend beyond the business of it all, drank some more wine, and took the train back upstate.

I was sitting once in the living room in the house where I grew up, with my father. This was in the last years of his life. It was late afternoon, and the light was coming into the room a bit too harshly. I didn't always like things too bright. I was home for a visit. We were sitting there talking, probably about things going on in my life, since my father was so very good at deflecting attention away from himself. I think I was probably trying very hard to seem relaxed, although I often wasn't as relaxed as I would've liked. There was so much love between us, but it was so very hard to acknowledge.

And then, almost out of nowhere, a very direct question from him. He asked me why I had moved away from the place where I had grown up. (By now it had been nearly twenty years.) He posed this question as though it were something he'd been wanting to ask for a very long time and had had to find great will to work up to. And I thought I detected an edge of anger in the question, although it was more likely injury. I think he had long mourned the fact that all his children had moved far away.

I had trouble finding the right words. "I guess I just wanted to see what it would be like to live in New York. I didn't necessarily think I would stay that long," I explained, struggling to make sense of it also for myself. "Things just started happening. And then I just kept . . . staying."

That was the thing about New York. For most people who moved there from a smaller place, the way I did, things were never the same afterward. It was like a great love in your life that you could never forget, whether it had gone sour or not. And my many years there prepared me for wanting something utterly different, a different extreme. It was true that New York lent you a certain toughness that made you think you could handle difficulty in all sorts of forms. Moving to a smaller city just didn't seem to be the answer. I wanted fields and winding roads. I wanted to see bearded guys in old trucks, to sit with an old woman in the general store and talk about how high the creeks had been looking lately. I wanted to walk out my door and not have to face a thousand strangers.

My father didn't say a lot. He looked as though he was trying hard to understand. Essentially, I was telling him I had to find a new place to live my life and that I was never able to come home. I was all grown up then anyway, and he was an old man. I wished I could've stayed and been more help to him, but I had to go, and I never did exactly apologize for that.

THE LION, THE PIG, AND THE WOLF AND OTHER THOUGHTS ABOUT NEW YORK

KAREN E. BENDER

I initially went to New York because I wanted to be able to think. I visited the city first when I was twenty-two years old, a junior at UCLA. Los Angeles, with its hard white light and its big skies, felt like a windowless box to me. It was the city where I had grown up, which meant that some thoughts felt unthinkable, merely because of the proximity of my loved ones. I wanted to get across the country because there, I felt, my mind would somehow be free.

I was interested in magazine writing, and the general consensus was that an internship at a magazine would open up doors. The UCLA summer internship program seemed to have no connections to any magazines I wanted to work at, but my boyfriend at the time was an L.A. correspondent for *Starlog*, a science fiction magazine, and convinced them to take me on for eight weeks. One June day in 1985, I flew with a handful of other interns from UCLA to my internship.

I remember standing in front of the *Starlog* building on Park Avenue South my first day. Even the light was different here, a heavier, more golden color than the bone-white brilliance in California. I went into the elevator and pressed the button; it shuddered and started to rise.

The *Starlog* office included several magazines, such as *Fangoria*, a magazine for horror movie fans, *Teen Idols Mania!*, *Black Hairstyles*, *Wrestling Scene*, and *Allure*, a knockoff of *Playgirl*. The *Starlog* office was one small room papered with posters of *Star Wars*, *E.T.*, *Star Trek*, and characters I could not yet identify from other science fiction stories. I was not a reader of sci-fi, and was doing this internship just because no one else would have me. However, the other staffers could, with encyclopedic expertise, catalogue every episode of *Star Trek* and, happily, educated me.

My first task was to answer reader letters. One man wrote a letter declaring that he knew "the secret of the universe." He added, "If it's not right and you publish it, it won't matter, because you're a science fiction magazine, but if I am right, think of the prestige!" There were exclamations of outrage from all corners of the nation. One reader said that he found *Mad Max III* terribly disappointing, and to "please direct these following suggestions for *Mad Max IV* to George Miller because no one will give me his address." There was one scandalous letter from a fan who claimed he had an "insider" photo of E.T. with his head cut off. After much discussion, it was decided that this photo should not be published, as it might cause too much distress to the readers.

I did not understand the mechanics of the dazzling world of editorial, but I hoped that these beginnings would be my entrée into the higher echelons of the magazine world, my bridge to *The New Yorker* or *Atlantic* or *Glamour* or *Vogue*. I tried to make my sentences shapely and perfect. Perhaps an editor from one of the magazines I aspired to would leaf through a copy of *Starlog*, find my short article on *Red Sonja*, and think, This *is a writer to watch*.

While I worked at *Starlog*, I lived in a state of great excitement and great fear, which made me utterly porous to everything in the city. I could not sleep in my tiny cell in the Barnard dorms. The noise was constant and unbelievable, and a bus screamed every five minutes outside my window; it felt as if each bus were parking in my ear. I slept a couple of hours each night, listening to the buses, and then, head heavy but sort of calm, went in to work. I missed my boyfriend back in Los Angeles. But I didn't *want* to miss anyone and so picked a fight when he came to visit. My short time in New York had made me understand this: at twenty-two, I felt most whole when I was alone.

I also liked being surrounded by strangers. I loved the whole concept of *rush hour*, the businessmen and -women in their suits, the messengers hurtling down the street, the idea that we were all rushing somewhere important. I didn't know where this important place was, exactly, but that made it more seductive and even possible—it could be anywhere. It could be in the taxis rushing through the summer rain, the headlights bright through the city's pale mist. It could be in the grand buildings, in one of the offices on the thirty-fifth floor or the seventy-seventh; it could be in the dark subway tunnel, which lit up as though god were approaching when the subway car grew close. I was in love with the city, though perhaps I was also in love with my sense of anticipation.

I returned to Los Angeles from my internship and realized that I had to get back to New York. I graduated from UCLA, saved some money, and heard that a friend I had met, Elisa, had a room available in her Park Slope apartment. I gripped the arms of my seat as we lifted off and headed toward the East Coast.

In 1987, I moved in with Elisa in a third-floor walk-up on 3rd Street. The first three weeks she was out of town for work, and I didn't know anyone in the city at all. This utter aloneness, in a city of millions, was disorienting. Each random thought echoed, like thunder, in my head. I wondered if I died suddenly, how long it would take for someone to find the body. I imagined it would take some time, and this realization was somehow focusing. I was here, and alone, and utterly myself; I felt untethered for the first time in my life.

I signed up at a job placement agency, and the long-golden-fingernailed placement rep sent me on interviews. "Come in for

your interview as an editorial assistant at *McCall's* . . . a fact checker for *Vanity Fair* . . . an assistant at Viking." A few weeks later, some friends moved to the city for school, and I got a job at a Fairchild magazine called *Travel Today!* that was aimed, as the publisher said, at "yuppies who want to go on weekend travel at the last minute." My first task was to learn how to successfully join the official workforce. I had somehow missed (or decided to ignore) the memo that I was not supposed to dress like a college student; the art director called me aside and told me that I had to stop coming to work in jeans that had holes in the knees. Embarrassed, I cried, and then went out and bought suit-y clothes, with padded shoulders that made me look like a mushroom. The worst defining characteristic of the job was that it paid $14,000 a year, a fact that even the editor who hired me apologized for.

This was 1987, our first full year in New York, and everything was new to us. I remember the first September day I walked down the street where I lived. There was a chill in the air, a change—yes, there were seasons here. And I remember walking down Broadway in November, looking up at a digital clock and thermometer at the top of a building and seeing the impossible number: 19. "Could it really be 19 degrees?" I asked my friend Margaret, walking with me. The cold made your mind blink; it was actually painful.

None of us had any money, but we didn't really need to spend much. We went out for Indian food on 6th Street, sat in our apartments eating popcorn and making fun of the men we deigned to date. We sometimes placed articles in magazines we liked, but sometimes had them rejected. We juggled our bill paying so the checks wouldn't bounce. The rest of our family members lived on the other side of the continent, but my friends and I created our own family in this new world.

I didn't know what it meant the day the stock market crashed in October 1987, but the older staff members of *Travel Today!* did—they gathered around the newspaper that day, blanched, shoulders hunched against a wind they had experienced before. The magazine staggered on for a few more months, and then, in the spring, we were summoned into the publisher's office. "There's no more magazine," the publisher said. We would get one more paycheck and that was that. The suddenness of the group firing stunned me, and the casual way the publisher told us we would be earning no more money filled me with fury. I did not want to feel helpless. I had kept meticulous records of my overtime; I went to Human Resources and somehow convinced them to fork over my seven hundred dollars for it. I felt airy with power—I had, briefly, in a small way, overcome the errant whims of the city.

I found a new position at Fairchild, at a magazine called *Travel Agent,* which was the industry newsletter for travel agents—I would work part-time, with no benefits, but I would have time to work on my fiction writing. Now when I walked through the city, I looked at the glowing lights in the offices and thought, more bitterly, about how I didn't know how to get in. I was trying to "freelance," which is how all of us who were underemployed referred to what we were doing. But calling up magazine editors was proving harder than I had anticipated; getting assignments was hard and then actually getting paid for them was even harder.

After Black Monday, the city plunged into recession; it was a good time to head out of town. I had been accepted to the program at the Iowa Writers' Workshop, and I headed there to work on my fiction writing. The night before I flew to Iowa, I walked with my friend Margaret around Chelsea, reluctant to go down the stairs to the train to leave her, to leave the city.

For three years, I lived in Iowa City, a city of stories and writers and cornfields and big sky. The New Yorkers who had come to the workshop stood out in the Midwest like loud, chattery birds. Robert was one of them, and I fell in love with him.

Robert had grown up in the city, and his New Yorker–ness was one reason I was first drawn to him. When he started to talk, he spoke so fast I sometimes had no idea what he was saying. He gestured, beautifully, with his hands. He wore a navy fedora to parties, which made him look like he had lived in New York in the 1940s. There were a hundred other reasons why I chose him that had nothing to do with New York but with something wonderful and unique about his essence; basically, I wanted to inhale him, and I wanted him to inhale me.

The second time I moved back to New York, after Iowa, I went, again, for an apartment. A friend of Robert's was moving out of an apartment in Williamsburg and wanted someone to take it over; it was a not-quite-to-code floor-through, and it was, astoundingly, $300 a month. The apartment was, essentially, a grant; it allowed me to work part-time while I worked as an adjunct instructor and wrote my first novel.

I loved Robert's family's New Yorker–ness, their confidence driving the highways that circled the city and that seemed to me like the Indy 500, the way takeout somehow appeared on his family's dining room table, his mother's knowledge of the discount department store Century 21, their easy eloquence. I worked on my novel, adjunct-taught classes, fact-checked, and did other freelance stuff. Two years later, in 1994, Robert and I moved into a one-bedroom apartment in a subsidized apartment building, one that he had gotten on a waiting list for twenty years earlier—Independence Plaza in Tribeca.

We now lived in a one-bedroom apartment that was, insanely, $650 a month, adjusted for your income. (You might see a crucial theme here about low rents enabling our lives in New York, which they did.) I had a card table in the bedroom and Robert had a desk in the living room, and we worked on our novels in our "offices" day after day.

We were trying to become "novelists," which meant that we were marching, breathless, determined, into, it seemed, nothing. We made a little money, we stared at our computers, and at night we went on long walks through Tribeca, Soho, the Village, or down through the Financial District. On bad days, when the concept of finishing a book seemed remote, impossible even, Robert suggested walking by one building on Wall Street that had three concrete faces molded into the side: a lion, a pig, and a wolf. The animal renderings were both absurd and oddly dignified. Why were these animals' profiles carved into this building? What did they mean? The sheer weirdness of those animals, the question of why they sat on the face of a financial institution, cheered us up. Those animal faces were why I loved New York, the strange beauty that could emerge at any moment.

"Look at them," he said, "and be brave."

We stood in the dark, silent caverns of Wall Street and tried to imagine what that would be like.

We needed a little luck, and then some came. Robert sold his novel, and then I did. We had a little money. We had published novels—could we call ourselves novelists? We got married and had our son, Jonah. We were still adjuncts and working part-time, but, suddenly we were this new entity in the city—a family. Now our lives revolved around a small, loud person who floated through the world, first strapped to our chests in the BabyBjörn and then pushed through the streets like a little rajah.

But the city was moving on without us. It was the late 1990s, and the old refrigerator building on our street was transformed into multimillion-dollar condos under the elegant name "The Ice House." Empty storefronts became stores that sold huge, antique furniture to fill up the fancy lofts. Celebrities were an exotic species whose presence began to ensure the end of our tenure here. Jonah was invited to birthday parties for toddlers, which were catered. We applied for teaching positions and got some interviews, but no job. Then I got a monthlong visiting writer position at a university in Wilmington, North Carolina. It seemed a great piece of luck. We did not understand how great a piece of luck it was.

This was in September 2001.

September 11 would have been Jonah's first day of preschool, which was about five blocks from the World Trade Center. At nine o'clock that morning, I think I would have been standing with the other parents, watching Jonah begin to meet the other children. The first plane would have hit the World Trade Center right when I was heading back to our apartment. Would I have turned around then and taken my son out of school? Would I have thought it a bizarre accident and headed home?

Instead, at nine in the morning on September 11, I was on the corner of Eastwood Road and Market Street in Wilmington, North Carolina, driving Jonah to a preschool play center called Fit for Fun.

There was a terrible disconnect those first slow days—to be somewhere not home, to be unable to reach family and friends in New York, to want to be there with them, to be in this sunny, unfamiliar place. "You would have been a couple of blocks away," people told us, when we mentioned where we would have been that morning, and my mind shut against that fact. The airline we had flown down went bankrupt; we rented a car and drove back to New York two weeks later, American flags hanging off the overpasses. We headed toward the Holland Tunnel and saw the smoke billowing from downtown.

We dropped off our rental car, got a taxi to Canal Street, and were stopped. The area was blocked from everyone but those who lived here. We looked at the smoke, the police, the blockades. Suddenly, we lived in a war zone.

"Do you live here, or do you have reservations?" a policeman asked.

We stared at him.

"For the restaurants," said the policeman. "You can cross the blockade if you have a reservation."

This was not a joke.

"We live here," we said, and I had never felt so strongly that I was home.

What I remember, those first weeks in fall 2001, was the politeness. You did not know who in the neighborhood would be alive. You went to the corner deli and you were glad to see the man behind the counter, the man whose name you did not know; you were just glad that he was here. "Hello," I said, and he brightened and said, "Hello."

There were so many people who were not here. They were the Missing. Their pictures were on the flyers that covered the lampposts, fences, any spaces they could fill in the neighborhood. I walked by them as I walked my son to preschool. The preschool was still open, near the rubble, the burning buildings, the police. The World Trade Center sat, a pile. I stared right at it every day and still could not believe it was what it was.

How did one go about a life? How did you value each day? What was the best thing to do next? How did you live without fear?

It was a surprisingly warm fall, and the fires didn't go out. They kept burning. We kept waiting for rain. The health authorities assured us that the air was fine, but told us to keep the windows closed and not to run the air conditioners.

It seemed that, during that terrible, anxious autumn, when no one knew what was going to happen, everyone was pretending—to work, to go about their days. One night during that time stands out to me. Traditionally at Halloween, a group from Tribeca hosted an annual costume party in Washington Market Park, but it was still closed because of the toxic dust. So this year, some local parents and children gathered on a side street in the neighborhood. The World Trade Center was still a smoking pile. The children filled the street, dressed as lions or tigers or fairies or dogs. A parent with connec-

tions had gotten the real Steve from Blue's Clues to sit at a table and shake hands. Jonah, who was, in fact, dressed as Blue, stared at him with awe. The real Steve looked at him with a kind of tenderness and sadness. He shook hands with Jonah and perhaps even gave him a sticker. We had our lives, these odd, precious things. We had to figure out how to best live the rest of them. There was no need to think anything else. We stood, watching the costumed children running with their beautiful, galling innocence. A few blocks south, the buildings burned, quietly, under the dark October sky.

September 11 didn't send us out of the city. The neighborhood slowly returned to a different sort of life: the hazardous waste team vacuumed the toxic dust out of the park, the rubble was slowly carted to the barges on the Hudson River, and the residents who had left briefly returned; but there was that terrible glaring space on Chambers Street that was there every time you looked.

What sent us out of New York City was the fact that the owners of Independence Plaza, where we lived, realized that their contract with the city had ended; they weren't legally obligated to offer subsidized housing anymore and were looking forward to hiking our rents to five thousand dollars a month. The tenants organized. They tried to push it back, but we knew our lives here were built on a fragile economy. We had to construct another sort of life. Jonah was growing, and our daughter Maia was on the way. We interviewed at different schools, and finally Robert was offered a job—back in Wilmington, North Carolina.

And so we left. It happened quickly, almost despite us, the way all this had happened. I don't remember much from our last days in New York City. I didn't want to think about our many years there because I didn't want there to be a past. There was the U-Haul that held all our boxes, our couches, our dishes. There was the way I looked back at the city skyline as we drove through New Jersey, heading south. There was the house we rented when we first got to Wilmington and the porch that I sat on our first night. It was a warm July night. I sat on our porch and waited for a car to drive by. I sat on the porch for a long time and waited to hear that sweet sound.

THE LOOSENING

RAYHANÉ SANDERS

I chose New York. I was seventeen and I had to go to college because that's what comes next. Since I have trouble with commitment, I had applied to over a dozen schools. I said "maybe" and they said "yes," and before I knew it I had a choice to make and I chose New York. I chose it because I couldn't possibly imagine myself in some Lands' End catalogue version of college—some northeastern, cozy-by-the-fire campus where everyone knows your name and boys wear boat shoes and blizzards keep you indoors, doing drugs and exchanging invites for summer stays on the Cape. And because my home state of California, which I have since grown to love, seemed at the time like a dry well—as dusty and brown and thirsty for action as its drought-plagued canyons, always catching on fire. I remember once my boyfriend and I driving the 10 east, leaving L.A. for New York in the middle of the Santa Ana season; the warm winds had set Malibu and the West Valley ablaze, and in the rearview mirror we could see the black smoke pluming, and I thought, eyes fixed east, *Let it burn*.

New York seemed to make some promises I couldn't refuse. I would have anonymity—my walk to class would be accompanied by fellow students, but also by East Village junkies and Baltic teenage models and finance sharks in their Italian suits, artists and hustlers, playwrights and bums, drag queens and book editors and the whole of humanity. I liked that. I liked that at any moment I could lose myself in the crowds, disappear from view, blend in and liquefy, cease being available. Something about living in the city—even in a room the size of a broom closet and with a shared bathroom down the hall or, later, in a neighborhood where the burgers were $15 but my boyfriend got held up at knifepoint at three in the afternoon putting quarters into a washing machine—felt decadent, luxurious even. Everyday things were thrilling. Leaving the house for a pack of cigarettes feels incredible when you do it at three-thirty in the morning, walking down Broadway in a negligee with a coat thrown over it. Meeting friends at the movies feels like a coup—victorious, like somehow you *won*—when instead of parking your car at the mall, you pass under the arch at Washington Square Park, where Harry chose Sally, on your walk over.

Fast as an L train approaching the station, seventeen turned into twenty turned into twenty-five turned into thirty. I remained in love, no doubt about it, but there were hints early on, cracks in the façade, that things in this fast-paced, mile-a-minute city could go from thrilling to dismal faster than you knew.

I remember sitting on my front stoop down by the Hudson River, smoking a cigarette, watching the towers burning and, yes, people jumping, nightmare-disbelief dawning to life, when the first tower just collapsed, one minute there, one minute gone, a free fall of dust and engineering and people and reality . . . all turned to ash. It sounded like one wail, like the whole city screamed at once, a grieving mother, her son dead in her arms. The hairs on my arms stood up. The second tower followed soon after and my street view, our skyline, was different, just like that. I sat there for a few hours—I couldn't get up, there was no way I was moving—watching all of surviving Wall Street heed Mayor Rudy Giuliani's simple missive and "head north," treading up my street wearing their suits and holding

their briefcases, painted, head to toe, in gray, like a zombie apocalypse movie, and it felt then like a giant warning: *Nothing is solid. Everything will change.*

There was the instant disaster, yes, but there would also be a slow burn. My boyfriend and I would break up. I'd get an evil bitch of a boss. I'd watch with balled-up fists as boys who had the same olive skin as my cousins back in Tehran got stopped, their backpacks rifled through, at the subway turnstiles. My subway rides would go from exchanging smiles with a mother and her sweet baby to holding my lower back in pain, weighed down by bags of manuscripts for work, while I reached the whole of my 5-foot-2-inch being for a sliver of pole to hold on to and even *more* people—was it possible?!—pushed their way into our cattle car, and I thought, *There's got to be another way.*

Friends started to leave—for Miami and L.A. and San Francisco and New Orleans and Austin, that millennial mecca. My God, even Boston. People were leaving for Boston. I started to have dreams in which I'd wake up in Los Angeles, look outside, and realize, with panic, that I had given it all up, that I'd gotten off the merry-go-round after working so hard to find a place on it and that my spot was surely now taken by some younger, fresher new arrival; I had left New York and made a ginormous mistake and ruined everything. I'd wake up in a sweat to the roar and squeal of ambulance sirens and sigh with relief at being safely ensconced in Brooklyn. Then I'd have the same dream in crafty reverse: there I'd be, sitting poolside, skin clear, hair done, rested, bouncing my baby on my knee, talking to some girlfriend about how leaving New York—avoiding a destiny of aging workhorse spinsterdom—was the best thing I could've done for my quality of life, for my future, when suddenly I'd wake up in some outerborough brick-and-steel industrial wasteland, the sky outside cold and dreary, the air toxic, rain rapping on the window. Then I'd wake up for real with a start, unsure of where I was, look outside, and cry, cry, because I was still here.

Things were starting to get to me.

What had once enticed me so much about living here, what had made me say yes and excitedly brought me to the altar—bishop's crook lampposts and cobblestone streets and wrought-iron fire escapes and late-night restaurants and all-night bars and Central Park and the Chrysler Building and Film Forum and summer concerts and the Brooklyn Bridge and flea markets and egg creams and Chinatown and cherry blossom trees and plays and brownstones and rooftop gardens and the Chelsea galleries and Grand Central's Oyster Bar and, my god, *people*, so many people, so interesting and inspirational and available you'd never feel lonely again—all that had started to feel like not enough.

I asked those on their way out why they were leaving—"How could you leave New York? Where do you go from here?"—and they told me they had never pictured themselves staying forever; it'd been nice and now they were done. But I had. I had pictured myself here forever. L.A. had been a place to leave for grander adventures, bigger horizons, smarter people, and fewer blonds, and New York had been a destination to reach and, once here, a star to follow, the dream always a little ahead, calling out to you, a siren song: this apartment, this job, this promotion, this reservation, this next goal to reach, this next hill to climb. We New Yorkers, we're like little striver-warriors, all of us, swords in hand, slashing dragons as we go. Tired but strong, worn-out but resourceful, resolute, steadfast. Determined to make it.

But I was starting to wonder what "it" really was. What was I proving with all of this? I was spending the equivalent of a mortgage on an 8-by-12 room in an apartment with three other busy shadows, passing ships in the night, whose names I often forgot, in a half-shady neighborhood where I was woken almost nightly by intoxicated masses pouring out of the bars and piling onto the street for a smoke. If it wasn't them, it was the ambulances or the garbage trucks or the impromptu rap battles. Contenders would actually pick my trash can up over the building gate and use the lid for percussion. I was waking up late for work, not showering (again), rushing to the train that would surely be "delayed due to train traffic ahead of us," elbowing some sleazy man behind me even as the MTA's automated message attested that "a crowded subway is no excuse for sexual misconduct." I was looking older than I was. I was finding gray hairs in numbers. I was gaining weight from sitting at my desk so much—there is no such thing as 9 to 5 in New York. The bags under my eyes, particularly the left one, I couldn't help but notice, were deepening and gaining in folds.

I had come to New York when I was seventeen because—and maybe I was not fully conscious of this then—the city had seemed like a great place to discover who you are. It just seemed that there was a lot to experience here, as if all you had to do was show up and the city would take care of the rest, making sure you got the education, the maturing, the wising-up you needed. Its crowds, the noise, the endlessness of it all, the perpetual motion, felt exciting then—revealing just the deep end I needed to jump into. There is something unique about New York, some quality, some matchless, pertinent combination of promise and despair, wizardry and counterfeit, abundance and depletion, that stimulates and allows for a reckoning to occur—maybe even forces it. The city pulls back the curtain on who you are; it tests you and shows you what you are made of in a way that has become iconic in our popular culture, and with good reason. In thirteen years, the city has kicked my ass and made me strong and served me well.

But thirty is not seventeen. You get older, certain things get satisfied, itches get scratched, and you find yourself wanting new things, new environments, better suited to who you are now, to who you hope to be. For all the construction and subway rate hikes, for all the gentrification and new-neighborhood labeling (DUMBO, BoCoCa, Nolita), New York never fundamentally changes; you do. The city is always here if you need it—one big giant laboratory, aflame with bright lights and tests and trials. And, for the most part, it's young people who need it—the next crop, in from the farms and the 'burbs and the mountains and the beaches. They gear up, slap on their goggles, pull on their rubber gloves, and take a deep breath. They don't know it yet, but they'll be deep-sea divers in no time, plumbing depths they didn't know existed, taking on shapes, moving in rhythms, along lines they couldn't anticipate crossing, let alone navigating. Those who make it, that is.

I left the City of Angels a long time ago to reach out and grab new angels, angels of my own making. To set them myself, hand to flesh, upon my shoulders. L.A.'s angels—its freeways, its smog, its culture of celebrity, its endless summer, its open sky void—would no longer do; they had nothing to offer me. I left thirteen years ago with an engine roaring in my belly and a hungry spark in my eye. I stayed away for a long time; when I would visit, I'd keep my head low, my eyes to the squeaky-clean pavement that had no stories to tell. I'd take note of its inconveniences—but what if I want soba noodles at 3 AM? I'd argue to friends—and steer clear of the beaches, where, I feared, the chant of the ocean might wipe my dreams clean. Back at JFK, off the plane, I'd quicken my pace, as if my legs always moved like that, as if because they did meant that I belonged, meant I was one of the city's own.

I stayed away for a good stretch. Like a good New Yorker, I got busier and busier and spent less and less time on myself—haircuts, exercise, thinking. I shut my eyes with the rest of them on the morning trains. It used to amaze me how commuters could keep a hot cup of coffee sturdy in their hand while they let out a little snore, clearly asleep; how they knew to wake up right before their stop. I became one of them. I was tired, depleted. The engine in my belly got me where I wanted to go, and now everything tasted like battery acid up and down my throat.

One summer, I passed by one of the brownstones I had fawned over when I first moved to Park Slope—Berkeley Place or Carroll Street, I can't remember now—one of those picture-perfect postcard-of-New-York ones, with the red door and the flower window boxes and the curved stone stoop, one of those that was still intact and hadn't been turned into oddly shaped studio apartments to maximize the

building's earnings. No, one family, one lucky family, lived here, stars on their foreheads.

There were kids running up and down the front steps chasing a dog; their feet, shoeless and wet, left prints. The mother was trying to pay a pizza-delivery guy; she reached over with a fistful of cash, as a couple of teenagers ducked out of the way, taking the box with them. The front door was open, and I slowed my pace, craning my neck to take a good look inside. The house probably cost a couple million at least—more than I'd ever dreamed of having. The plastic bags I was carrying home from the market had branded red lines into my wrists (I lost circulation blocks ago); moist Band-Aids covered half of my blistered, pulsing feet; the burn between my legs was visceral, my thighs chafed and raw from the constant burn of sweat, the constant friction of walking in 90-plus-degree heat and 90 percent humidity. I was, as usual, exhausted. But as I watched the domestic scene play out before me, peering inside my dream Brooklyn-Barbie home—the apex, the diamond, of the dream itself—something truly amazing happened: I didn't want it. Truth be told, it looked cramped; I could see that the staircase rising from the ground floor was not much wider than my hips, that it would be difficult to carry laundry up and down its steps. The mom looked tired—beaten, actually. I knew that in the back the neighbors' gardens would be squeezing in from either side, rectangular plots rubbing up on each other like sticks of gum. I walked on, stunned by my own feelings, feeling like a traitor, wanting nothing more than to ignore what I just felt—but finding myself unable to.

If we are transplants, we say we came to New York for its "energy," but the truth is, that energy doesn't come from the streets or the stores or the buzzy power-lunch restaurants. It's not here because of the subways or the block parties or the Puerto Rican Day Parade. *We* brought it here. It's just the collective energy of us—the by-product and the fumes of the ambition we lugged with us when we came. Ambition: our bright bird-dream and our heavy load.

What I realized that afternoon in Park Slope—and many after-

noons since—is that I had come here so many moons ago to find out who I was, to qualify, to prove things to myself I didn't even have names for yet, to test my worth. And it occurred to me that I had gotten what I came for—I *had* it, like a quarter in my palm. I understood then that "the city"—even what we call it honors the mythic site that it is, more symbol than place—had served its purpose: I knew exactly who I was, precisely what I was worth, and it was now time to find a more conducive place to enjoy her.

I said goodbye to New York not because anything got bad or went sour. I didn't have a moment, as Joan Didion did, when I realized that I had "stayed too long at the Fair." I left New York because I wanted more. I wanted space and silence, mountains and sky—the calm to appreciate my life, a life that, I now knew, had already begun and didn't need to "get started." I left New York and returned to L.A. because I had entered into a new reckoning, a different kind of inventory, and when I wake up to a morning full of rolling fog off the coast and open my eyes to the pink shock of bougainvillea outside my window and take in the smell of eucalyptus that just permeates the air here, medicine in every breath, I know that I am right where I need to be. I said goodbye to all that and left New York because I, like Didion, "am not that young any more." I just never dreamed what good that would signal, what joy that would mean.

CAPTIVE

DANA KINSTLER

I practiced leaving at certain times. In the summer, I approached the roof of our apartment building, walked the three flights up from the tenth floor where we lived, past 11, 12, to 14, skipping over the phantom 13, to the place where the staircase narrowed, curled tighter, pushed toward the light that beamed from a narrow window I couldn't reach, not even on tiptoe. There was an opening that promised unobstructed sky. Here was the roof! Relieved, I pushed open the heavy metal door and stepped outside. I was thirteen. It was 1975.

No one else was ever there. This is where I brought my solitary party: a can of Tab, a transistor radio, a rolled-up neon green quilt; this was where I would camp out for the night.

This is where I saw the sky, the trees of Gramercy Park, the hotel across the park, the tops of buildings I learned to name as a child. At night the top of the Met Life building burned like a golden pyramid. With the uneven asphalt underneath my towel and the tops of the buildings lit up over the four-foot edge of the barricade, I imagined I dwelled in a forest. I brought an airline mask to block the glare, Con Edison's pink four-sided clock tower behind me, the Chrysler's fish-scale body and spire ahead, the Empire State presiding over them all like a silver fairy. I put my transistor radio by my head, propped the bottle of baby oil for the morning tan, scanned a copy of J.D. Salinger's *Franny and Zooey* to read by skyscraper light. Before me was the open green expanse of the park.

But even with the eye mask on, I couldn't transcend the city. There were windows to the east, west, and south, and each apartment emanated artificial light—lampshade glow and ceiling light shine and candlelight flicker, radiating from metal frames inside concrete buildings. The edges of the adjacent corner building were buttressed with gargoyles; these stone-winged creatures perched over their roof, at eye level, looking over onto Irving Place. One of them peered over its long curled nose, studying and correcting me, as if it saw deep into my conflict. I was here. I wished I were somewhere else. There were other eyes I couldn't see behind opaque window glass. Everyone was staring down at me.

I often saw the walk up to the roof as the trajectory for the princess Aurora heading for the spindle in the fairy tale *Sleeping Beauty*; there, she'd prick her finger and fall into a century-long slumber to fulfill her destiny. That was my fear and my hope, both. I wanted to be stunned into staying. I wanted someone to make the decision for me. My tortured state of longing was always a part of me; I longed to leave the city, and I needed to reside there and belong, rent for as long as my father and grandmother and great-grandmother had before me. A lifetime—that long.

Growing up, I learned which historic events shaped my building and block and neighborhood: my building, the National Arts Club on Gramercy Park, had been the home of Samuel Tilden, a former New York governor, who lost the presidential election. Next door was the Player's Club, started by actor Edwin

Booth, brother of assassin John Wilkes Booth. Edwin's statue is in the center of the park. Once, I climbed up into his metal lap with my teenage boyfriend, who lived next to the hotel, and we faced uptown, smoking cigarettes, cradling beers, watching the traffic zoom down Lexington Avenue, which began or ended, depending on how you saw it, just on the other side of the park, at the sideways entrance to the Gramercy Park Hotel. My friend's theory: that you only belonged if you had crawled this park's paths, shoved a fistful of pebbles in your mouth.

The hotel would change, later, become unrecognizable, trendy, and chic, a room slept in to the tune of $2,872.26 a night. But back then, my family ate in the dining room, which was papered with equestrian murals of riders on a hunt that never resolved; this old world image comforted me as we ate slabs of well-done meat in that genteel shabby abode. As a teenager, I frequented the phone booth in the lobby where I could sink in with a stack of quarters, pretending to leave home, in order to call someone, anyone, in my stakeout, usually the boyfriend next door. I sat in the hotel lobby for three hours, hoping to meet the Clash after my second night of seeing them on their five-night run in 1980 at the Bond on Times Square. Then I went home. I could always just go home.

It's impossible to talk about leaving New York City without talking about leaving home. I mean, depart from that first apartment where I was conceived and raised, an abode my father started renting in 1946, when he was twenty, and where he still lives and paints? In 1992, my grandmother's furniture came downtown from East 77th Street on a truck, after she passed away.

After college, I came home, returning to sleep on a single mattress in my childhood bedroom. When my father, recently divorced, told me to move out, I was shocked, but not surprised. I was distract-

ing him, he said; he could feel my presence, sleeping in until noon, while he paced in front of the easel in his studio at the end of the hall. Couldn't I keep regular hours?

No. I could not. I wanted to write and dance. I waited tables, I cooked for a caterer, and when I wasn't at work, I got out of bed at lunchtime. The lounging disturbed him. He wanted his apartment back. A pair of leopard-print panties fell out of a manila envelope addressed to him, one I opened by mistake. Who might move in to take my place? It was hard to be semi-grown-up, still living at home. But could I pay the rent? I was terrified and excited. I was twenty-four.

I moved into a six-floor walk-up on 11th Street and Avenue A. This was 1986. I had a room in an apartment. Each time I moved, after that initial departure from home, my apartment got a little bigger. The next one was just a tiny room with a toilet and sink, but it was all mine. Always, I faced an air shaft. Each move felt like going from one grade school wooden cubbyhole to another, until I obtained the full-length high school metal locker. This made you feel you'd reached the last rung—you could lock it, decorate it with posters of David Bowie, or if you were skinny enough, step inside. You had arrived. Once I moved into a one-bedroom in Brooklyn in 1991, as far from Gramercy Park as I had ever lived—across a river—I was ready to go.

Each of my grandmothers left Manhattan by boat. My maternal grandmother set sail for Europe after her wedding in the Little Church Around the Corner on West 29th Street. She married in a purple velvet flapper dress, drank at a speakeasy, and then slept at the Plaza. Later, she moved to Vermont, where she built a house nestled against the Green Mountains in a valley. We collected ferns and moss and planted terrariums, which I carried home and put on my sooty windowsill in our city apartment.

My father's mother, Hazel, had ridden the ferry up the Hudson to work in a Catskills hotel every summer, starting at age six. She boarded the ferry at Gansevoort Street with her mother and four siblings, leaving their tenement apartment on Henry Street and returning every fall. My great-grandmother, who'd arrived in New York Harbor in the 1890s from Russia with her four children and her husband, had not known what was in store for her. Widowed seven years later, still she saw the island as a sliver of hope, a place to land and start anew and where she could hack away at her dreams.

I'd never known that—the exhilaration of landing and arriving and a place of possibility and opportunity and hope. My experience was of the smoldering variety—living in adoration of an island that contained all my family history while still full of mystery. It was edgy and decrepit, but as essential and vital to me as it had been when I was a teenager.

But then my city changed. It became a rich person's game, a chessboard of real estate pieces that, once moved, reconfigured neighborhoods, stripped them of history and ethnicity, transfigured the island from a variegated city into something else. It made people move out to Brooklyn. It made them move to New Jersey. It made them move to California.

In the 1980s, the buildings transitioned as if under a spell, woken up from a hundred-year slumber: bank became chain store, office building became restaurant. Max's Kansas City, my haunt, became a Korean grocery. I moved to Brooklyn myself, switched zip codes and area codes, but it didn't change my city back when I set foot in its streets; it was under an enchantment, I was sure, and although I hoped it would one day be broken, I feared otherwise.

In Brooklyn, I met my husband. He lived on DeGraw; I lived on Henry Street. He was from Minnesota. I was writing a novel set in Minnesota. With wheat-hued hair and green eyes, he exuded Midwestern calm and kindness—very exotic. We lay on a plaid blanket in the Brooklyn Botanic Garden, underneath crooked boughs; creamy pink magnolia petals fluttered to the thawing earth. I felt

sleepy. He told me stories. He dreamed of living in a house, maybe in Vermont. He wanted to leave. So did I.

One year later, newly married, we loaded a van and drove seven hours north to Vermont to start a new life.

My grandmother was born in 1899 on Henry Street on the Lower East Side, the youngest of five; her four siblings were born in Russia and came over on the boat with her mother and father. Named Hazel but dubbed "Essie," she was six when her father died. She spoke of it often; it was the beginning of her devotion to labor. She retold the story as she folded and tucked hospital corners, as if that could bring order to my life as it was then. I was often between jobs. She and my grandfather had been neighbors in Harlem when it was a Jewish neighborhood; together, they made first aid kits during World War II, diversifying my grandfather's lingerie business. She was a hat model and seamstress, and when she died, I collected all evidence of what New York City had meant to her—labels, eye hooks, zippers, brocade frog clasps, spools of thread and bobbins, a business card with a name, *Hazel Kay*, a kind of pen name that I found mysterious, with an address in the Garment District where she'd gone to work. She was not beautiful, she told us, but she knew how to wear a hat. Her style became part of mine—1940s gabardine dresses and high-waisted pants, big buttons, elbow-length gloves, and suede pumps. She embodied 1940s glamour—the blowsy, capable sensibility of Carole Lombard combined with the dusky, velveteen sultriness of Myrna Loy. She favored silk, rhinestones, and mink. Her sister married a furrier; they had ridden the trolley car and the elevated train up over Manhattan. This train line would, one day, become the fashionable High Line, attracting tourists from around the world.

Irony was not lost on Hazel Kay. She knew that the city would keep changing, in ways she could neither comprehend nor prevent.

"This city's not the same," my grandmother cried, and moved into a deep place in her apartment; she also slipped on sidewalk ice and fell and refused to leave her building again. She didn't exit for eight and a half years, until she was buried in the Brooklyn cemetery. My cousin Jacqueline said, "Finally, Aunt Essie got out of her apartment."

I wanted more from my city; I had hoped it would be something else, not an end point but a starting point, but it felt as if the work my grandmother did for her son and that he, in turn, did for me and my sister is for this. So I could safely cross over and leave Manhattan and move up the Hudson and have my babies, just as once my great grandmother had to bring her brood over and build their roots in the city and up the river, in a new world. So that I might leave.

When I think about home, I remember riding the subway in silence, saved from unwanted conversation, or hailing a cab and confessing, revealing a weakness to the driver, protected behind the Plexiglas divider, extracting an unsolicited awareness from a stranger I might never see again.

Or maybe I would.

There is that ache of not having another place in the world where I might ever feel so alive and alone, invisible while visible, ever again. Alone in exactly the right kind of way.

My relationship to New York City—*home*—is and has always been about my relationship to yearning.

But this is what I understand about leaving New York: I have to leave, or I will never be able to restore my own capacity to write about home. I need to enter the land of longing, as if viewing my city through the tunnel underground at the 58th Street subway stop, as if through tunnels with curves, and tunnels of length, and up and down flights of stairs—stairs that appear to never end—in order to reach the stop where, finally, I can step out and regard, with deep reverence, that place that buried my grandmother and loved me enough so that I might, too, get on a boat and leave. On this boat, of the figurative variety.

Everything I long for in New York City is all still here; it is with me. Not in the apartments where we all were once but on a bench in the park, with the spring heat up around my ankles and the tulips in full gaudy pink display, that saucy arm around my waist—it's still here. I just have to leave in order to take it all with me, again.

I leave in order to preserve the past—so that I might remember it and recall it and use it. The stories my grandmother told—her stories became my stories, and then I added more—how I climbed the fence into Gramercy Park just because; how I lived in a six-floor walk-up across from a crack den during that shiny, dark era in the East Village; how I rode my bicycle uptown on Saturday mornings to Central Park and then back down, sometimes against traffic, and sold T-shirts at concerts in the park and then threw roof parties with pitchers of Bloody Marys; how I saved to make ends meet so I could land my own studio apartment on St. Mark's Place—a last-minute, illegal sublet from a waitress I met catering a wedding on the Hudson. Carried trays of shrimp skewers at film wrap parties, typed cover letters, shipped books, rode elevators in this building and that one, slid into subway cars just before the door closed. Pigeons cooed on my windowsill in the mornings on Avenue A. I can't tell all these stories, not yet. So I write them down, I bring my daughters in to show them my city, but they can't know what it once was. In Gramercy Park, my daughter runs to find the gold plaque on the bench honoring my now-deceased boyfriend; he died young, years after I left. I try to tell them what it was like, but they can only see it as it is now. This elaborate, layered, brimming metropolis. Metallic and leafy. Steam heat in every room. So that they can imagine, as I once did, when my grandmother would say "This city is not the same anymore" and start to tell me one of her tales.

MY MISSPENT YOUTH

MEGHAN DAUM

"My Misspent Youth" was first published in the October 18, 1999, issue of *The New Yorker*.

To read it fourteen years later is to look at a time capsule. There's talk of $18,000 salaries and $1,055 rents for one-bedroom apartments. Tuition at Columbia ran me $20,000 per year; today it's more than twice that much. The fresh-cut flowers I insisted on buying from the Korean grocer surely cost more now than the eight or ten dollars a week I shelled out back then. "My Misspent Youth" is a Manhattan-centric story; instead of experiencing Brooklyn as the center of the literary universe, I haunted the bars of the Lower East Side and coveted an apartment in a grand Edwardian building in Morningside Heights.

The essay had its share of detractors back in its day. Adjectives like "whiny," "entitled," and "shallow" were in heavy rotation. "Why can't you enjoy things like walking in the park, which is free?" an indignant caller asked me during an interview on WNYC. But its audience seems to have snuck up on it over time. Today, scarcely a week goes by that I do not hear from someone who, upon discovering it in the recesses of the Internet or in the 2001 book that bore its name, has felt it to be describing his or her own life, has recognized those foolish, delicious fantasies involving prewar apartments with chipping paint and clanking radiators and grieved alongside me for a version of New York—and, by extension, a version of adulthood, of being human, of being *alive*—that was discontinued long ago and may have, in fact, never been the commodity we like to crack it up to be.

The essay has made me into something of a reluctant advice lady. *Is an MFA worth it? Should I turn down the job in Indianapolis and go to New York? Will I regret it forever if I don't? Will I regret it forever if I do?* I nearly always say yes, *go*. I nearly always say buy your ticket and don't look back— at least not until it's time to look back. Because when you leave, chances are the thing you'll be looking back on for the rest of your life is New York. I have now been gone for more years than I was ever there. I have lived on the Midwestern prairies and in the Santa Monica Mountains. I have managed to get out of debt. I have a house, a car, and health insurance. I don't really know my way around Brooklyn. But, still, New York is the foundation. New York is the place I am from, even though I was never from there to begin with.

I got married (to a man who'd lived just blocks away from me in Manhattan, a man I wouldn't meet until we'd both logged thousands of miles hopping from place to place) in Central Park, near the entrance at West 86th Street. It was late October 2009, an unseasonably warm day that, now that I think of it, essentially marked the ten-year anniversary of my essay's appearance in *The New Yorker*. The sky, a cloudless and almost cartoonish shade of blue, had loosened itself from a night of thunderstorms and held us in the kind of enormous, intoxicating embrace you can only get from a perfect New York day. The gargoyles

and cornices of the buildings of Central Park West looked down on us like wise and crotchety angels. The people on the street cheered us and ignored us in equal measure. Life wasn't solved or certain or even especially stable. But it was financially sound for the moment. Things were as grown-up as they were probably ever going to get. I carried fresh-cut flowers from the Korean market. Whatever they cost, they were worth it.

18 OCTOBER 1999

Earlier this summer I was walking down West End Avenue in Manhattan and remembered, with a sadness that nearly knocked me off my feet, just why I came to New York seven years ago and just why I am now about to leave. Certain kinds of buildings seem almost too gorgeous to belong to the actual world, or at least the present-day world. Given the aluminum siding and brickface that proliferates throughout most of the United States, I'm always amazed that massive, ornate residences like 838 West End Avenue, with its yellow façade and black hieroglyphics, or 310 Riverside Drive, with its gargoyles and cornices, are still standing and receiving mail delivery and depositing kids in and out of the front doors like pretty much any domicile anywhere. When I was growing up in northern New Jersey, just twenty-five miles away from Manhattan, I had no concept that actual people could live in such places. My first inkling came when I was seventeen. I walked into an apartment on the Upper West Side of Manhattan and decided, within two minutes, what the controlling force of my life would be.

It was the summer of 1987, and I was in the process of learning how to drive a stick shift. My father is a composer and he allowed me to drive him to Manhattan in our Plymouth Horizon in order to drop off some lead sheets to a music copyist he worked with. The

music copyist lived on West End Avenue and 104th Street, in a modest four-room apartment in a 1920s-era building. The moment the rickety elevator lurched onto the sixth floor and the copyist opened the door, life for me was never the same.

There was nothing particularly fancy about the place. It was a standard prewar with moldings around the ceilings and, most likely, porcelain hexagonal bathroom tiles that were coming loose. Although I'm not sure if there were faded Persian rugs on the floors and NPR humming from the speakers, it was just the sort of place for that. The music copyist and his wife had lived there for almost twenty years and although rent was the furthest thing from my mind at the time, I can now surmise, based on what they probably earned, that the apartment was rent controlled, perhaps $300 per month. It's now difficult to imagine a time when I didn't walk into someone's apartment and immediately start the income-to-rent ratio calculations. But on that summer night, standing in the living room of this apartment, looking down on the streets whose voluptuous, stony buildings formed the shore to the river that so famously keeps here safely away from there, my life was changed forever. I mean no melodrama in this. From that moment on, everything I did, every decision I made, every college applied to or not applied to, every job taken or not taken, was based on an unwavering determination to live in a prewar, oak-floored apartment, on or at least in the immediate vicinity of 104th Street and West End Avenue.

I've always been somebody who exerts a great deal of energy trying to get my realities to match my fantasies, even if the fantasies are made from materials that are no longer manufactured, even if some governmental agency has assessed my aspirations and pronounced them a health hazard. Lately, my New York fantasy has proven a little too retro for my own good. Though I did come to New York immediately after college and lived, believe it or not, within four blocks of 104th Street and West End Avenue, it wasn't until recently that I began to realize that I wasn't having quite as good a time here as I once did. I say this as someone who has had a very, very good

time in New York. I say this also as someone who has enjoyed a good deal of professional success here, particularly considering that I am young and committed to a field that is notoriously low paying and unsteady. But low pay and unsteadiness never really bothered me all that much. I've historically been pretty good at getting by on what I have, especially if you apply the increasingly common definition of "getting by," which has more to do with keeping up appearances than keeping things under control. Like a social smoker whose supposedly endearing desire to emulate Marlene Dietrich has landed her in a cancer ward, I have recently woken up to the frightening fallout of my own romantic notions of life in the big city: I am completely over my head in debt. I have not made a life for myself in New York City. I have purchased a life for myself.

As I write this, I owe $7,791 to my Visa card. To be fair (to whom? Myself? Does fairness even come into play when one is trying to live a dream life?), much of those charges are from medical expenses, particularly bills from a series of dental procedures I needed last year. As a freelance person, I'm responsible for buying my own health insurance, which is $300 per month for basic coverage in New York State. That's far more than I can afford, so I don't have any. Although I try to pay the $339 per quarter charge to keep a hospitalization insurance policy that will cover me if some major disaster befalls, I am often late in paying it and it gets canceled. But lest this begin to sound like a rant about health care, I will say that medical expenses represent only a fraction of my troubles. I need to make an estimated quarterly tax payment next month of $5,400, which is going to be tough because I just recently paid back $3,000 to my boyfriend (now ex) who lent me money to pay last year's taxes, and I still owe $300 to the accountant who prepared the return. My checking account is overdrawn by $1,784. I have no savings, no investments, no pension fund, and no inheritance on the horizon. I have student loans from graduate school amounting to $60,000. I pay $448.83 per month on these loans, installments which cover less than the interest that's accruing on the loan; despite my

payments, the $60,000 debt seems to actually be growing with each passing month.

It's tempting to go into a litany of all the things on which I do not spend money. I have no dependents, not even a cat or a fish. I do not have a car. I've owned the same four pairs of shoes for the past three years. Much of the clothing in my closet has been there since the early 1990s, the rare additions usually taking the form of a $16 shirt from Old Navy, a discounted dress from Loehmann's, or a Christmas sweater from my mother. At twenty-nine, it's only been for the last two years that I've lived without roommates. My rent, $1,055 a month for a four-hundred-square-foot apartment, is, as we say in New York City when describing the Holy Grail, below market. I do not own expensive stereo equipment, and even though I own a television I cannot bring myself to spend the $30 a month on cable, which, curiously, I've deemed an indulgence. With one exception, I have not spent money on overseas travel. All of this is true, just as it is true to say that there have been times when I haven't hesitated to buy things for my home—some rugs, a fax machine, a $200 antique lamp. There are even more times—every week, for instance—that I don't hesitate to spend money in a social capacity, $45 on dinner, $20 on drinks. I make long-distance phone calls almost daily with no thought to peak calling hours or dime-a-minute rates. I have a compulsive need to have fresh-cut flowers in my apartment at all times, and I'll spend eight or ten dollars once or twice a week at the Korean market to keep that routine going. This behavior may be careless, but it is also somewhat beside the point. In the grand scheme of things, the consumer items themselves do not factor heavily; it's easier to feel guilt over spending $60 on a blender, as I did last month, than to examine the more elaborate reasons why I reached a point where I found it impossible to live within my means.

Once you're in this kind of debt, and by "kind" I'm talking less about numbers than about something having to do with form, with the brand of the debt, all those bills start not to matter anymore. If I allowed them to matter I would become so panicked that I wouldn't

be able to work, which would only set me back further. I've also noticed that my kind of debt takes a form that many people find easier to swallow than, say, the kind of debt that reflects overt recklessness. I spent money on my education and my career. These are broad categories. There's room here for copious rationalizations and I'll make full use of them. I live in the most expensive city in the country because I have long believed, and had many people convinced, that my career was dependent upon it. I spend money on martinis and expensive dinners because, as is typical among my species of debtor, I tell myself that martinis and expensive dinners are the entire point—the point of being young, the point of living in New York City, the point of living. In this mind-set, the dollars spent, like the mechanics of a machine no one bothers to understand, become an abstraction, an intangible avenue toward self-expression, a mere vehicle of style.

I grew up in the kind of town that probably comes as close to defining a generalized notion of the American Dream as any. It's an affluent, New Jersey suburb whose main draw is its good public school system. As in many well-to-do suburbs, if you're not in need of K–12 services, there's not much in it for you, and so virtually no one between the ages of eighteen and thirty-five can afford or has reason to live there. The result is that the teenager is king. He sets the cultural and intellectual standard for the community. Moreover, he does so without the benefit of any adult influence other than his parents.

As I try to sort out the origins of my present financial situation, I always come back to the feelings I had as a teenager in the suburbs and the ineffable hankering I felt to access some kind of earthier, more "intellectual" lifestyle. When I was growing up in the 1980s, the cultural hegemony of my world was mired in a 1950s sensibility that came directly out of the parents' nostalgia about their youths. I went to parties in junior high school where we actually danced to *The Big Chill* soundtrack. Kids wore Bermuda shorts and seersucker shirts. Unlike the self-conscious vibe of the world I entered later in college, there was nothing ironic in any of this. We knew no one older than ourselves or younger than our parents—no college or graduate students, no single professionals, barely anyone who worked outside of a corporate structure. Therefore the teen agenda looked a lot like the parental agenda, which was, even though it was the late 1980s, pretty much an Eisenhower-era paradigm: college, work, marriage, return to suburbs. As adolescents we were, for better or worse, the staple crop and chief export of the place. Realtors have been known to drive prospective home buyers throughout the town and point out houses in which kids have gone to Ivy League colleges.

My family was in a unique situation because we lived off of my father's income as a freelance composer. Although I never had the sense that we were poor, I now realize that we must have, at certain times anyway, come pretty close to it. The main reason I never felt poor was that my parents, who had experienced their own kind of lifestyle epiphany when they were first exposed to academic settings, had an aesthetic value system that was less a reflection of having or not having money than with, in our opinion anyway, good taste. Unlike the neighbors, who had expensive wall-to-wall carpet and furniture sets from Seaman's, we had wood floors and oriental rugs, and I grew up believing that we were superior because of it. Even when I got older and began to run into my financial problems, I never had a conscious desire for a lot of money. I was never interested in being rich. I just wanted to live in a place with oak floors.

In what emerged as the major misconception of the subsequent twelve years, I somehow got the idea that oak floors were located exclusively in New York City. This came chiefly from watching Woody Allen movies. I wanted to live someplace that looked like Mia Farrow's apartment in *Hannah and Her Sisters* (little did I know that it was Mia Farrow's apartment). To me, this kind of space did not connote wealth. These were places where the paint was peeling and the rugs were frayed, places where smart people sat around drinking gin and tonics, having interesting conversations, and living, according to my logic, in an authentic way. As far as I was aware at seventeen, rich was something else entirely. Rich meant monstrous Tudor-style houses in the ritzy section of my town. Rich were the handful of kids who drove BMWs to school. I had the distinct feeling that my orthodontist, whose sprawling ranch house had front steps that were polished in such a way that they looked like they were made of ice, was rich. None of these particular trappings of wealth held my attention. In fact, nothing outside of the movies really held my attention until that night in 1987 when I saw the apartment on 104th Street.

How different the ride down that clanking elevator was from the ride up! Like a lover to whom you suddenly turn one morning and feel nothing but loathing, my relationship to my suburban town went, in the time it took that elevator to descend six floors, from indifference to abhorrence. With all the drama and preciousness of a seventeen-year-old girl, I now realized the pathetic smallness of my world. I now saw the suburbs, as I announced to my father, "for what they really are." The suburb/city alliance was, in my opinion, an unequal partnership between parasite and host, a dynamic permanently tainted by a sense that although the suburbs cannot live without the city, the city would hardly notice if the suburbs were all spontaneously irradiated by a tyrannical dictator of a distant star system.

Worst of all, the suburbs were a place from which escape held little romance. Unlike the kid from the small midwestern or southern town who saves up for bus money to come to the big town, the suburban New Jersey teenager who sits in her bedroom, listening to 1980s Suzanne Vega records and longing for some life that is being vaguely described in the songs—"my name is Luka, I live on the second floor" (could this be on 104th Street?)—doesn't elicit much sympathy. But I persevered, planning my escape through the standard channels: college selection. I'd seen the music copyist's apartment during the summer between my junior and senior years of high school and so applying to college that fall became a matter of picturing the apartment and wondering what kind of college an inhabitant of such an apartment would have attended.

My logic, informed by a combination of college guidebooks and the alma maters of those featured in the *New York Times* wedding announcements, went something like this: Bryn Mawr rather than Gettysburg, Columbia rather than N.Y.U., Wisconsin rather than Texas, Yale rather than Harvard, Vassar rather than Smith. My ranking system had nothing to do with the academic merits of the schools. It was more a game of degrees of separation from Upper West Side house plants and intellectualism. Somehow, Vassar emerged as the most direct route. After all, Meryl Streep, a girl from suburban New Jersey, had gone there (and later played Woody Allen's ex-wife in Manhattan), as well as the Apthorp-dwelling Rachel Samstadt in *Heartburn,* a character based on Nora Ephron, a personal role model of mine, not to mention a real life resident of the Apthorp. I also had some vague notions about getting myself into a position where I could become a writer, and this had something to do with being "artsy." So in a manner particular to restless suburban girls who consider themselves "different" and "unconventional" in much the same way that protagonists in young adult novels are portrayed, I was so consumed with going to a particular kind of artsy college and mixing with a particular kind of artsy crowd that I could do nothing during my entire senior year of high school but throw wads of paper into a wastebasket from across the room and say "If I make this shot, I get into Vassar."

I made the shot. I went to Vassar. It was either the best move of my life or the biggest mistake. I'm still not sure which. Though it would be five years until I entered my debt era, my years at Vassar did more than expand my intellect. They expanded my sense of entitlement so much that, by the end, I had no ability to separate myself from the many extremely wealthy people I encountered there. For the record, let me say that a large part of that sense of entitlement has been a very good thing for me. Self-entitlement is a quality that has gotten a bad name for itself and yet, in my opinion, it's one of the best things a student can get out of an education. Much of my success and happiness is a direct result of it. But self-entitlement has also contributed to my downfall, mostly because of my inability to recognize where ambition and chutzpah end and cold, hard cash

begins. Like the naïve teenager who thought Mia Farrow's apartment represented the urban version of middle-class digs, I continued to believe throughout college that it wasn't fabulous wealth I was aspiring to, merely hipness.

Though there were lots of different kinds of kids at Vassar, I immediately found the ones who had grown up in Manhattan, and I learned most of what I felt I needed to know by socializing with them. In this way, my education was primarily about becoming fully versed in a certain set of references that, individually, have very little to do with either a canon of knowledge as defined by academia or preparation for the job market. My education had mostly to do with speaking the language of the culturally sophisticated, with having a mastery over a number of points of cultural trivia ranging from the techniques of Caravaggio to the discography of The Velvet Underground. This meant being privy to the kind of information that is only learned from hours spent hanging out with friends in dorm rooms and is therefore unavailable to those buried in the library trying to keep their scholarships or working at Stereo World trying to pay the bills. It is to have heard rumors that Domino's Pizza has ties to the pro-life movement, that Bob Dylan's mother invented White-Out and that Jamie Lee Curtis is a hermaphrodite. It is to never wear nude panty hose, never smoke menthol cigarettes, never refer to female friends as "girlfriends," and never listen to Billy Joel in earnest. It is to know at least two people featured in the *New York Times* wedding pages on any given Sunday and to think nothing of putting $80 towards a bridal shower dinner at a chic restaurant for one of these people. It is to know that anyone who uses the word "chic" is anything but. It is to know arugula from iceberg lettuce, Calder from Klimt, Truffaut from Cassavetes. It is to be secure in one's ability to grasp these comparisons and weigh one against the other within a fraction of a second, to know, as my Jewish Manhattanite friends put it, "from stuff"—to know from real estate, from contemporary fiction, from clothing designers and editors of glossy magazines and Shakespearean tragedies and skirt lengths. Name-dropping was my drug

of choice and I inhaled the stuff. By the time graduation came, I'd earned a degree in English, but that seemed incidental to my stellar achievements in the field of "from stuff."

I still wanted to be a writer. And with my ever-evolving sense of entitlement, that seemed more possible than ever. When I graduated in 1992, I followed a herd of my classmates into Manhattan, many of whom moved back in with their parents on Park Avenue. I got myself an entry-level job in publishing, and, along with a couple of friends, rented a five-room, prewar apartment with chipping paint on 100th Street and Riverside Drive, a mere four blocks from the scene of my 1987 epiphany. I was ecstatic. Such expert marksmanship! Such rich rewards for thorough research and careful planning. My job, as an editorial assistant at a glossy fashion magazine, paid $18,000 a year. The woman who hired me, herself a 1950s-era Vassar gradu- ate, told me that she hoped I had an independent source of income, as I surely wouldn't be able to support myself on my salary. But I did support myself. My roommates, an elementary school teacher who was making $19,000 a year and a film student who worked part-time at a non-profit arts organization, supported themselves too. We each paid around $550 per month and lived as recent graduates should, eating ramen noodles and $.99 White Rose macaroni and cheese.

Looking back, I see those years as a cheap, happy time. It was a time at which a certain kind of poverty was appropriate; anything ritzier would have been embarrassing. Our neighborhood was a place for people who knew the city, for people from the city. Unlike the west seventies and eighties, which I've always experienced as slightly ephemeral, mall-like and populated by those who've come from elsewhere, the residents of this neighborhood seem to give off a feeling of being very deeply rooted into the ground. It's also a place that has absolutely no investment in fashion. No matter what the decade, there's an odd 1970s quality to the neighborhood. It's a place where you can still find people wearing corduroy blazers, a place that has always made me think of both the television show *Taxi* and the cover of Carole King's *Tapestry* album. Though I was living completely hand-to-mouth, I loved my neighborhood and looked forward to moving ahead in my career and one day being able to afford my own place in roughly an eight-block radius. From my position at the time, that seemed well within the range of feasibility. It was 1993, I was twenty-three, and I'd received a raise so that I was earning $21,000. I had no idea it was the closest I'd be to financial solvency for at least the next decade.

I'd been told I was lucky to get a job at a magazine—I had, after all, graduated into what was being called the worst job market in twenty years—and even though I had little interest in its subject matter, I didn't dare turn down the position. Within my first week on the job, I found myself immersed in a culture that was concerned entirely with money and celebrity. Socialites sat on the editorial board in order to give input on trends among the extremely wealthy. Editorial assistants who earned $18,000 managed to wear Prada, rent time-shares in the Hamptons, have regular facials, and pay thousands of dollars a year for gym memberships and personal trainers. Many of them lived in doorman buildings in the West Village or Upper East Side, for which their parents helped foot the bill.

This wasn't my scene. I felt as far away from my *Hannah and Her Sisters* fantasy as I had in the suburbs. I didn't want to be rich. I just wanted to live in New York and be a writer. Moreover, I wanted to be a writer in New York immediately. After a year of office work, I decided that an M.F.A. program in creative writing would provide the most direct route to literary legitimacy. I applied to exactly one program, Columbia, which, not coincidentally, happened to be located in my neighborhood. It's also the most expensive writing program in the country, a fact I ignored because the students, for the most part, seemed so down-to-earth and modest. Unlike my Prada-wearing, Hamptons-going colleagues from the magazine,

Columbia students, in their flannel shirts and roach-infested student housing, seemed as earnest and unrich as I was, and I figured that if they could take out $20,000-a-year loans, so could I. Even as I stayed at Columbia for three years and borrowed more than $60,000 to get my degree, I was told repeatedly, by fellow students, faculty, administrators, and professional writers whose careers I wished to emulate, not to think about the loans. Student loans, after all, were low interest, long term, and far more benign than credit-card debt. Not thinking about them was a skill I quickly developed.

If there is a line of demarcation in this story, a single moment where I crossed the boundary between debtlessness and total financial mayhem, it's the first dollar that I put toward achieving a life that had less to do with overt wealth than with what I perceived as intellectual New York bohemianism. It seems laughable now, but at the time I thought I was taking a step down from the Chanel suits and Manolo Blahniks of my office job. Hanging out at the Cuban coffee shop and traipsing over the syringes and windblown trash of upper Broadway, I was under the impression that I was, in a certain way, slumming. And even though I was having a great time and becoming a better writer, the truth was that the year I entered graduate school was the year I stopped making decisions that were appropriate for my situation and began making a rich person's decisions. Entering this particular graduate program was a rich person's decision. But it's hard to recognize that you're acting like a rich person when you're becoming increasingly poor. Besides, I was never without a job. I worked for an anthropology professor for $9 an hour. I read manuscripts at $10 a pop for a quack literary agent. I worked at a university press for $10 an hour. Sometimes I called in sick to these jobs and did temp work in midtown offices for $17 an hour. A couple of times I took out cash advances on my credit cards to pay the rent.

There were a handful of us who were pulling these kinds of stunts. My roommate had maxed out her credit cards in order to finance a student film. I knew several women and even a few men who were actively looking for rich marriage partners to bail them

out of their debt. One aspiring novelist I know underwent a series of drug treatments and uncomfortable surgical procedures in order to sell her eggs for $2,500. A couple of promising writers dropped out of the program and left the city. These days, when I talk to the people who left, they give off the sense of having averted a car crash but by the same token, they wonder if they'd be farther along in their careers had they stuck it out. But this question of sticking it out has less to do with M.F.A. programs than with the city in general. Whether or not one is paying $20,000 a year to try to make it as a writer, New York City has become a prohibitively expensive place to live for just about anyone. Although I've devoted a lot of energy to being envious of Columbia classmates whose relatives were picking up the tab for their educations, it's now becoming clear to me that assuming the presence of a personal underwriter is not limited to entry-level jobs at glossy magazines or expensive graduate programs. These days, being a creative person in New York is, in many cases, contingent upon inheriting the means to do it.

But the striver in me never flinched. As I was finishing at Columbia, my writing career was giving off signs that it might actually go somewhere. If I hadn't been doing so well I might have pulled out of the game. I would have gotten a job, started paying my bills, and averted my own impending car crash. Instead, I continued to hedge my bets. I was publishing magazine articles regularly and, after a few months of temping at insurance companies and banks, scored some steady writing gigs that, to my delight, allowed me to work as a full-time freelance writer. After five years and eight different roommates in the 100th Street apartment, I was earning enough money to move to my own place and, more importantly, had garnered enough contacts with established Manhattanites to find myself a two-year sublet in a rent-stabilized apartment. The fact that I got this sublet through a connection from a Columbia professor has always struck me as justification enough for the money I spent to go to school; as we all know by now, the value of a rent-stabilized one-bedroom is equal to if not greater than that of a master's degree or even the sale of a manuscript to a publisher. And though I still had not hit the literary jackpot by producing the best-seller that would pay off my loans and buy me some permanent housing, I still felt I'd come out ahead in the deal.

So it's not that I was sold a complete bill of goods. Things were going well. In 1997 I was twenty-seven, teaching a writing course at N.Y.U., publishing in a variety of national magazines, and earning about $40,000 a year after taxes. (The teaching job, incidentally, paid a paltry $2,500 for an entire semester but I was too enamored with the idea of being a college teacher to wonder if I could afford to take it.) Neither clueless suburbanite nor corporate, subsidized yuppie, I could finally begin practicing the life I'd spent so long studying for. I had a decent-sized apartment with oak floors and porcelain hexagonal bathroom tiles that were coming loose. Like an honest New Yorker, I even had mice lurking in the kitchen. I bought the rugs and the fax machine. I installed a second telephone line for fax/data purposes.

Soon, however, I had some hefty dental bills that I was forced to charge to Visa. I tried not to think about that too much until I ended up making a few doctor's visits that, being uninsured, I also charged to Visa. When April rolled around, I realized my income was significantly higher that year than any previous year and that I had woefully underestimated what I owed the IRS. Despite a bevy of the typical freelancer's write-offs—haircuts, contact lenses, an $89.99 sonic rodent control device—I was hit with a tax bill of over $20,000. And although the IRS apparently deemed sonic rodent control devices an acceptable deduction, it seemed that I'd earned too much money to be eligible to write off the nearly $7,000 (most of it interest) I'd paid to the student loan agency or the $3,000 in dental bills. Most heartbreaking of all, my accountant proffered some reason that my $60 pledge to WNYC—my Upper West Side tableau couldn't possibly be complete without the NPR coffee mug—was not tax deductible as advertised. In the months it took me to assemble that $20,000 I had to reduce my monthly student loan payments from the suggested

$800 per month to the aforementioned $448.83 per month, a reduction that effectively ensured that I wouldn't touch the principal for years. I continued to pay my $1,055 per month rent, and made every effort to pay the phone, gas, and electric bills, the American Express bills, and the hospitalization-only medical coverage.

It was around this time that I started having trouble thinking about anything other than how to make a payment on whatever bill was sitting on my desk, most likely weeks overdue, at any given time. I started getting collection calls from Visa, final disconnection notices from the phone company, letters from the gas company saying "Have you forgotten us?" I noticed that I was drinking more than I had in the past, often alone at home where I would sip Sauvignon Blanc at my desk and pretend to write when in fact I'd be working out some kind of desperate math equation on the toolbar calculator, making wild guesses as to when I'd receive some random $800 check from some unreliable accounting department of some slow-paying publication, how long it would take the money to clear into my account, what would be left after I set aside a third of it for taxes and, finally, which lucky creditor would be the recipient of the cash award. There's nothing like completing one of these calculations, realizing that you've drunk half a bottle of $7.99 wine, and feeling more guilt about having spent $7.99 than the fact that you're now too tipsy to work. One night I did a whole bunch of calculations and realized that despite having earned a taxable income of $59,000 in 1998, despite having not gone overboard on classic debtor's paraphernalia like clothes and vacations and stereo equipment, despite having followed the urban striver's guide to success, I was more than $75,000 in the hole.

There are days when my debt seems to be at the center of my being, a cancer that must be treated with the morphine of excuses and rationales and promises to myself that I'm going to come up with the big score—book advance, screenplay deal, Publishers Clearing House prize—and save myself. There are other days when the debt feels like someone else's cancer, a tragedy outside of myself, a con-

demned building next door that I try to avoid walking past. I suppose
that's why I'm even able to publicly disclose this information. For me,
money has always, truly, been "only money," a petty concern of the
shallower classes, a fatuous substitute for more important things like
fresh flowers and "meaningful conversations" in the living room. But
the days when I can ignore the whole matter are growing further and
further apart. My rent-stabilized sublet is about to expire, and I now
must find somewhere else to live. I have friends getting rich off the
stock market and buying million-dollar houses. I have other friends
who are almost as bad off as I am and who compulsively volunteer
for relief work in Third World countries as a way of forgetting that
they can't quite afford to live in the first world.

But New York City, which has a way of making you feel like
you're in the Third World just seconds after you've thought you conquered all of western civilization, has never really been part of the
rest of the world. In that sense, I suppose it's foolish to believe that
one can seek one's fortune, or at least one's sustenance, through
rational means. I suppose that part of the city's magical beastli-
ness is the fact that you can show up with the best of intentions, do
what's considered to be all the right things, actually achieve some
measure of success and still find yourself caught inside a financial
emergency.

I have to be out of my sublet by September 1. Even if I tried to
assume control of the lease, the landlord will renovate the apartment
and raise the rent to $2,000. I told a friend about this the other day,
hoping she would gasp or give me some sort of reaction. Instead
she said, "That's cheaper than our place." A two-bedroom apartment
down the street rented for $4,500 a month. A studio anywhere in
Manhattan or the "desirable" parts of Brooklyn will go for an
average of $1,750. West 104th Street is totally beyond my means.
Worse, 104th Street is now beyond the means of most of the people
that made me want to live there in the first place. The New York that
changed my life on that summer night when I was seventeen simply
no longer exists.

Now, having taken all of this apart, I am determined to not put it back together the same way. Several months ago, on a day when the debt anxiety had flared up even more than usual, I arrived at the idea of moving to Lincoln, Nebraska. I'd been to Lincoln on a magazine assignment twice before, met some nice people, and found myself liking it enough to entertain the notion of moving there. But both times I'd discarded the idea of moving there the minute the wheels hit the tarmac at LaGuardia. Surely I'd never be able to live without twenty-four-hour take-out food and glitzy Russian martini bars. On this latest round of panic, however, I chewed on the idea for a while, decided that it was a good plan, and have pretty much continued to feel that way ever since. I can rent an apartment there for $300 a month. I can rent an entire house, if I want one, for $700. Full coverage health insurance will cost me $66 a month. Apparently, people in Nebraska also listen to NPR, and there are even places to live in Lincoln that have oak floors. Had I known that before, I might have skipped out on this New York thing altogether and spared myself the financial and psychological ordeal. But I'm kind of glad I didn't know because I'm someone who has had a very, very good time here. I'm just leaving the party before the cops break it up.

MINNESOTA NICE

CHERYL STRAYED

I saw a man get stabbed on a sunny afternoon in the West Village on my twenty-fourth birthday. He didn't die. He didn't even call out for help. He just cursed the man who'd attacked him in a language I could neither understand nor identify while clutching the place on his thigh where the knife had entered it, his palms smeared with blood. I was sitting alone at a little wooden table on the sidewalk across the street, drinking coffee and eating a slice of cake in the warm September sun.

"Someone just stabbed that man," I said loudly to the waiter, who emerged from the café doors moments after the attack.

He turned to glance at him. The injured man remained in the spot where he'd been stabbed, across the narrow street from us on the edge of a small park I didn't know the name of. He'd run there in the moments before the assault, attempting to shield himself with a metal bike rack. In a last-ditch effort he'd tried to lift the entire impossible apparatus, hoping to topple it onto his assailant. He'd hoisted it perhaps two feet before it crashed back onto the pavement with a frightful clatter. In the next instant the knife was in his leg. In spite of the assailant's force, his delivery was almost delicate, the deed done in one elegant jab, as if he were popping a balloon. Then, without a sound, he ran, knife in hand.

That's when the victim cried out in the language I didn't understand and the waiter came outside.

"I wouldn't worry about it," he said to me now, languidly refilling my coffee cup from the pot he carried.

"You wouldn't?" I asked.

Of all the things to worry about, it seemed a man getting stabbed a dozen yards away would be the thing. And yet, how strange it was that it appeared I was the only one who was alarmed—there'd been other witnesses to the stabbing, the dozen or so people who'd been walking along the sidewalk when the clamor began. Some had paused to watch, others had crossed the street to avoid it, but they'd all continued on their way once it was over.

"Hey!" I hollered to the injured man after the waiter went back inside the café. "Do you need help?"

He looked in my direction and shook his head vaguely, then rambled away in a limping fashion as if I'd chased him off, his jeans bloody and torn where he'd been wounded.

I'd been living in New York City for little more than a month by then. I was renting an apartment on Seventh Avenue in Park Slope with the man who was then my husband and waitressing at a place ten blocks away. It was 1992, a time when unknown writers who were married to even more unknown musicians and paid the bills waiting tables could still afford to rent an apartment on Seventh Avenue in Park Slope. On my days off I roved the city like a gleeful tourist, feeling important simply to be there. I went to the tops of the Empire State Building and the Statue of Liberty. I wandered Central Park and the Brooklyn Botanic Garden. I waited in line for nosebleed tickets to the opera and off-Broadway plays. I visited MOMA and the Whitney and the Met. I poked around the East Village and Soho. I hung out at the Strand and CBGBs and strolled meaningfully past the Chelsea Hotel thinking of all the glorious and fucked-up people who'd stayed there.

I am in New York City! I couldn't help but exclaim silently in my head every now and then, country bumpkin from Minnesota that I was. I couldn't keep myself from thinking everything in New York was superior to every other place I'd ever been, which hadn't been all that many places. I was stunned by New York. Its grand parks and museums. Its cozy cobbled streets and dazzlingly bright thoroughfares. Its alternately efficient and appalling subway system. Its endlessly gorgeous women clad in slim pants and killer shoes and interesting coats.

And yet something happened on my way to falling head over heels in love with the place. Maybe it was the man getting stabbed that no one worried about. Or maybe it was bigger than that. The abruptness, the gruffness, the avoid-eye-contact indifference of the crowded subways and streets felt as foreign to me as Japan or Cameroon, as alien to me as Mars. Even the couple who owned the bodega below our apartment greeted my husband and me each day as if we were complete strangers, which is to say they didn't greet us at all, no matter how many times we came in to buy toilet paper or soup, cat food or pasta. They merely took our money and returned our change with gestures so automatic and faces so expressionless they might as well have been robots.

"Do they really not *recognize* us?" I asked my husband on a regular basis, both of us mildly outraged by this tiny thing that grew to feel like the greatest New York City crime of all, to be denied the universal silent acknowledgment of familiarity, the faintest smile, the hint of a nod.

Maybe it was the way my customers at the place where I waited tables always knew I wasn't from there because I was "too nice"— "Minnesota Nice," one group of regulars had nicknamed me—much as I attempted to seem like a harder, cooler, more dazzling thing: a New Yorker.

In the end, I had to realize it was never meant to be. It wasn't New York. It was me..I'd entered the city the way one enters any grand love affair: with no exit plan. I went willing to live there forever,

to become one of the women clad in slim pants and killer shoes and interesting coats. I was ready for the city to sweep me into its arms, but instead it held me at a cool distance. And so I left New York the way one leaves a love affair too: because, much as I loved it, I wasn't truly in love. I had no compelling reason to stay.

On a cold afternoon in February, my husband and I loaded our things into a pickup truck that was double-parked on the street on Seventh Avenue, each of us taking turns alternately guarding the truck from would-be thieves and going up and down the stairs with boxes. Past dark, our work done hours later than we'd hoped, we got into the cab with our two cats in their kennels squeezed between us. Just as my husband started the engine, there was a loud rapping on the window a few inches from my head. I turned with a start and saw the man who owned the bodega. The one who'd never once shown us a glimmer of recognition. He was beaming now and holding a bag of tangerines. I stared at him for a moment, startled and uncertain, until he made a motion with his hand for me to roll down the window and I did.

"For you," he said and handed me the tangerines. "Good luck."

ABOUT THE CONTRIBUTORS

ELISA ALBERT ("Currency") is the author of *The Book of Dahlia* and *How This Night Is Different*, and the editor of the anthology *Freud's Blind Spot*. Her fiction and nonfiction have appeared in *Commentary*, *Tin House*, *Salon*, *Gulf Coast*, *Washington Square*, *Five Chapters*, *Post Road*, and on NPR. Her novel, *After Birth,* will be published by Houghton Mifflin Harcourt in Fall 2014.

KAREN E. BENDER ("The Lion, the Pig, and the Wolf and Other Thoughts About New York") is the author of the novels *A Town of Empty Rooms* and *Like Normal People.* Her short fiction has appeared in magazines, including *The New Yorker*, *Granta*, *Zoetrope*, *Ploughshares*, *Story*, *Narrative*, and *The Harvard Review;* has been reprinted in *Best American Short Stories*, *Best American Mystery Stories,* and *New Stories from the South: The Year's Best;* and has won two Pushcart Prizes. Her story collection, *Refund*, is forthcoming. Visit her at karenbender.com.

CHLOE CALDWELL ("Leaving My Groovy Lifestyle") is the author of the essay collection *Legs Get Led Astray* (Future Tense Books). Her nonfiction has appeared in *Salon*, *Nylon*, *The Rumpus*, *The Sun*, *Thought Catalog*, and more. She lives in Portland, Oregon.

EMILY CARTER ROIPHE ("Transport") is a freelance writer and cultural critic currently living in New Haven. In 2008 she returned to the Northeast after twenty years in the Twin Cities. Her work has been included in *Best American Short Stories* and won a National Magazine Award. She has appeared on the cover of *Poz Magazine* and the *Minneapolis City Pages*. Her 2001 novel *Glory Goes and Gets Some* received a Whiting Foundation award. She currently does cultural criticism for the *Minneapolis Star Tribune* and is pondering adding another brick to the Tower of Babble by reading her reviews aloud on YouTube.

RUTH CURRY ("Out of Season") lives in Brooklyn and is the co-founder of Emily Books.

MEGHAN DAUM ("My Misspent Youth") has been an opinion columnist at *The Los Angeles Times* since 2005. She has written for numerous publications, including *The New Yorker*, *Harper's*, and *Vogue*, and is the author of three books: the essay collection *My Misspent Youth*, the novel *The Quality of Life Report*, and the memoir *Life Would Be Perfect If I Lived in That House*. She lives in Los Angeles with her husband and sheepdog.

MARCY DERMANSKY ("Maybe I Loved You") is the author of the critically acclaimed novels *Bad Marie* and *Twins*. Marcy's short fiction has been published widely in literary journals and anthologies, including *Salon*, *Five Chapters*, and *McSweeney's*. Find out more about Marcy at her website, marcydermansky.com, or follow her on Twitter at @mdermansky.

VALERIE EAGLE ("View from the Penthouse") is an actress and writer living in Kingston, New York. She writes and performs monologues about her many years as a homeless crack addict and prostitute in New York City, her diagnosis as HIV-positive while in jail, and her four and a half years in recovery. At fifty-one, Valerie is a full-time student at Ulster Community College. She is working on a book and a one-woman show.

HOPE EDELMAN ("You Are Here") is the author of six nonfiction books, including the bestsellers *Motherless Daughters, Motherless Mothers*, and *The Possibility of Everything*. Her essays and articles have appeared in numerous magazines and newspapers, including *The New York Times*, *The Los Angeles Times*, the *Chicago Tribune*, *Glamour, Self, Real Simple, Writer's Digest, The Huffington Post,* and *Parade*. She lives in Topanga Canyon, California, with her husband and two daughters and teaches in the MFA program at Antioch University–Los Angeles.

LAUREN ELKIN ("Losing New York") is the author of *Une Année à Venise* (Editions Héloïse d'Ormesson) and coauthor of *The End of Oulipo? An Attempt to Exhaust a Movement*. She lives in Paris and London.

MAGGIE ESTEP ("Think of This as a Window") has published seven books and recorded two spoken-word CDs. Her work has been translated into four languages, optioned for film, and frequently stolen from libraries. She lives in Hudson, New York, with her partner and two rescued pit bulls.

MELISSA FEBOS ("Home") is the author of the memoir *Whip Smart* (St. Martin's Press, 2010). Her work has been widely anthologized and appeared in publications including *Glamour, Salon, Dissent, The Southeast Review, The New York Times, Bitch Magazine, The Rumpus, Drunken Boat, Hunger Mountain*, and *The Chronicle of Higher Education Review*. She has been featured on NPR's *Fresh Air*, CNN's *Dr. Drew, Anderson Cooper Live,* and elsewhere. The recipient of MacDowell Colony fellowships in 2010 and 2011, and a 2012 Bread Loaf nonfiction fellowship, Melissa co-curates the Mixer Reading and Mu-

sic Series in Manhattan, teaches creative writing at Sarah Lawrence College, and lives in Brooklyn.

ROXANE GAY ("Strange Lands") lives and writes in the Midwest.

EMILY GOULD ("Russia, with Love") is the cofounder of Emily Books and the author of *And the Heart Says Whatever* and a forthcoming novel, *Friendship*. She lives in Brooklyn.

ANN HOOD ("Manhattan, Always Out of Reach") is the author of the bestselling novels *Somewhere Off the Coast of Maine, The Red Thread*, and *The Knitting Circle* as well as the memoir *Comfort: A Journey Through Grief*, which was a *New York Times* Editor's Choice and chosen as one of the top ten nonfiction books of 2008 by *Entertainment Weekly*. She has won two Pushcart Prizes as well as Best American Spiritual Writing, Food Writing, and Travel Writing awards. A regular contributor to *The New York Times*, Hood's short stories and essays have appeared in many publications, including *Ploughshares, Tin House, Traveler, Bon Appetit, O, More, The Paris Review*.

DANA KINSTLER ("Captive") has won fiction prizes from *Glimmer Train, Gulf Coast, Southern Indiana Review*, and *The Missouri Review* and has been published in the *Mississippi Review, The Green Mountain Review*, and *Salamander*. Her essays have appeared in *The Sunday London Telegraph* and the anthologies *Feed Me, About Face, Mr. Wrong*, and *My Father Married Your Mother: Dispatches from the Blended Family*. A third-generation native of Manhattan, she now lives with her family in the Hudson River Valley, New York.

EMILY ST. JOHN MANDEL's ("Long Trains Leaving") most recent novel is *The Lola Quartet*. She lives in Brooklyn. Visit her at emilymandel .com.

LIZA MONROY ("A War Zone for Anyone Looking for Love") is the author of the novel *Mexican High* and the memoir *The Marriage Act: The Risk I Took to Keep My Gay Best Friend in America . . . And What It Taught Us About Love*. She has written for *The New York Times*, *The New York Times Magazine*, *The LA Times*, *Newsweek*, *Self*, *Poets & Writers*, and various anthologies, and coauthored the *MTV/Frommer's Guide to Mexico*.

MARIE MYUNG-OK LEE ("Misfits Fit Here") is the author of the novels *Somebody's Daughter* and *The Infinite Futures of Einstein Alfred Nobel Kwok, MD* (forthcoming). Her essays have appeared in *The New York Times*, *Slate*, *Salon*, the *Washington Post*, and *The Nation*, and she is a regular contributor to *The Atlantic*.

MIRA PTACIN ("Homecoming") is a creative nonfiction and children's book writer and founder of the Freerange Nonfiction Reading Series & Storytelling Collective. She teaches writing at the Salt Institute for Documentary Studies in Portland, Maine. She recently completed a memoir about the uterus and the American Dream, and lives on Peaks Island with her husband and two dogs Maybe and Huckleberry. You can visit her at miraptacin.com.

RAYHANÉ SANDERS ("The Loosening") is a literary agent, freelance editor, and sometimes-writer based in Los Angeles and New York.

DANI SHAPIRO ("My City") is the author of the bestselling memoirs *Devotion* and *Slow Motion*, and five novels, including *Black & White* and *Family History*. Her work has appeared in *The New Yorker*, *Granta*, *Tin House*, *Ploughshares*, *n+1*, *Vogue*, *Elle*, *The New York Times Book Review*, and many other publications. Her new book, *Still Writing: The Pleasures and Perils of a Creative Life*, has just been published. She lives with her family in Litchfield County, Connecticut.

JANET STEEN ("Heedless, Resilient, Gullible, and Stupid") worked in New York City for magazines such as *Esquire*, *Time Out New York*, and *Details*. She now edits novels, memoirs, and various kinds of nonfiction, and is an editor and regular essayist for the arts-and-culture website The Weeklings. She lives in a hollow in the mountains of upstate New York.

EMMA STRAUB ("Someday, Some Morning, Sometime") is the author of the novel *Laura Lamont's Life in Pictures* and the short story collection *Other People We Married*. She is a native New Yorker.

CHERYL STRAYED ("Minnesota Nice") is the author of No. 1 *New York Times* bestseller *Wild*, the New York Times bestseller *Tiny Beautiful Things*, and the novel *Torch*. Strayed's writing has appeared in *The Best American Essays*, *The New York Times Magazine*, the *Washington Post Magazine*, *Vogue*, *Allure*, *The Missouri Review*, *The Sun*, *The Rumpus*—where she has written the popular "Dear Sugar" column since 2010—and elsewhere. Her books have been translated into twenty-eight languages around the world. She holds an MFA in fiction writing from Syracuse University and a bachelor's degree from the University of Minnesota. She lives in Portland, Oregon, with her husband and their two children.

EVA TENUTO ("Crash and Burn") studied acting at the American Academy of Dramatic Arts and went on to found The Women's Experimental Theater Group, which performed at various venues in New York City and East Coast colleges for over a decade. She most recently developed the nonprofit TMI Project, a memoir-writing workshop in which real-life stories are shaped into well-crafted monologues and performed by the people who lived them. Visit TMIproject.org.

REBECCA WOLFF ("So Long, Suckers") is the author of three collections of poetry (*Manderley*, *Figment*, and *The King*) and a novel,

The Beginners (Riverhead, 2011), as well as numerous pieces of occasional prose. Her fourth poetry book and second novel are in process. Wolff is the editor of Fence and Fence Books and the publisher of The Constant Critic, a site for poetry criticism. She is also a doula. She is the mother of two children, with whom she lives in Hudson, New York, and is a fellow at the New York State Writers Institute at the University at Albany.

ABOUT THE EDITOR

© Brad DeCecco

SARI BOTTON ("Real Estate") is a writer and editor whose work
has appeared in *The New York Times*, *New York Magazine*, *The Sun*,
The Village Voice, *Harper's Bazaar*, *More*, *Marie Claire*, *The Rumpus*,
Memoirville, *This Recording*, *xojane*, assorted anthologies, and other
publications. She is the editorial director of the TMI Project (tmiproject
.org), a nonprofit organization that holds memoir and true storytelling workshops in jails, shelters, veterans' hospitals, cancer wards,
schools, and other places where people don't usually get to tell their
stories or be heard.

ACKNOWLEDGEMENTS

ere's a little secret: editing an anthology is a great way to get your name on the cover of a book without having to write the whole damn thing—or even much of it, actually—which is awesome for a writer who has so far been too traumatized by fear to complete a book of her own.

It's also a great way to position yourself among a coterie of writers who are way out of your league. I cannot express enough gratitude to all the great and accomplished authors in this collection who were kind enough to appear here with me. An extra-special thank-you to the talented and kind-hearted Cheryl Strayed, who made good on her promise to contribute to the collection even though she was in the midst of the craziest year of her life and battling pneumonia.

Thanks, too, to Stephen Elliott, Isaac Fitzgerald, and the whole Rumpus family, without whom I might not have connected with several of the contributors to this collection. Ditto, my friend Emily St. John Mandel.

Deep gratitude goes out to my savvy agent, Rayhané Sanders of WSK Management, who forgave me not only for disregarding her advice to eschew anthologies, but also for going behind her back to get a deal on my own; she also contributed a wonderful essay.

Thanks to my smart editor, Laura Mazer, and also to Brooke Warner, who acquired the book, and Rachel Kramer Bussel, who referred me and gave me some pointers on editing anthologies.

Eva Tenuto, talented founder of—and my partner in—TMI Project .org, has by example helped me broaden my scope and develop new skills as a writer and editor. (Plus she's kept me gainfully employed!) I can't thank her enough. And thanks to Julie Novak, who co-founded TMI Project, and suggested that Eva bring me on board.

Thanks to my parents, who first brought me to New York City. And to my late grandparents, who took me to the restaurant where I spotted that woman contentedly eating and writing by herself.

If I hadn't met my sweet husband, Brian Macaluso, in 2003, I might never have up and said goodbye to all that. And I couldn't have pulled this together without his love, encouragement, and support. Thank you, Loveypie.

SELECTED TITLES FROM SEAL PRESS

Drinking Diaries: Women Serve Their Stories Straight Up, edited by Caren Osten Gerszberg and Leah Odze Epstein. $15.00, 978-1-58005-411-9. Celebrated writers take a candid look at the pleasures and pains of drinking, and the many ways in which it touches women's lives.

No Kidding: Women Writers on Bypassing Parenthood, edited by Henriette Mantel. $16.00, 978-1-58005-443-0. This fascinating collection features a star-studded group of contributors—including Margaret Cho, Wendy Liebman, Laurie Graff, and other accomplished, funny women—writing about why they opted out of motherhood.

Wanderlust: A Love Affair with Five Continents, by Elisabeth Eaves. $16.95, 978-1-58005-311-2. A love letter from the author to the places she's visited—and to the spirit of travel itself—that documents her insatiable hunger for the rush of the unfamiliar and the experience of encountering new people and cultures.

Dancing at the Shame Prom: Sharing the Stories That Kept Us Small, edited by Amy Ferris and Hollye Dexter. $15.00, 978-1-58005-416-4. A collection of funny, sad, poignant, miraculous, life-changing, and jaw-dropping secrets for readers to gawk at, empathize with, and laugh about—in the hopes that they will be inspired to share their secret burdens as well.

Fast Times in Palestine: A Love Affair with a Homeless Homeland, by Pamela Olson. $16.00, 978-1-58005-482-9. A powerful, deeply moving account of the time Pamela Olson spent in Palestine—both the daily events that are universal to us all (house parties, concerts, barbecues, and weddings) as well as the violence, trauma, and political tensions that are particular to the country.

www.SealPress.com
www.Facebook.com/SealPress
Twitter: @SealPress